The 'STAN

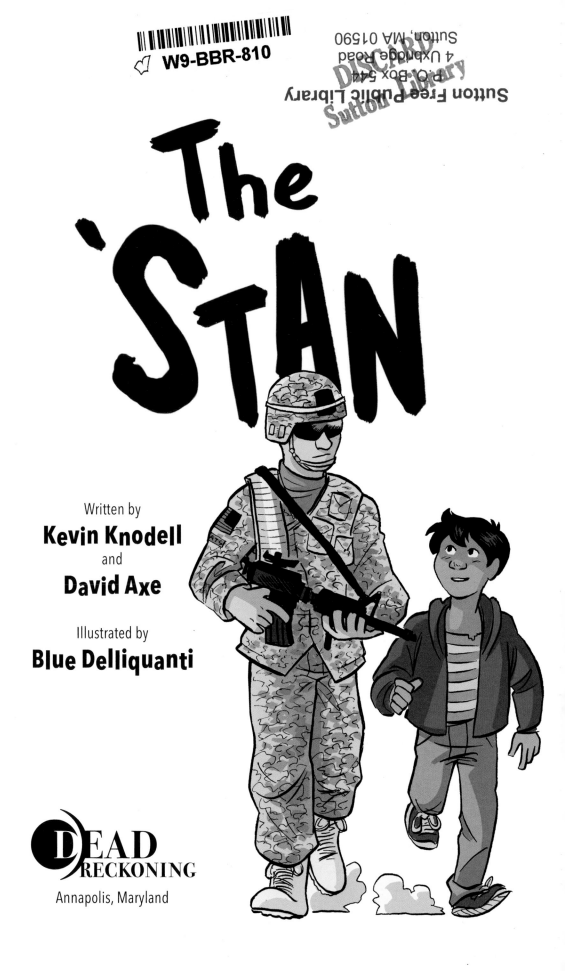

Written by
Kevin Knodell
and
David Axe

Illustrated by
Blue Delliquanti

DEAD RECKONING
Annapolis, Maryland

Published by Dead Reckoning
291 Wood Road
Annapolis, MD 21402

Library of Congress Cataloging-in-Publication Data

Names: Knodell, Kevin, date, author. | Axe, David, author. | Delliquanti, Blue, illustrator.
Title: The 'Stan / written by Kevin Knodell and David Axe ; illustrated by Blue Delliquanti.
Description: Annapolis, MD : Dead Reckoning, an imprint of the Naval Institute Press, 2018.
Identifiers: LCCN 2018018722 (print) | LCCN 2018028625 (ebook) | ISBN
    9781682470992 (ePDF) | ISBN 9781682470985 (pbk. : alk. paper)
Subjects: LCSH: Afghan War, 2001---Comic books, strips, etc. | LCGFT: Comics
    (Graphic works)
Classification: LCC DS371.412 (ebook) | LCC DS371.412 .K56 2018 (print) | DDC
    958.104/70222--dc23
LC record available at https://lccn.loc.gov/2018018722

♾ Print editions meet the requirements of ANSI/NISO z39.48-1992
(Permanence of Paper).
Printed in the United States of America.

26 25 24 23 22 21 20 19 18   9 8 7 6 5 4 3 2 1
First printing

This is a work of nonfiction. Some names have been changed to protect the privacy of individuals.

CONTENTS

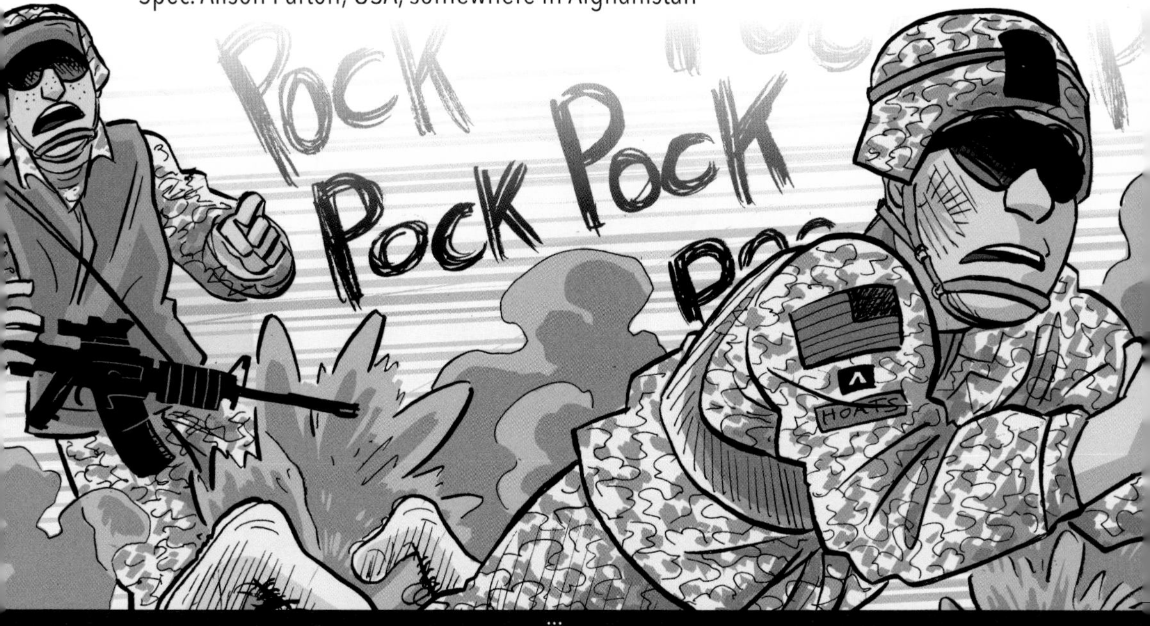

Pock
Pock Pock

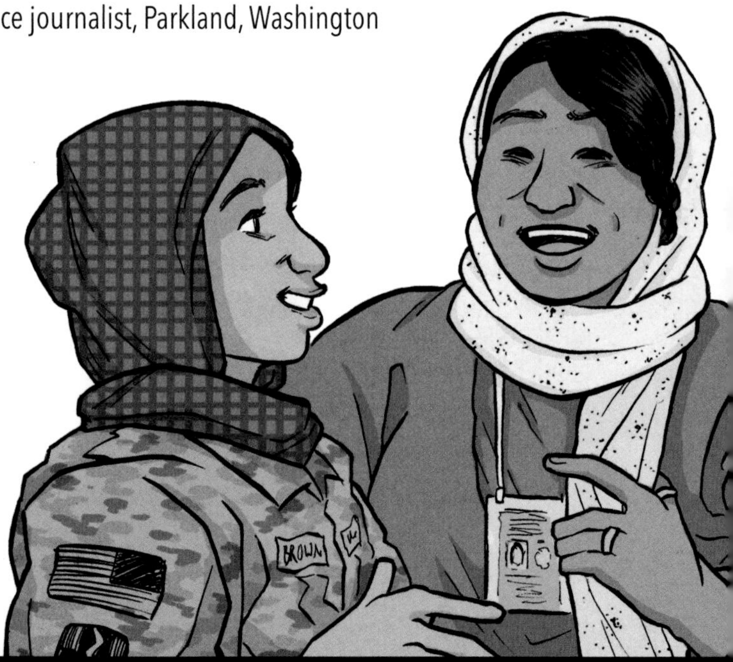
BROWN

PREFACE

There was a time, around 2013 or so, that I secretly worried that the Afghanistan war might end.

Yeah, that's an odd concern for a political liberal and self-avowed pacifist. One who, to boot, had by that time been a war correspondent for eight long years in conflict zones all over the world. I'd spent months in combat across Afghanistan since 2007.

I'd seen people suffer horrible injuries. I'd talked to desperate, impoverished, and terrified Afghans and traumatized, disillusioned soldiers. In Logar Province in March 2011, I narrowly survived the explosion of a massive improvised explosive device that struck the U.S. Army vehicle I was riding in.

Still, two years later, I quietly worried that the war would end. President Barack Obama had pledged to shrink, and eventually halt, the conventional U.S.-led combat mission in the country.

In 2013 the withdrawal was well under way. Twelve years after U.S. Special Forces invaded the landlocked Central Asian country in pursuit of the terror group Al Qaeda—and by extension Afghanistan's brutal ruling regime the Taliban—it truly seemed like the war was ending.

For Americans, at least.

I should have been relieved. The United States had invested hundreds of billions of dollars in Afghanistan. More than a thousand Americans had died. And yet the country remained poor, uneducated, violent, and politically corrupt.

But in my selfishness, I feared losing my easy access—via the U.S. military—to Afghanistan's most dangerous districts. The war had defined my young adulthood. The closer it came to killing me, the deeper my connection with the conflict. For better or worse, the Afghanistan war had made me who I was and am. I treasured that.

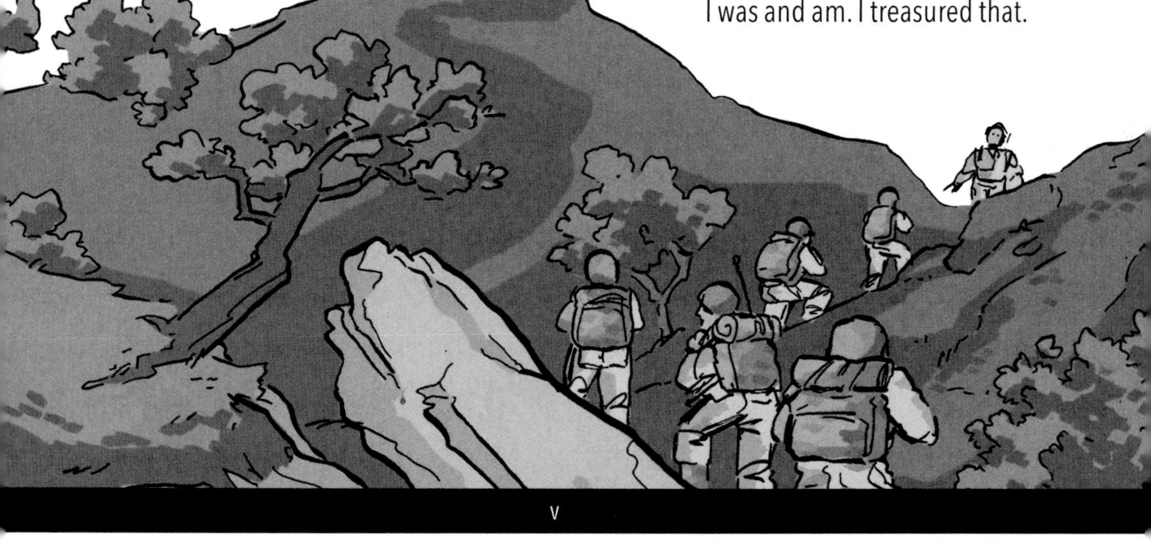

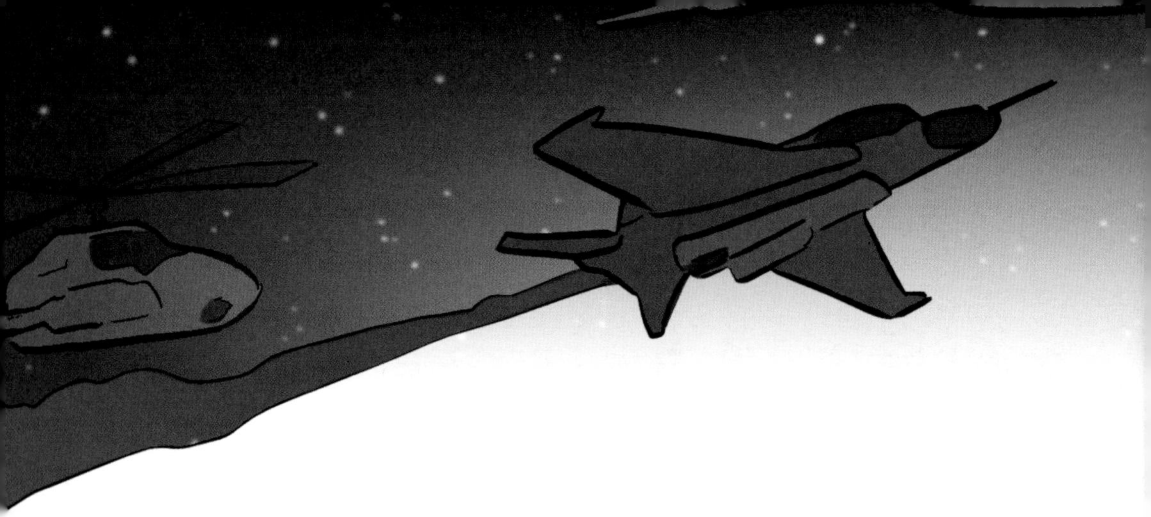

It had also made the United States what it was . . . and still is. An angry, resentful, increasingly powerless superpower. A country where, to many millions, killing foreigners, and especially Muslim foreigners–however pointless their deaths might be–somehow represents a political end unto itself. As long as the United States can still slaughter brown people, America is still great. Right?

In 2013 I squeezed in one last trip to southern Afghanistan with the U.S. Army, patrolling a desolate corner of Kandahar Province that coalition air strikes and artillery had all but destroyed. It was peaceful because it was lifeless.

But elsewhere, the war still raged and politics roiled. I should have known that Obama's drawdown wouldn't stick. I should have known that resurgent militant groups, enduring corruption in Kabul, and regime change in my own country would reverse the war's halting progress toward some kind of tense resolution.

Afghanistan has long known war. Afghanistan long will know war. I could take weird comfort in that unhappy truth. I might never lose my connection to the fighting, because the fighting might never stop.

The 'Stan is a collection of short comics about a long war. The following tales are all true. They're based on my reporting and reporting by Kevin Knodell and a few others. When we began writing the stories–and Blue Delliquanti began drawing them–it was possible to believe our book, once it hit shelves, would look back on a war that was in America's past.

Instead, it's a book that's still very much about Afghanistan's, and America's, present. And likely future.

David Axe
Columbia, South Carolina
October 2017

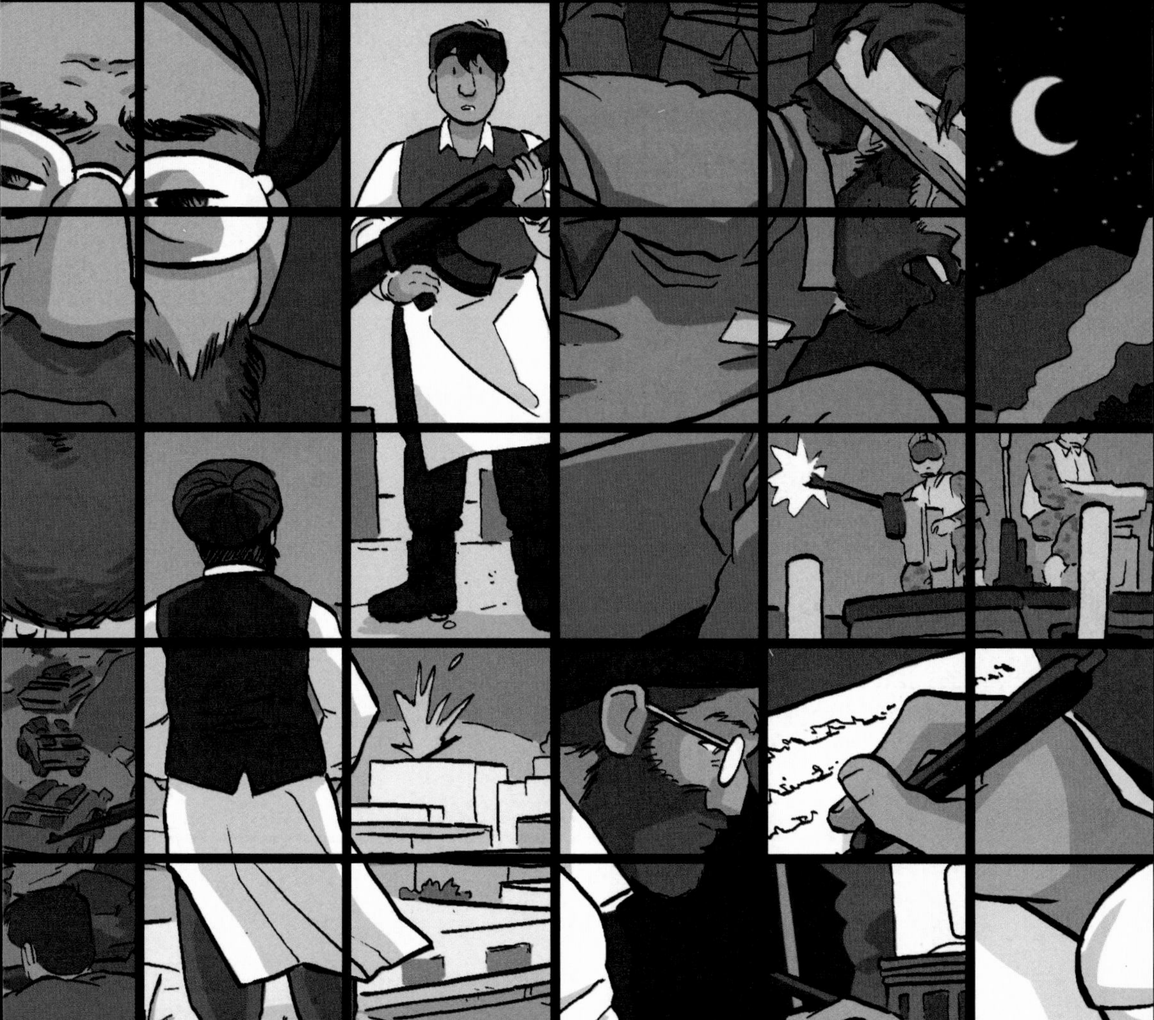

Abdul Salam Zaeef,
Taliban ambassador to Pakistan, Kandahar

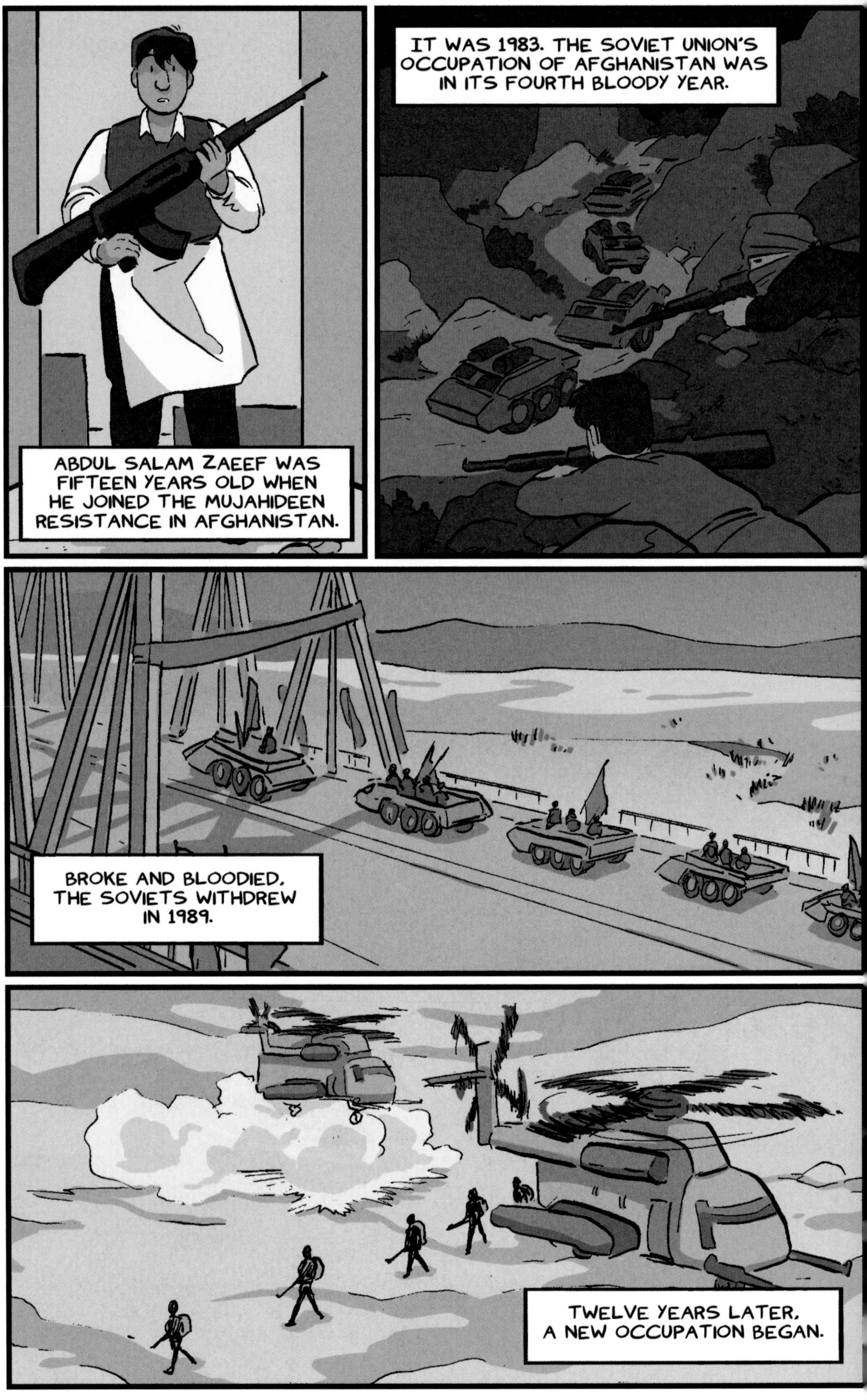
ABDUL SALAM ZAEEF WAS FIFTEEN YEARS OLD WHEN HE JOINED THE MUJAHIDEEN RESISTANCE IN AFGHANISTAN.
IT WAS 1983. THE SOVIET UNION'S OCCUPATION OF AFGHANISTAN WAS IN ITS FOURTH BLOODY YEAR.
BROKE AND BLOODIED, THE SOVIETS WITHDREW IN 1989.
TWELVE YEARS LATER, A NEW OCCUPATION BEGAN.

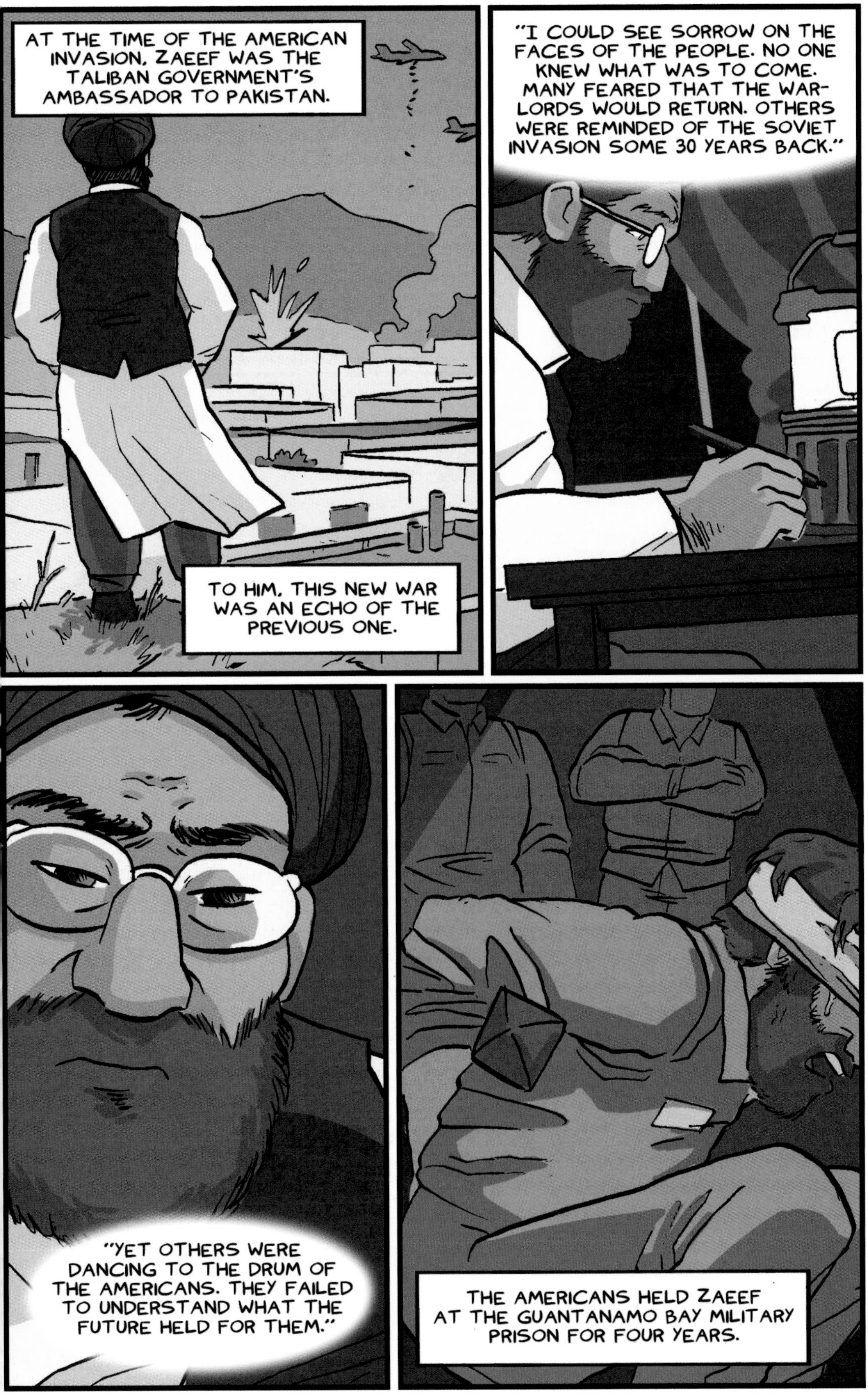
AT THE TIME OF THE AMERICAN INVASION, ZAEEF WAS THE TALIBAN GOVERNMENT'S AMBASSADOR TO PAKISTAN.
TO HIM, THIS NEW WAR WAS AN ECHO OF THE PREVIOUS ONE.
"I COULD SEE SORROW ON THE FACES OF THE PEOPLE. NO ONE KNEW WHAT WAS TO COME. MANY FEARED THAT THE WAR-LORDS WOULD RETURN. OTHERS WERE REMINDED OF THE SOVIET INVASION SOME 30 YEARS BACK."
"YET OTHERS WERE DANCING TO THE DRUM OF THE AMERICANS. THEY FAILED TO UNDERSTAND WHAT THE FUTURE HELD FOR THEM."
THE AMERICANS HELD ZAEEF AT THE GUANTANAMO BAY MILITARY PRISON FOR FOUR YEARS.

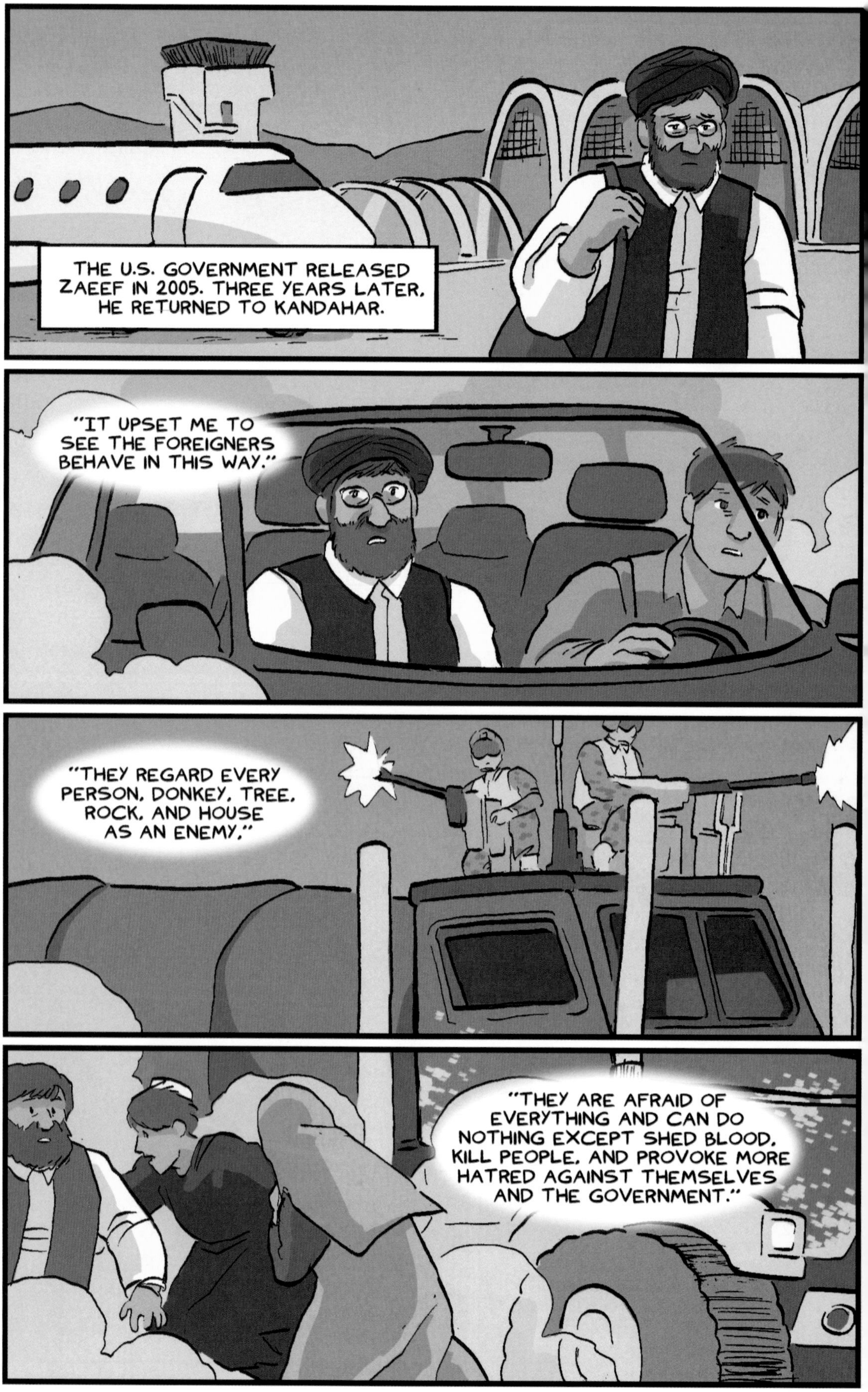
THE U.S. GOVERNMENT RELEASED ZAEEF IN 2005. THREE YEARS LATER, HE RETURNED TO KANDAHAR.
"IT UPSET ME TO SEE THE FOREIGNERS BEHAVE IN THIS WAY."
"THEY REGARD EVERY PERSON, DONKEY, TREE, ROCK, AND HOUSE AS AN ENEMY."
"THEY ARE AFRAID OF EVERYTHING AND CAN DO NOTHING EXCEPT SHED BLOOD, KILL PEOPLE, AND PROVOKE MORE HATRED AGAINST THEMSELVES AND THE GOVERNMENT."

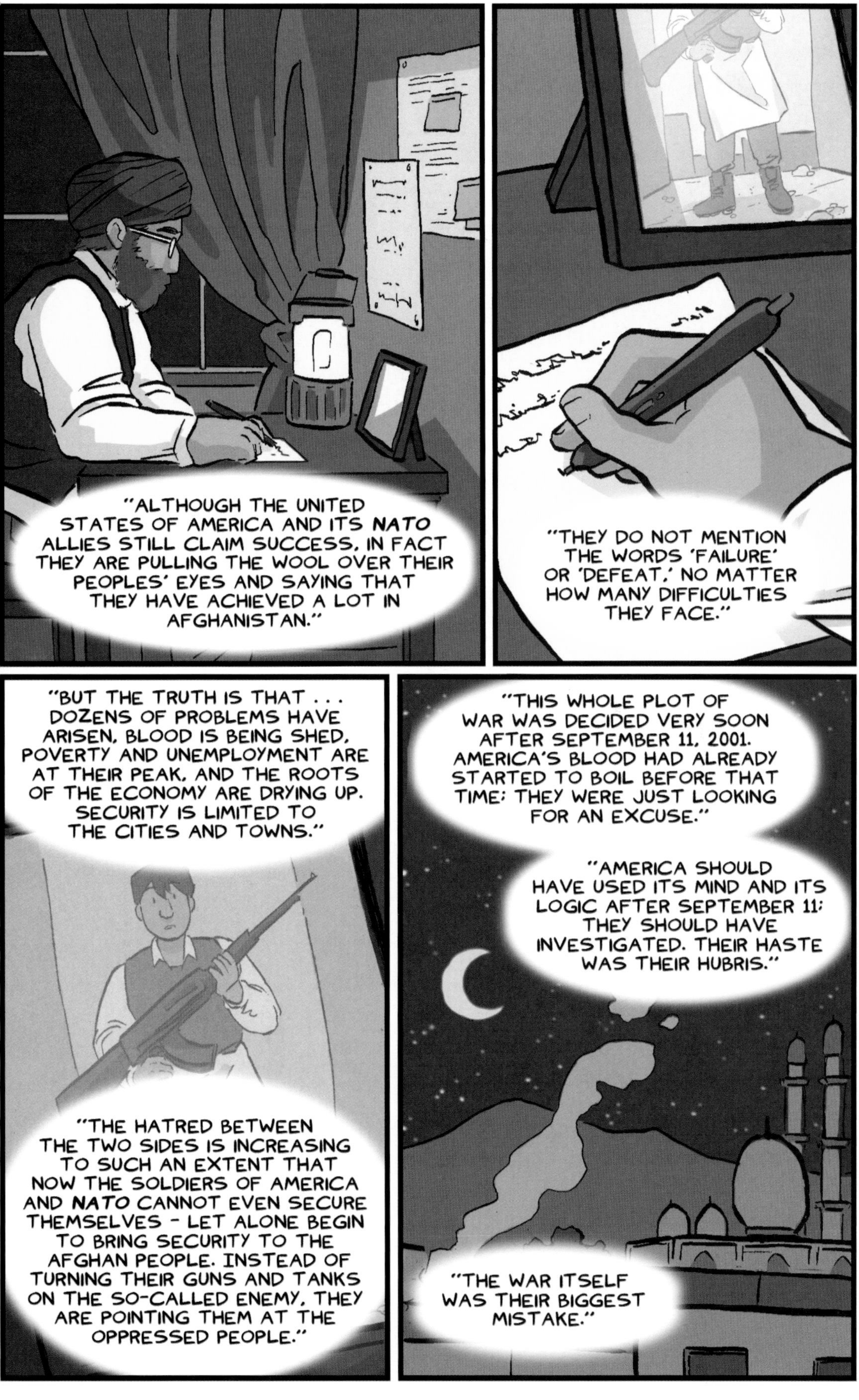
"ALTHOUGH THE UNITED STATES OF AMERICA AND ITS NATO ALLIES STILL CLAIM SUCCESS, IN FACT THEY ARE PULLING THE WOOL OVER THEIR PEOPLES' EYES AND SAYING THAT THEY HAVE ACHIEVED A LOT IN AFGHANISTAN."
"THEY DO NOT MENTION THE WORDS 'FAILURE' OR 'DEFEAT,' NO MATTER HOW MANY DIFFICULTIES THEY FACE."
"BUT THE TRUTH IS THAT . . . DOZENS OF PROBLEMS HAVE ARISEN, BLOOD IS BEING SHED, POVERTY AND UNEMPLOYMENT ARE AT THEIR PEAK, AND THE ROOTS OF THE ECONOMY ARE DRYING UP. SECURITY IS LIMITED TO THE CITIES AND TOWNS."
"THE HATRED BETWEEN THE TWO SIDES IS INCREASING TO SUCH AN EXTENT THAT NOW THE SOLDIERS OF AMERICA AND NATO CANNOT EVEN SECURE THEMSELVES - LET ALONE BEGIN TO BRING SECURITY TO THE AFGHAN PEOPLE. INSTEAD OF TURNING THEIR GUNS AND TANKS ON THE SO-CALLED ENEMY, THEY ARE POINTING THEM AT THE OPPRESSED PEOPLE."
"THIS WHOLE PLOT OF WAR WAS DECIDED VERY SOON AFTER SEPTEMBER 11, 2001. AMERICA'S BLOOD HAD ALREADY STARTED TO BOIL BEFORE THAT TIME; THEY WERE JUST LOOKING FOR AN EXCUSE."
"AMERICA SHOULD HAVE USED ITS MIND AND ITS LOGIC AFTER SEPTEMBER 11; THEY SHOULD HAVE INVESTIGATED. THEIR HASTE WAS THEIR HUBRIS."
"THE WAR ITSELF WAS THEIR BIGGEST MISTAKE."

2 "COMMANDO SHOPPING SPREE"

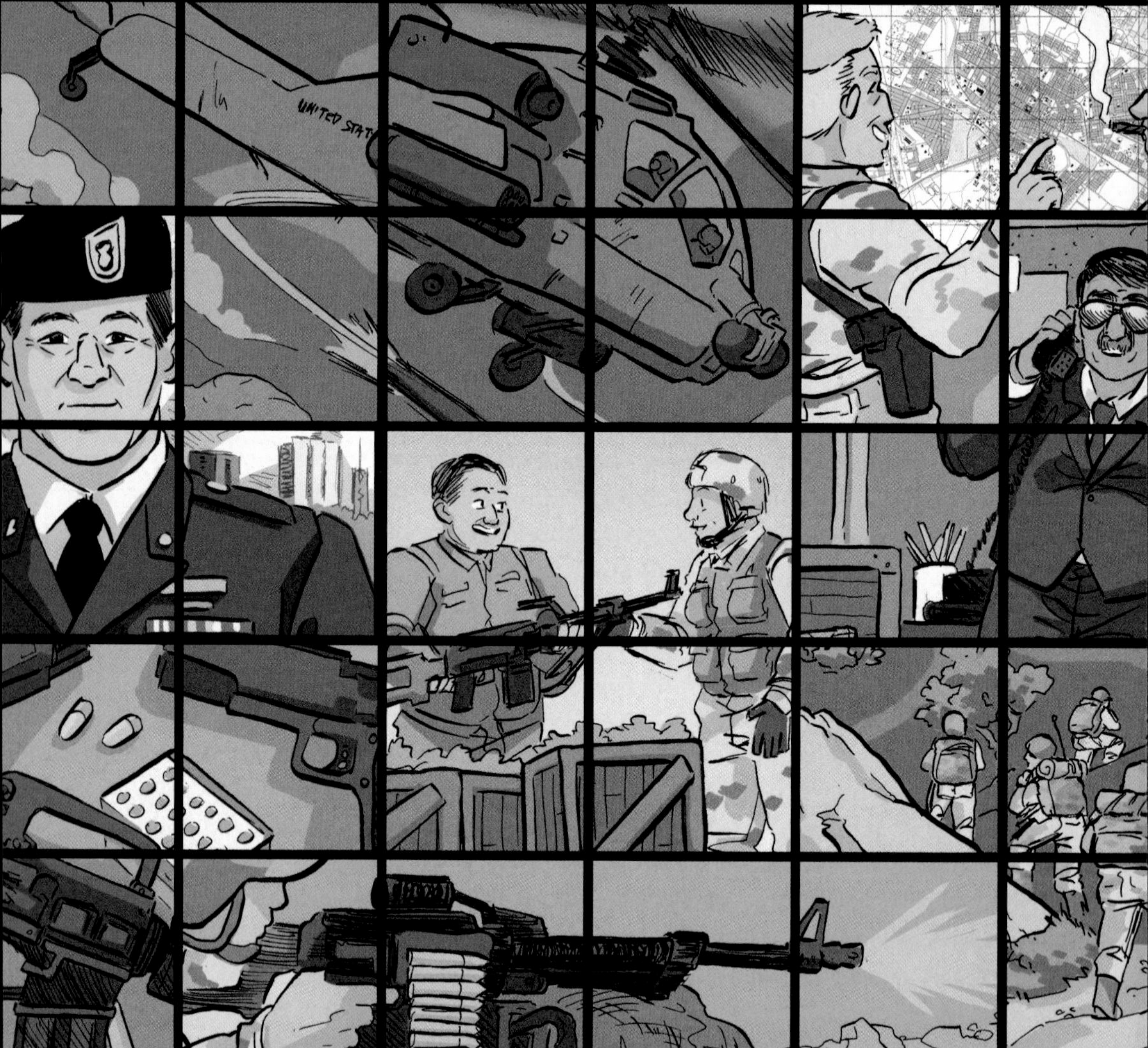

MSgt. Scott Satterlee, USA, Khost Province

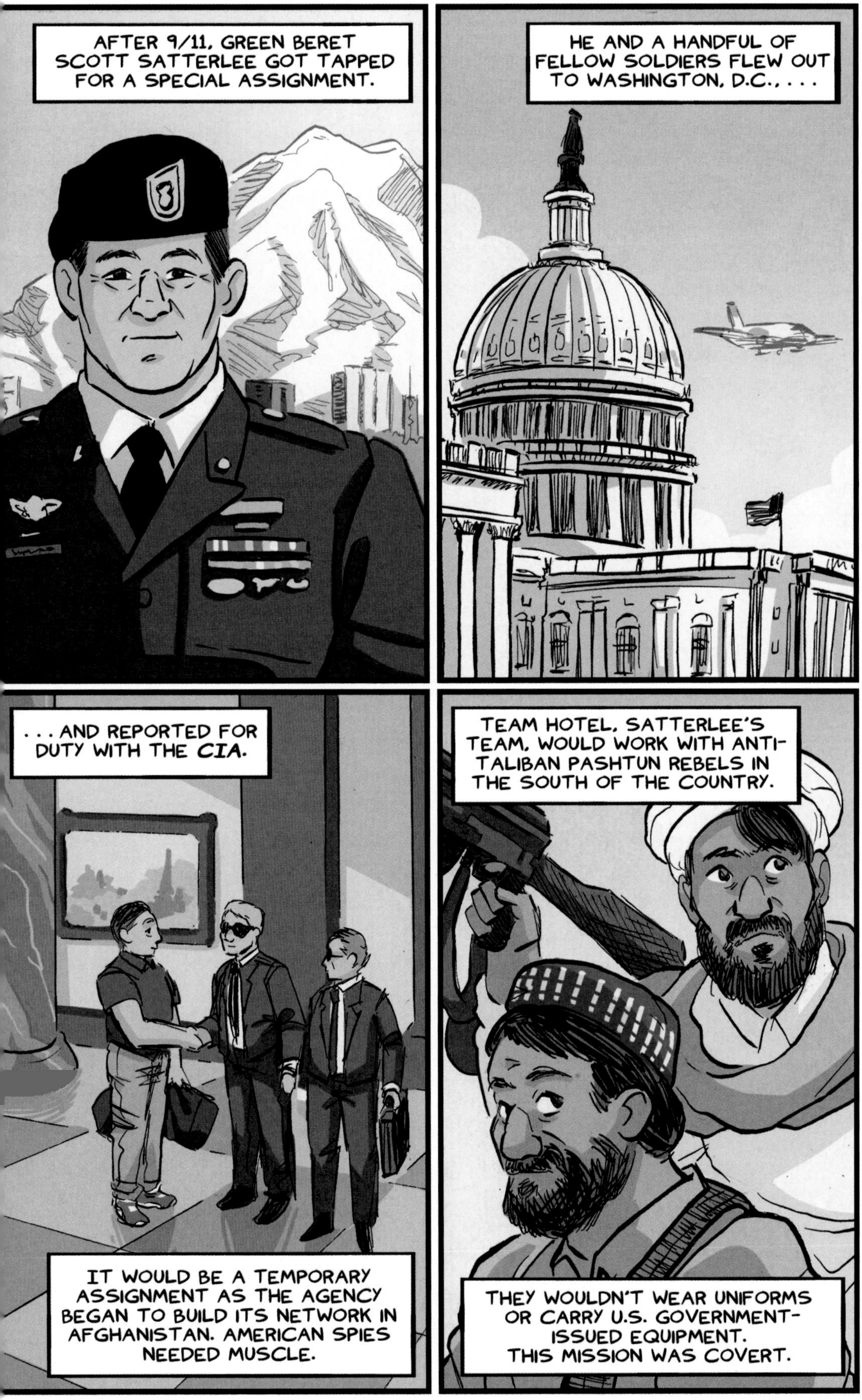
AFTER 9/11, GREEN BERET SCOTT SATTERLEE GOT TAPPED FOR A SPECIAL ASSIGNMENT.
HE AND A HANDFUL OF FELLOW SOLDIERS FLEW OUT TO WASHINGTON, D.C., . . .
. . . AND REPORTED FOR DUTY WITH THE *CIA*.
IT WOULD BE A TEMPORARY ASSIGNMENT AS THE AGENCY BEGAN TO BUILD ITS NETWORK IN AFGHANISTAN. AMERICAN SPIES NEEDED MUSCLE.
TEAM HOTEL, SATTERLEE'S TEAM, WOULD WORK WITH ANTI-TALIBAN PASHTUN REBELS IN THE SOUTH OF THE COUNTRY.
THEY WOULDN'T WEAR UNIFORMS OR CARRY U.S. GOVERNMENT-ISSUED EQUIPMENT.
THIS MISSION WAS COVERT.

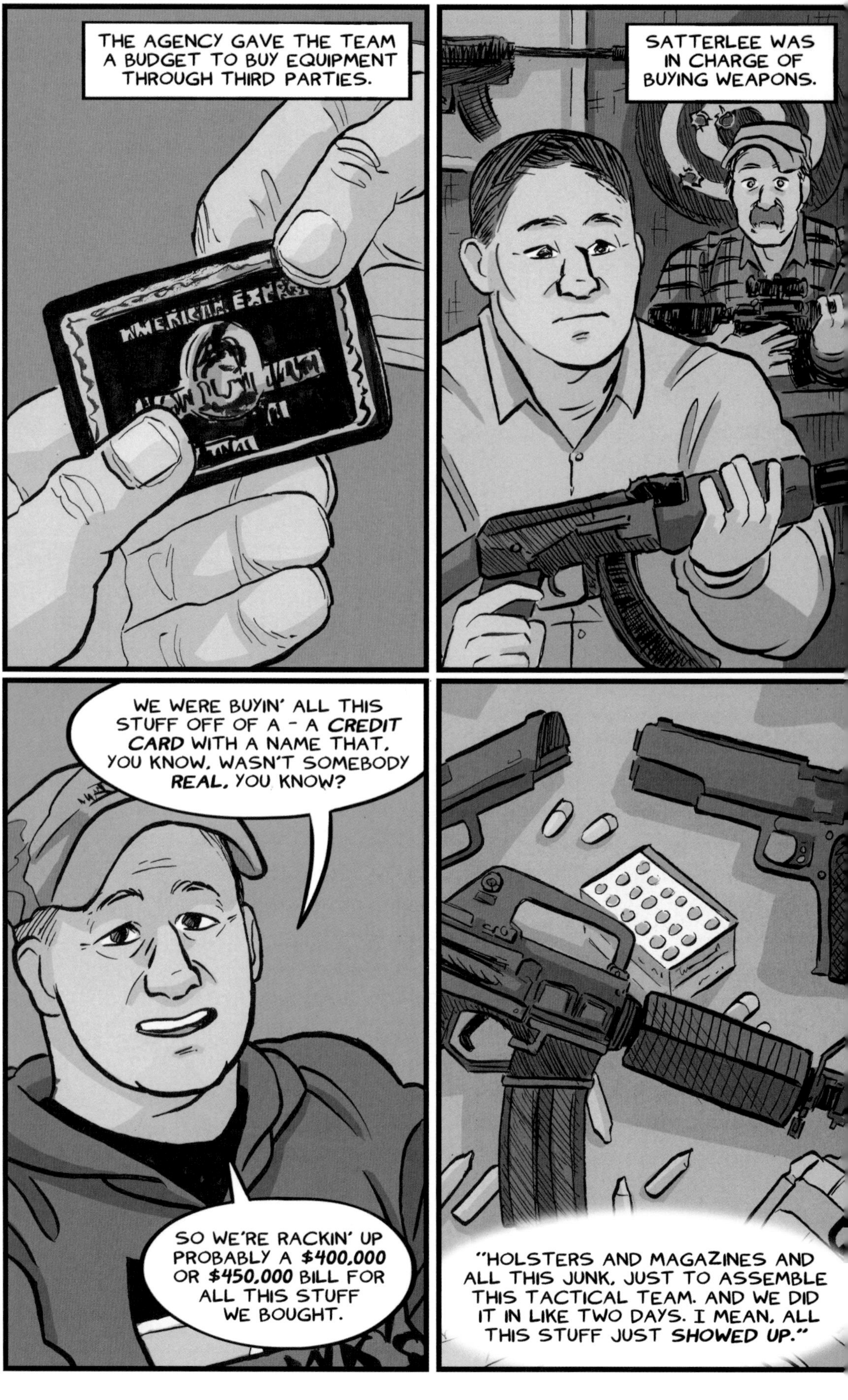
THE AGENCY GAVE THE TEAM A BUDGET TO BUY EQUIPMENT THROUGH THIRD PARTIES.
SATTERLEE WAS IN CHARGE OF BUYING WEAPONS.
WE WERE BUYIN' ALL THIS STUFF OFF OF A - A *CREDIT CARD* WITH A NAME THAT, YOU KNOW, WASN'T SOMEBODY *REAL,* YOU KNOW?
SO WE'RE RACKIN' UP PROBABLY A *$400,000* OR *$450,000* BILL FOR ALL THIS STUFF WE BOUGHT.
"HOLSTERS AND MAGAZINES AND ALL THIS JUNK, JUST TO ASSEMBLE THIS TACTICAL TEAM. AND WE DID IT IN LIKE TWO DAYS. I MEAN, ALL THIS STUFF JUST *SHOWED UP.*"

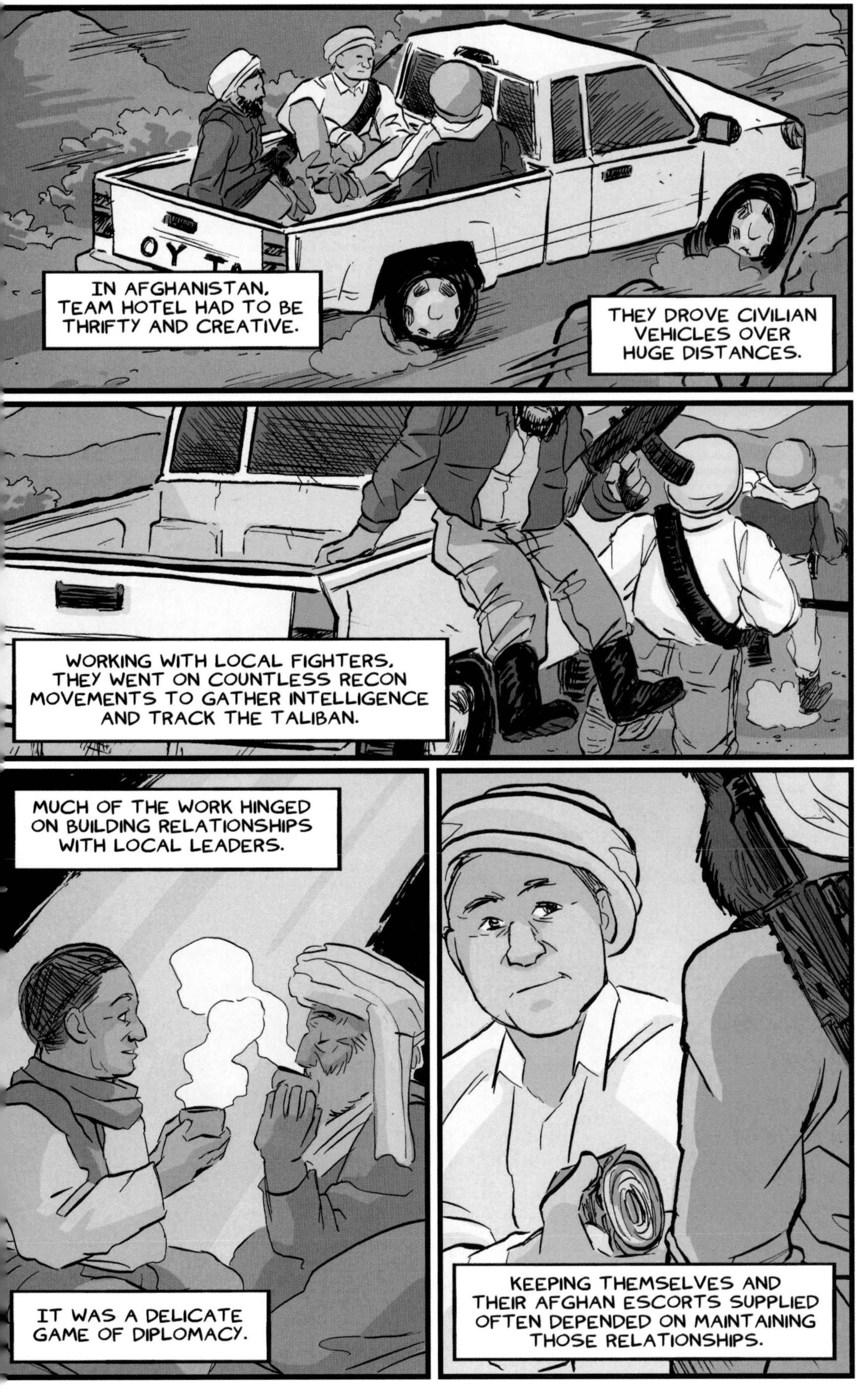
IN AFGHANISTAN, TEAM HOTEL HAD TO BE THRIFTY AND CREATIVE.
THEY DROVE CIVILIAN VEHICLES OVER HUGE DISTANCES.
WORKING WITH LOCAL FIGHTERS, THEY WENT ON COUNTLESS RECON MOVEMENTS TO GATHER INTELLIGENCE AND TRACK THE TALIBAN.
MUCH OF THE WORK HINGED ON BUILDING RELATIONSHIPS WITH LOCAL LEADERS.
IT WAS A DELICATE GAME OF DIPLOMACY.
KEEPING THEMSELVES AND THEIR AFGHAN ESCORTS SUPPLIED OFTEN DEPENDED ON MAINTAINING THOSE RELATIONSHIPS.

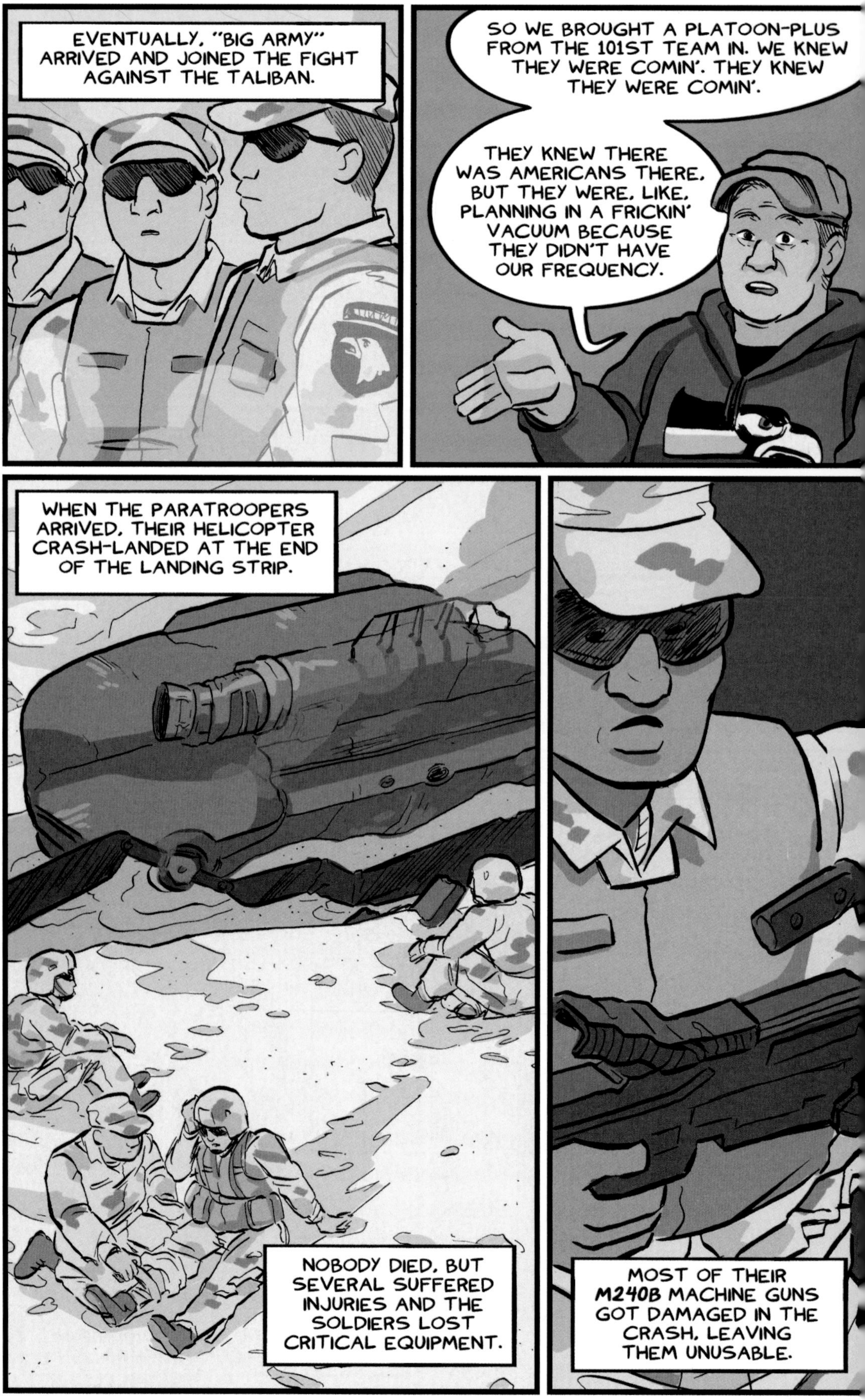
EVENTUALLY, "BIG ARMY" ARRIVED AND JOINED THE FIGHT AGAINST THE TALIBAN.
SO WE BROUGHT A PLATOON-PLUS FROM THE 101ST TEAM IN. WE KNEW THEY WERE COMIN'. THEY KNEW THEY WERE COMIN'.
THEY KNEW THERE WAS AMERICANS THERE, BUT THEY WERE, LIKE, PLANNING IN A FRICKIN' VACUUM BECAUSE THEY DIDN'T HAVE OUR FREQUENCY.
WHEN THE PARATROOPERS ARRIVED, THEIR HELICOPTER CRASH-LANDED AT THE END OF THE LANDING STRIP.
NOBODY DIED, BUT SEVERAL SUFFERED INJURIES AND THE SOLDIERS LOST CRITICAL EQUIPMENT.
MOST OF THEIR M240B MACHINE GUNS GOT DAMAGED IN THE CRASH, LEAVING THEM UNUSABLE.

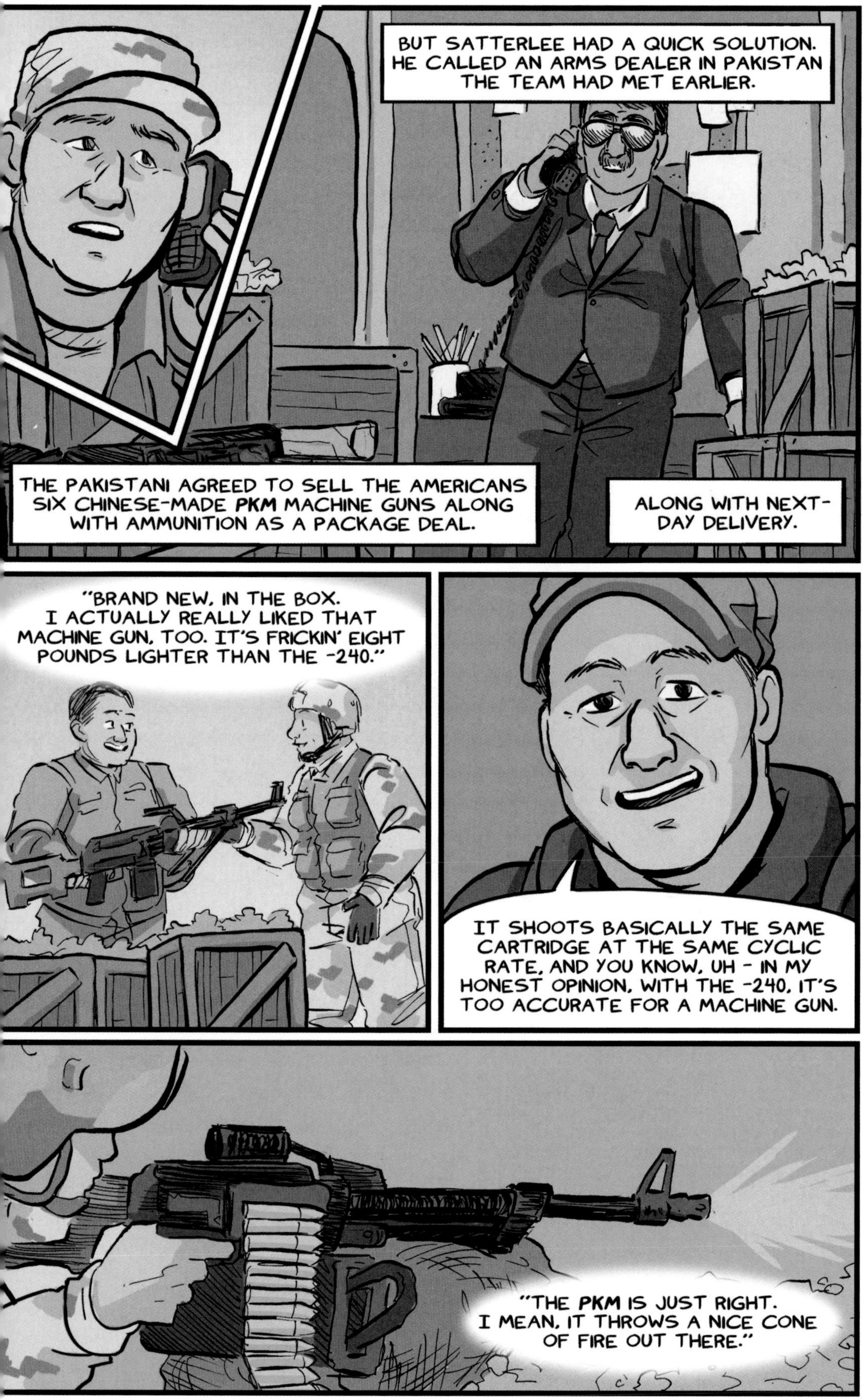

BUT SATTERLEE HAD A QUICK SOLUTION. HE CALLED AN ARMS DEALER IN PAKISTAN THE TEAM HAD MET EARLIER.
THE PAKISTANI AGREED TO SELL THE AMERICANS SIX CHINESE-MADE **PKM** MACHINE GUNS ALONG WITH AMMUNITION AS A PACKAGE DEAL.
ALONG WITH NEXT-DAY DELIVERY.
"BRAND NEW, IN THE BOX. I ACTUALLY REALLY LIKED THAT MACHINE GUN, TOO. IT'S FRICKIN' EIGHT POUNDS LIGHTER THAN THE -240."
IT SHOOTS BASICALLY THE SAME CARTRIDGE AT THE SAME CYCLIC RATE, AND YOU KNOW, UH - IN MY HONEST OPINION, WITH THE -240, IT'S TOO ACCURATE FOR A MACHINE GUN.
"THE **PKM** IS JUST RIGHT. I MEAN, IT THROWS A NICE CONE OF FIRE OUT THERE."

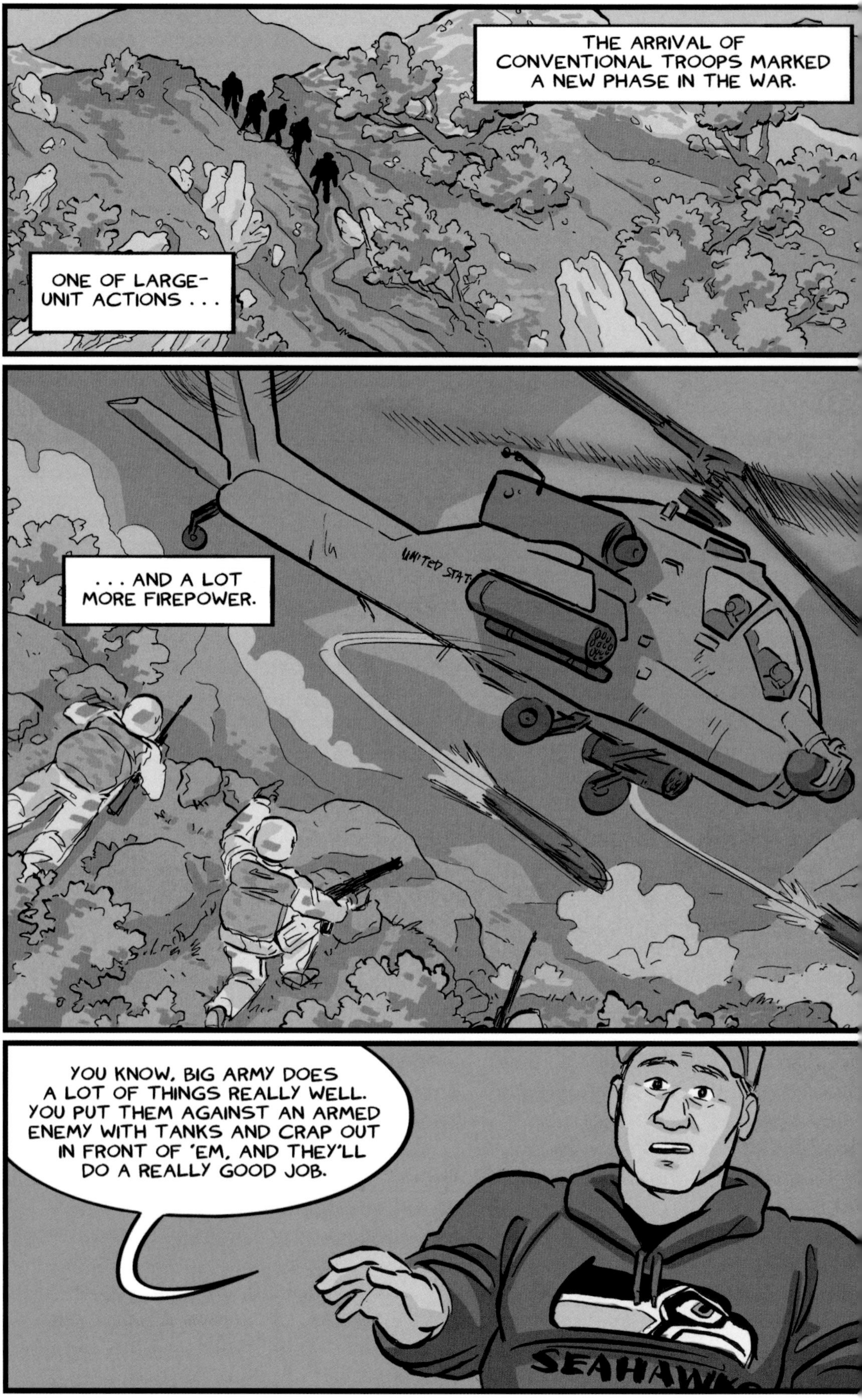
THE ARRIVAL OF CONVENTIONAL TROOPS MARKED A NEW PHASE IN THE WAR.
ONE OF LARGE-UNIT ACTIONS . . .
. . . AND A LOT MORE FIREPOWER.
YOU KNOW, BIG ARMY DOES A LOT OF THINGS REALLY WELL. YOU PUT THEM AGAINST AN ARMED ENEMY WITH TANKS AND CRAP OUT IN FRONT OF 'EM, AND THEY'LL DO A REALLY GOOD JOB.

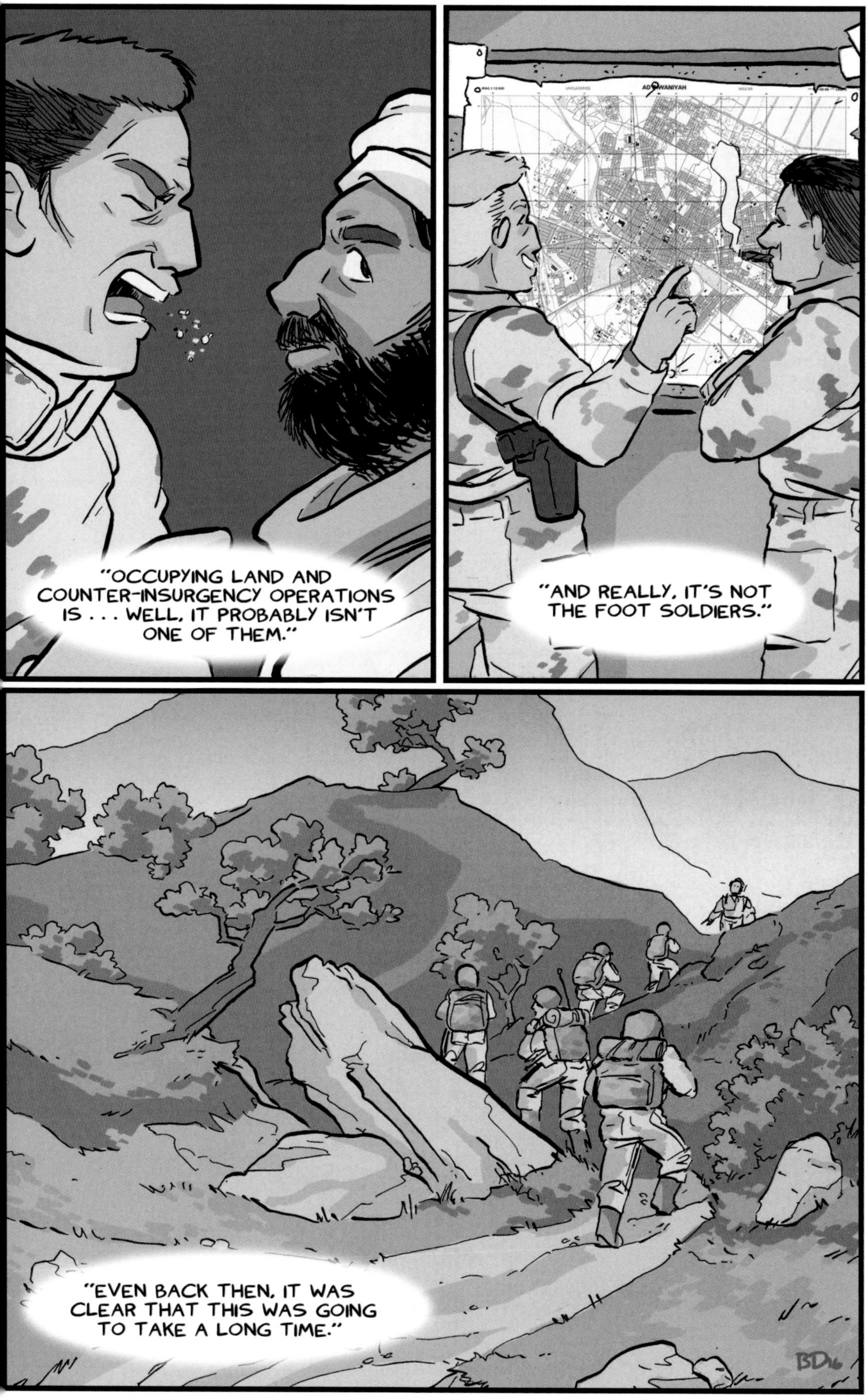
"OCCUPYING LAND AND COUNTER-INSURGENCY OPERATIONS IS . . . WELL, IT PROBABLY ISN'T ONE OF THEM."
"AND REALLY, IT'S NOT THE FOOT SOLDIERS."
"EVEN BACK THEN, IT WAS CLEAR THAT THIS WAS GOING TO TAKE A LONG TIME."
BD16

3 "WINTER IN KORENGAL"

Spec. Donald Lee, USA,
Korengal Valley

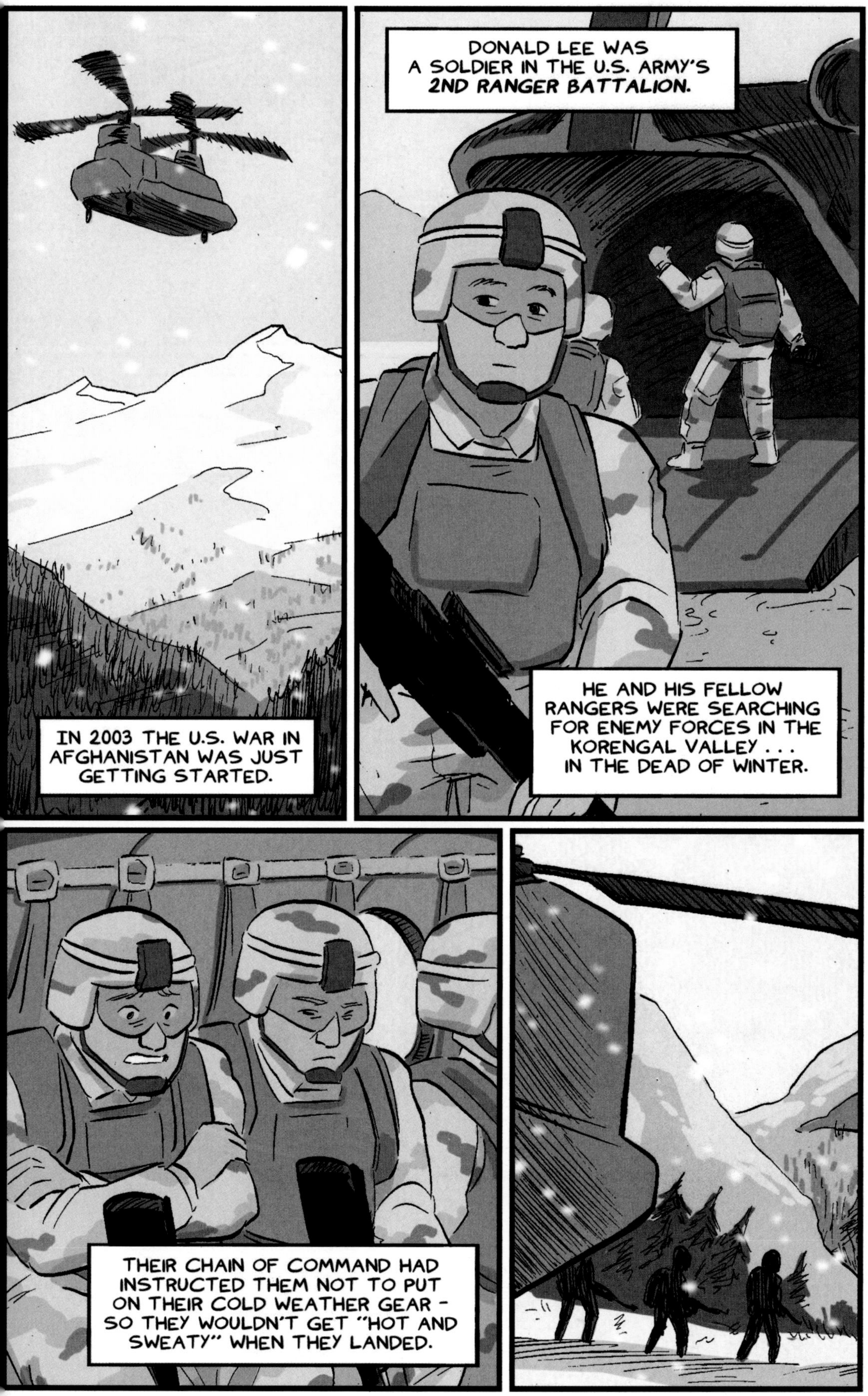
IN 2003 THE U.S. WAR IN AFGHANISTAN WAS JUST GETTING STARTED.
DONALD LEE WAS A SOLDIER IN THE U.S. ARMY'S 2ND RANGER BATTALION.
HE AND HIS FELLOW RANGERS WERE SEARCHING FOR ENEMY FORCES IN THE KORENGAL VALLEY . . . IN THE DEAD OF WINTER.
THEIR CHAIN OF COMMAND HAD INSTRUCTED THEM NOT TO PUT ON THEIR COLD WEATHER GEAR - SO THEY WOULDN'T GET "HOT AND SWEATY" WHEN THEY LANDED.

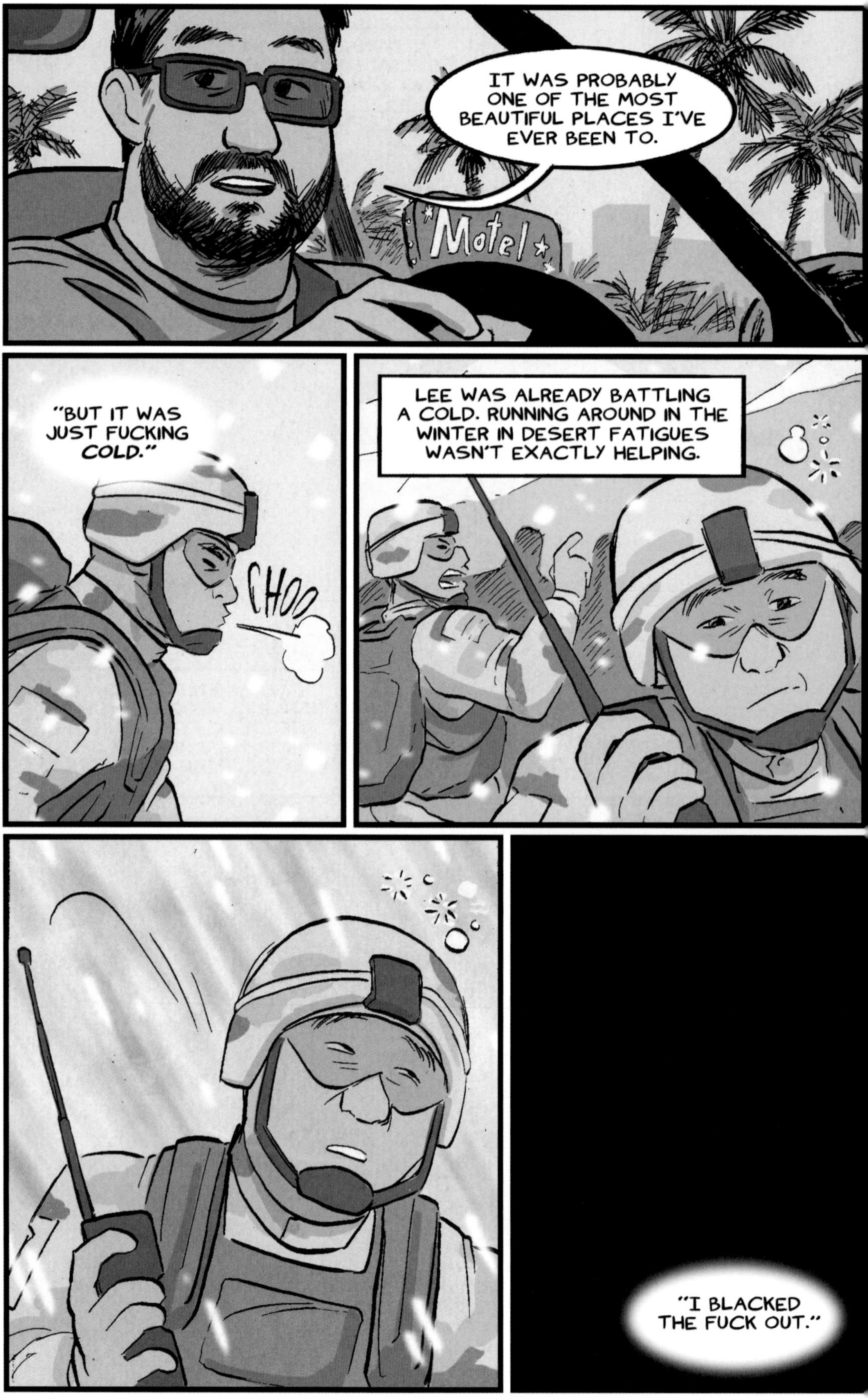

IT WAS PROBABLY ONE OF THE MOST BEAUTIFUL PLACES I'VE EVER BEEN TO.
Motel
"BUT IT WAS JUST FUCKING COLD."
CHOO
LEE WAS ALREADY BATTLING A COLD. RUNNING AROUND IN THE WINTER IN DESERT FATIGUES WASN'T EXACTLY HELPING.
"I BLACKED THE FUCK OUT."

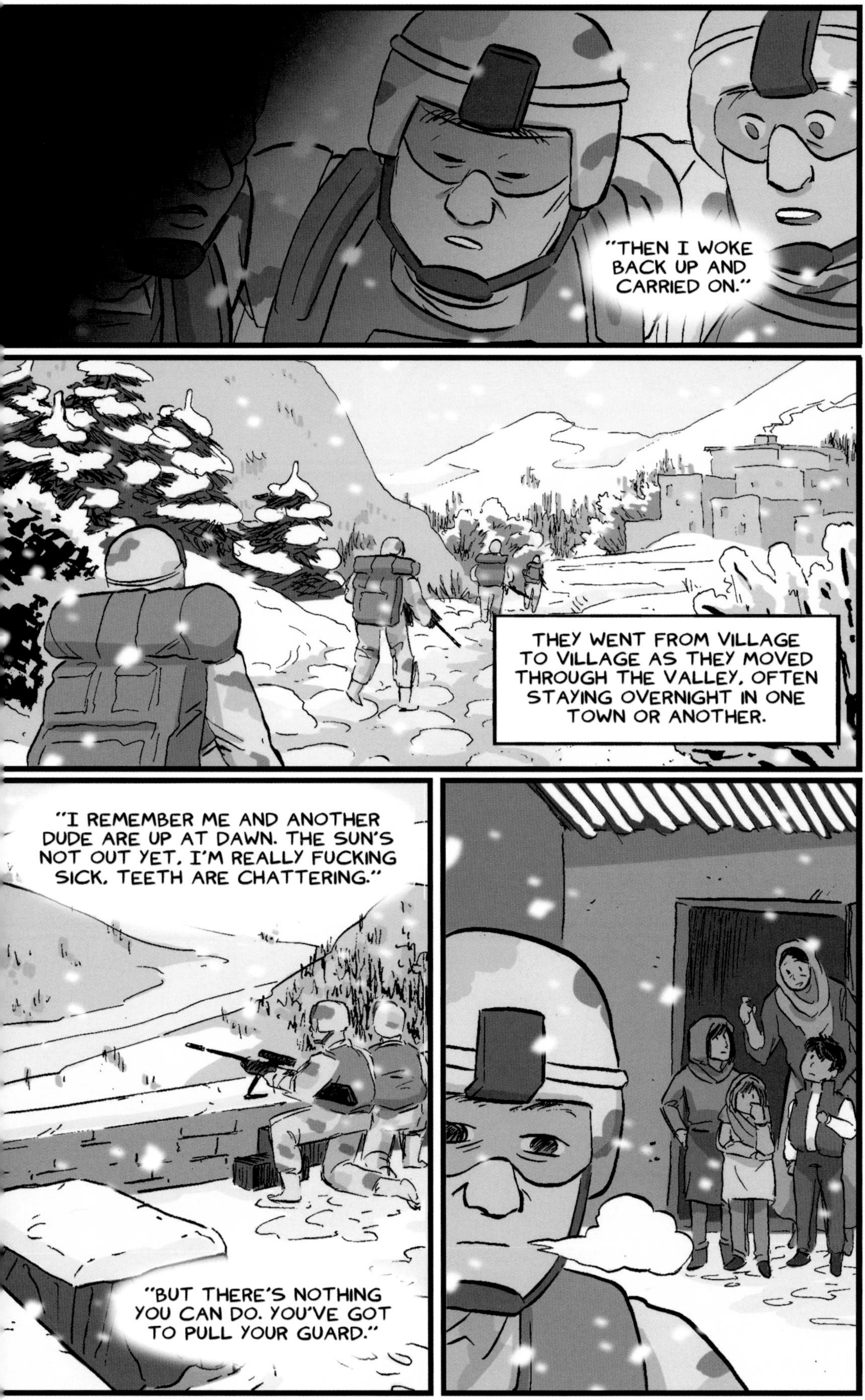
"THEN I WOKE BACK UP AND CARRIED ON."
THEY WENT FROM VILLAGE TO VILLAGE AS THEY MOVED THROUGH THE VALLEY, OFTEN STAYING OVERNIGHT IN ONE TOWN OR ANOTHER.
"I REMEMBER ME AND ANOTHER DUDE ARE UP AT DAWN. THE SUN'S NOT OUT YET, I'M REALLY FUCKING SICK, TEETH ARE CHATTERING."
"BUT THERE'S NOTHING YOU CAN DO. YOU'VE GOT TO PULL YOUR GUARD."

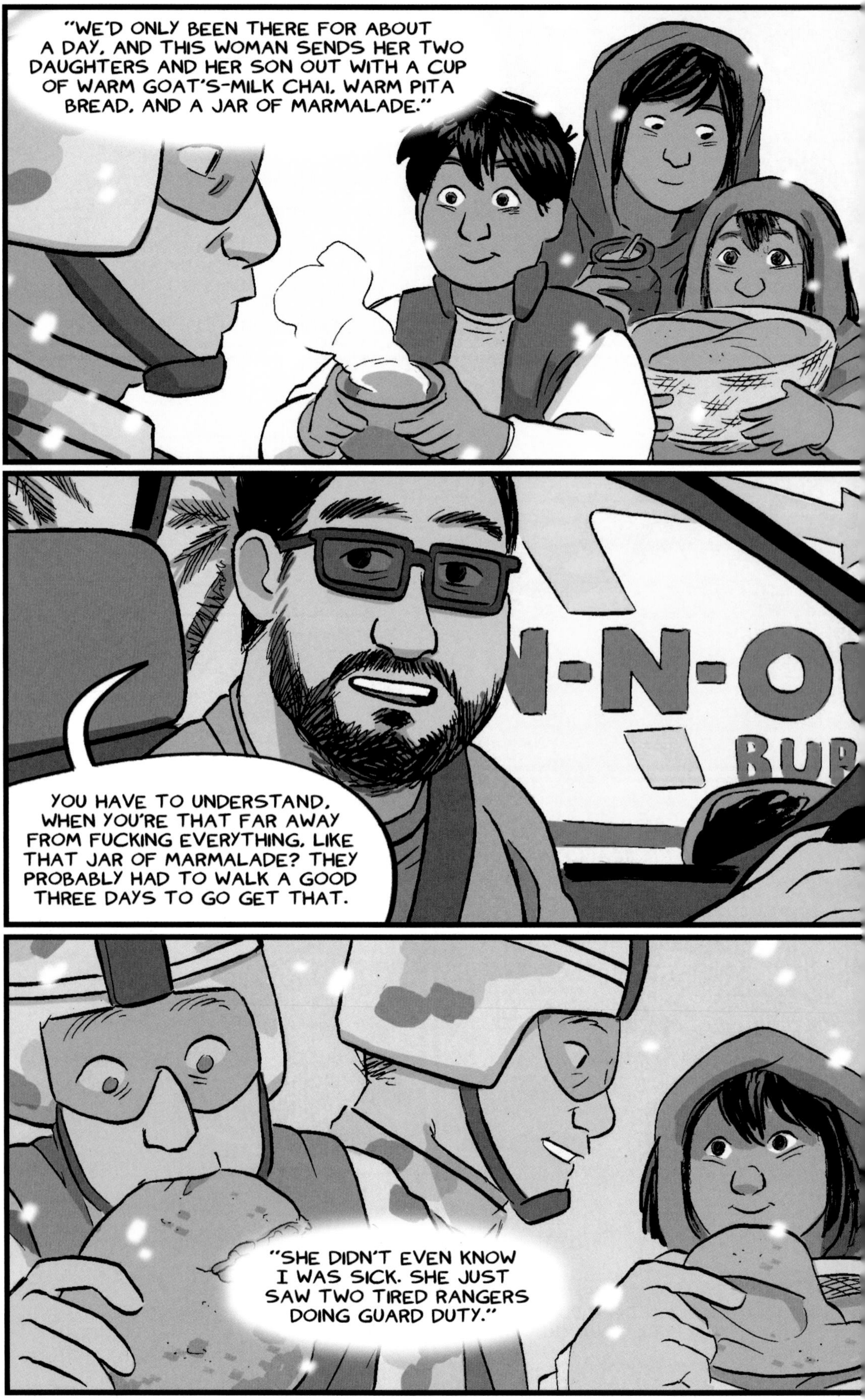
"WE'D ONLY BEEN THERE FOR ABOUT A DAY, AND THIS WOMAN SENDS HER TWO DAUGHTERS AND HER SON OUT WITH A CUP OF WARM GOAT'S-MILK CHAI, WARM PITA BREAD, AND A JAR OF MARMALADE."
YOU HAVE TO UNDERSTAND, WHEN YOU'RE THAT FAR AWAY FROM FUCKING EVERYTHING, LIKE THAT JAR OF MARMALADE? THEY PROBABLY HAD TO WALK A GOOD THREE DAYS TO GO GET THAT.
"SHE DIDN'T EVEN KNOW I WAS SICK. SHE JUST SAW TWO TIRED RANGERS DOING GUARD DUTY."

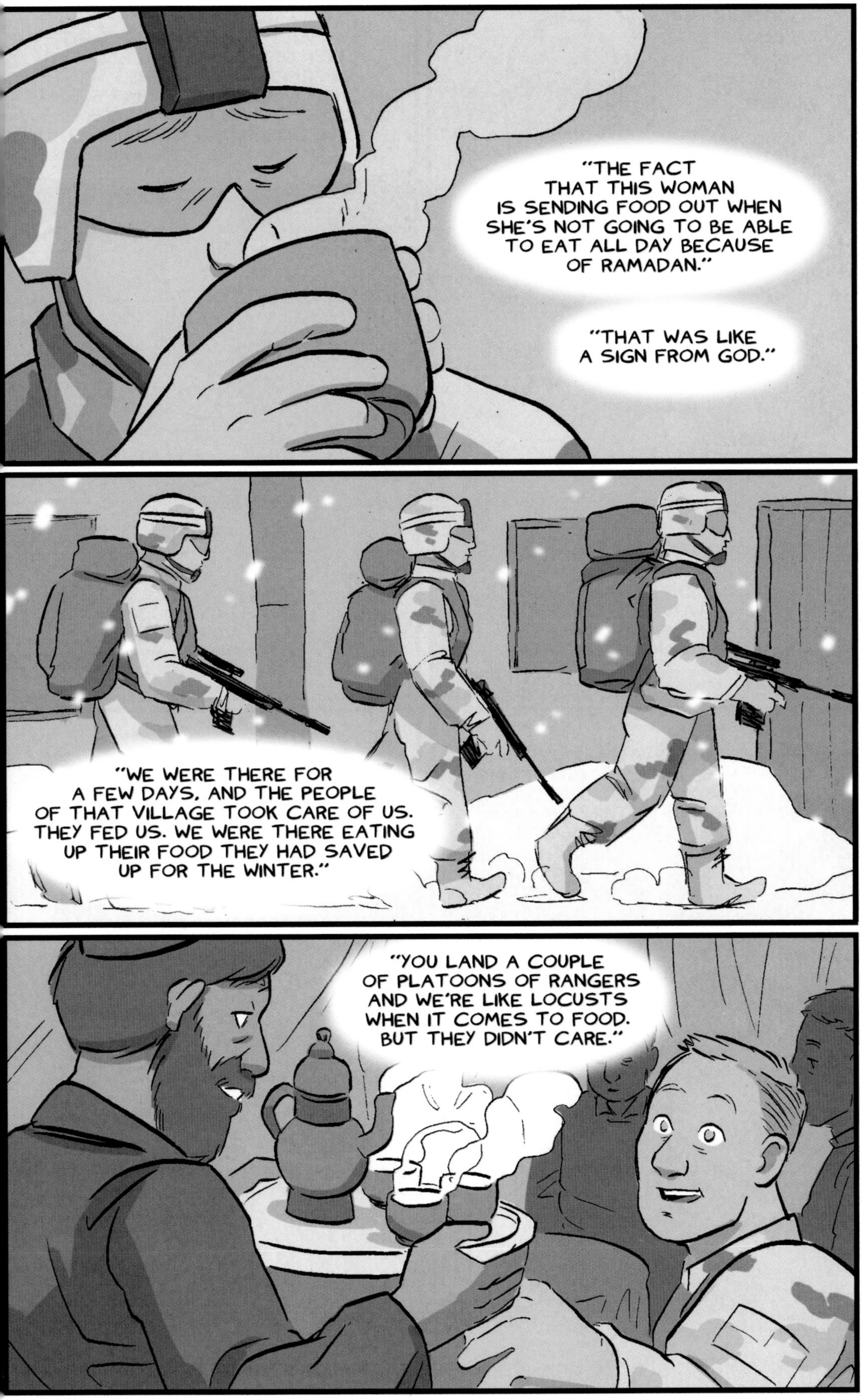
"THE FACT THAT THIS WOMAN IS SENDING FOOD OUT WHEN SHE'S NOT GOING TO BE ABLE TO EAT ALL DAY BECAUSE OF RAMADAN."
"THAT WAS LIKE A SIGN FROM GOD."
"WE WERE THERE FOR A FEW DAYS, AND THE PEOPLE OF THAT VILLAGE TOOK CARE OF US. THEY FED US. WE WERE THERE EATING UP THEIR FOOD THEY HAD SAVED UP FOR THE WINTER."
"YOU LAND A COUPLE OF PLATOONS OF RANGERS AND WE'RE LIKE LOCUSTS WHEN IT COMES TO FOOD. BUT THEY DIDN'T CARE."

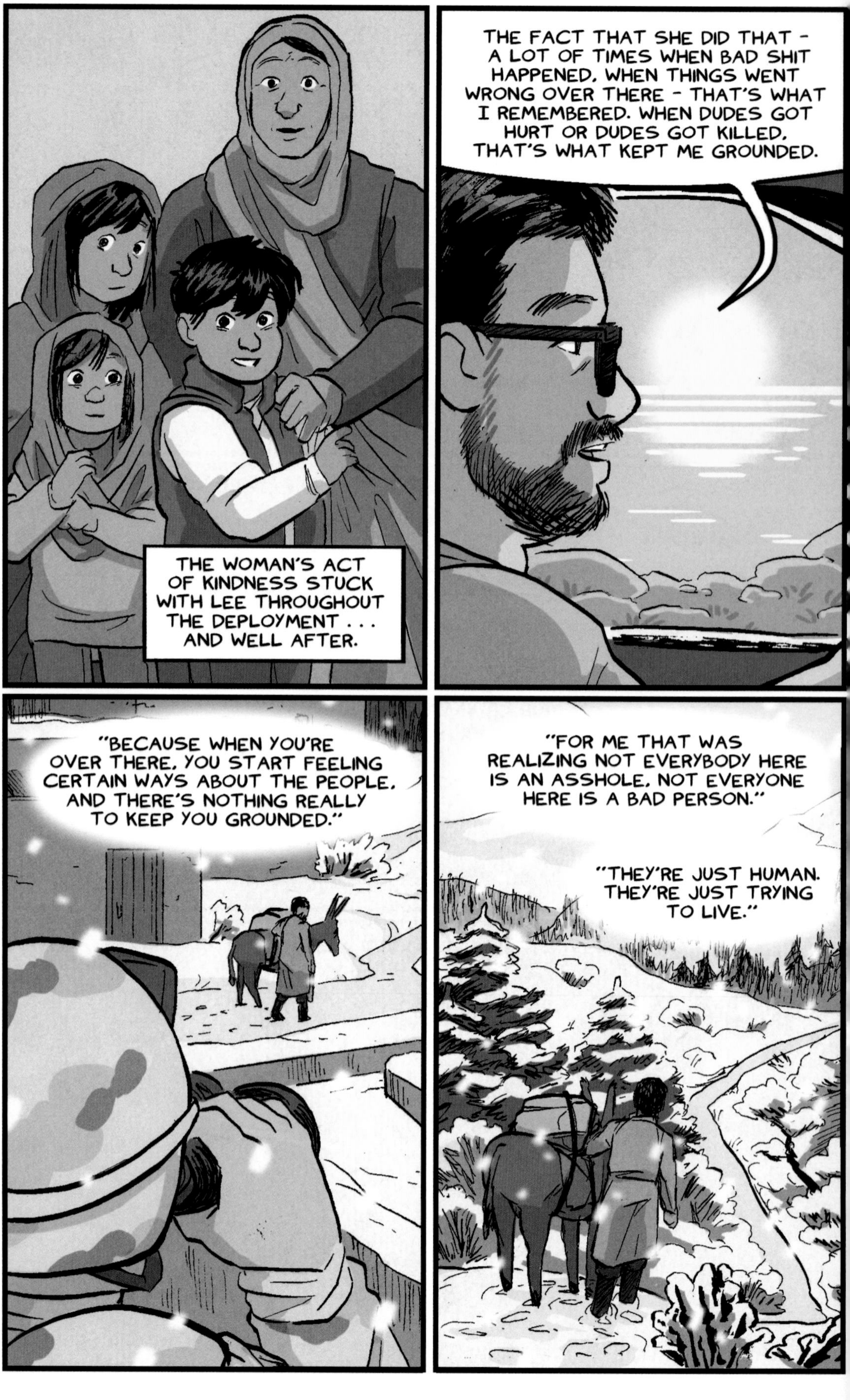
THE WOMAN'S ACT OF KINDNESS STUCK WITH LEE THROUGHOUT THE DEPLOYMENT . . . AND WELL AFTER.
THE FACT THAT SHE DID THAT - A LOT OF TIMES WHEN BAD SHIT HAPPENED, WHEN THINGS WENT WRONG OVER THERE - THAT'S WHAT I REMEMBERED. WHEN DUDES GOT HURT OR DUDES GOT KILLED, THAT'S WHAT KEPT ME GROUNDED.
"BECAUSE WHEN YOU'RE OVER THERE, YOU START FEELING CERTAIN WAYS ABOUT THE PEOPLE, AND THERE'S NOTHING REALLY TO KEEP YOU GROUNDED."
"FOR ME THAT WAS REALIZING NOT EVERYBODY HERE IS AN ASSHOLE, NOT EVERYONE HERE IS A BAD PERSON."
"THEY'RE JUST HUMAN. THEY'RE JUST TRYING TO LIVE."

4 "HOATS' WAR"

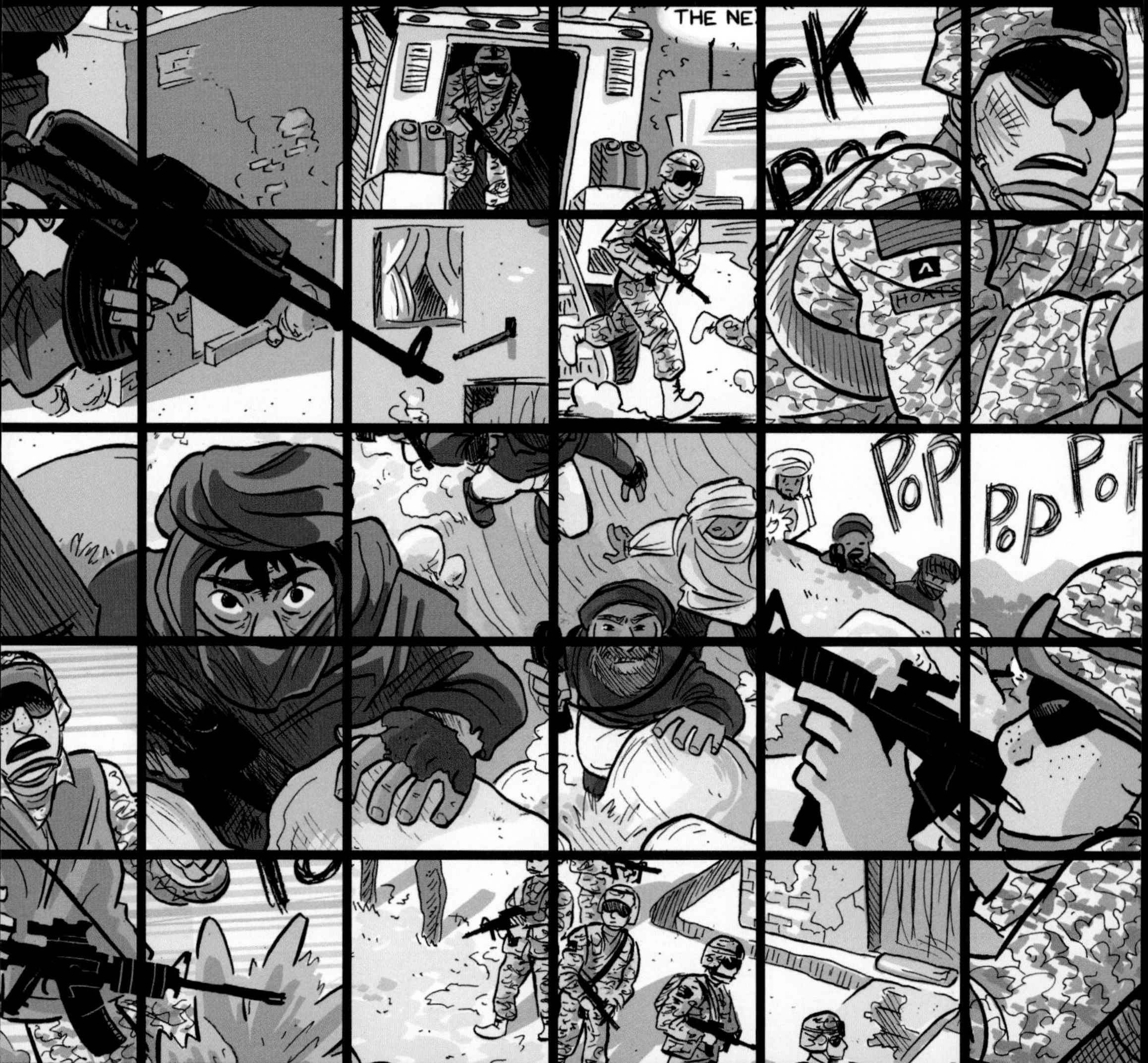

THE NE
CK
HOATS
POP
POP POP

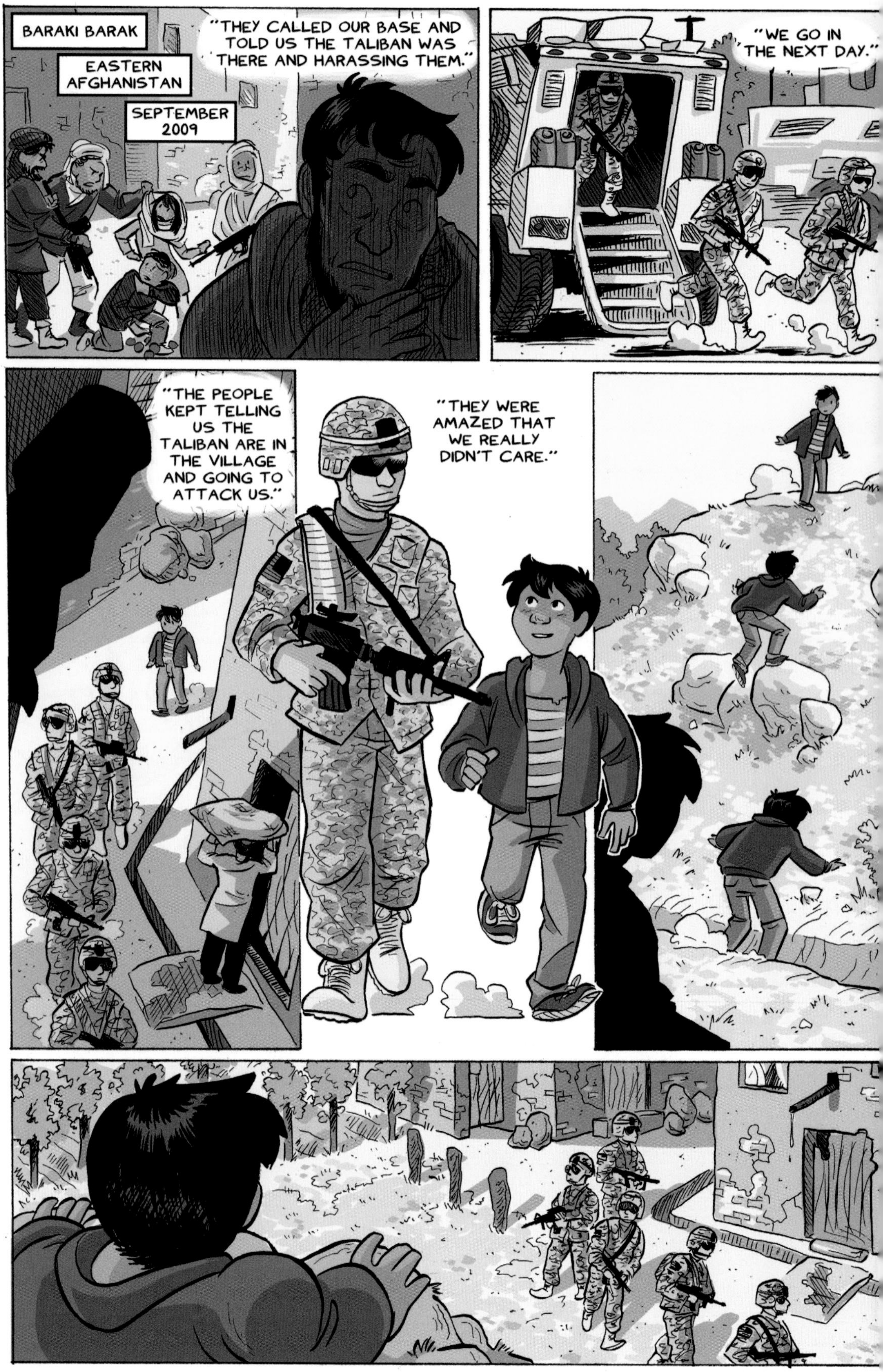
BARAKI BARAK
EASTERN AFGHANISTAN
SEPTEMBER 2009
"THEY CALLED OUR BASE AND TOLD US THE TALIBAN WAS THERE AND HARASSING THEM."
"WE GO IN THE NEXT DAY."
"THE PEOPLE KEPT TELLING US THE TALIBAN ARE IN THE VILLAGE AND GOING TO ATTACK US."
"THEY WERE AMAZED THAT WE REALLY DIDN'T CARE."

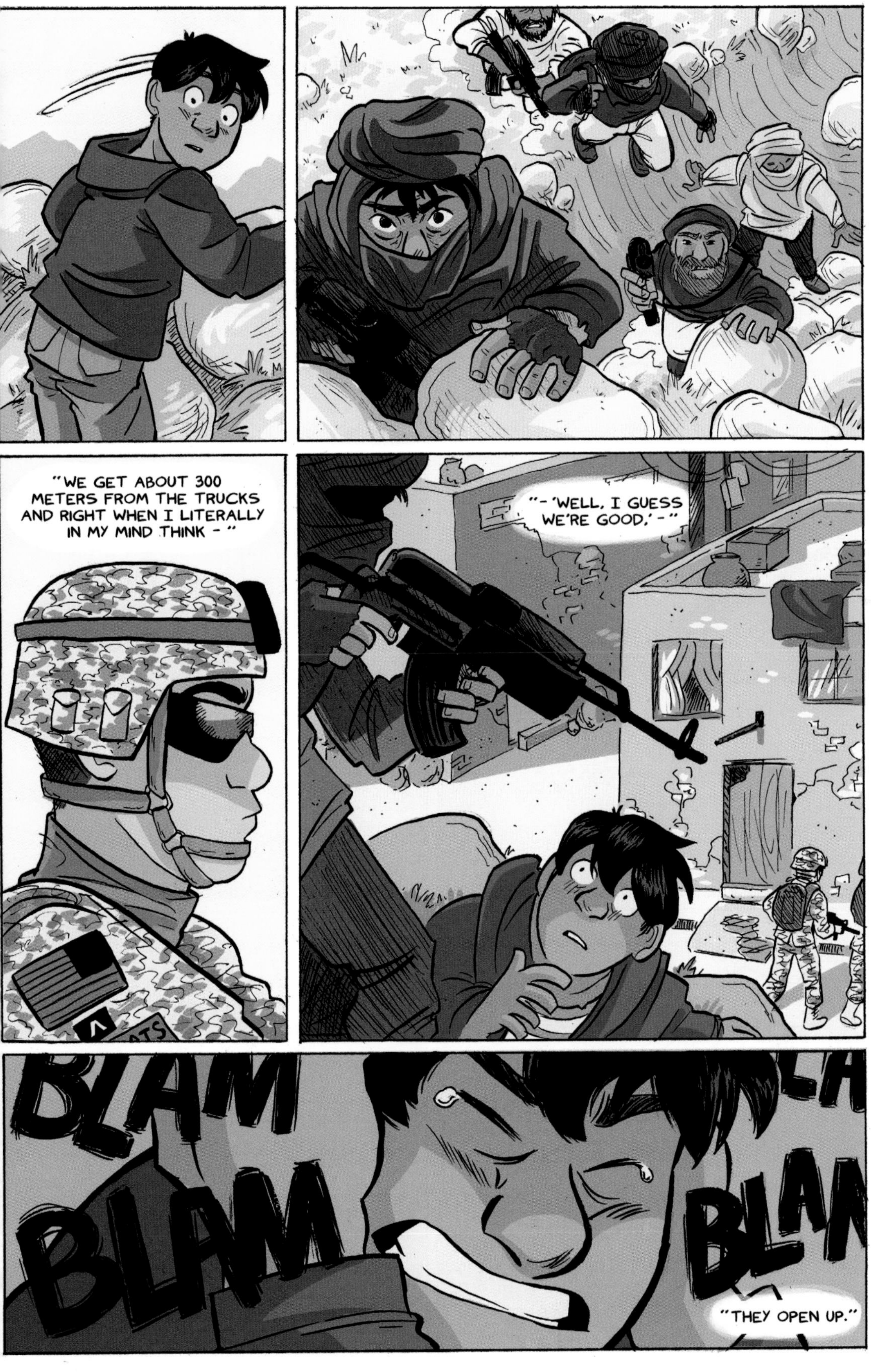
"WE GET ABOUT 300 METERS FROM THE TRUCKS AND RIGHT WHEN I LITERALLY IN MY MIND THINK - "
"- 'WELL, I GUESS WE'RE GOOD,' - "
BLAM
BLAM
BLAM
"THEY OPEN UP."

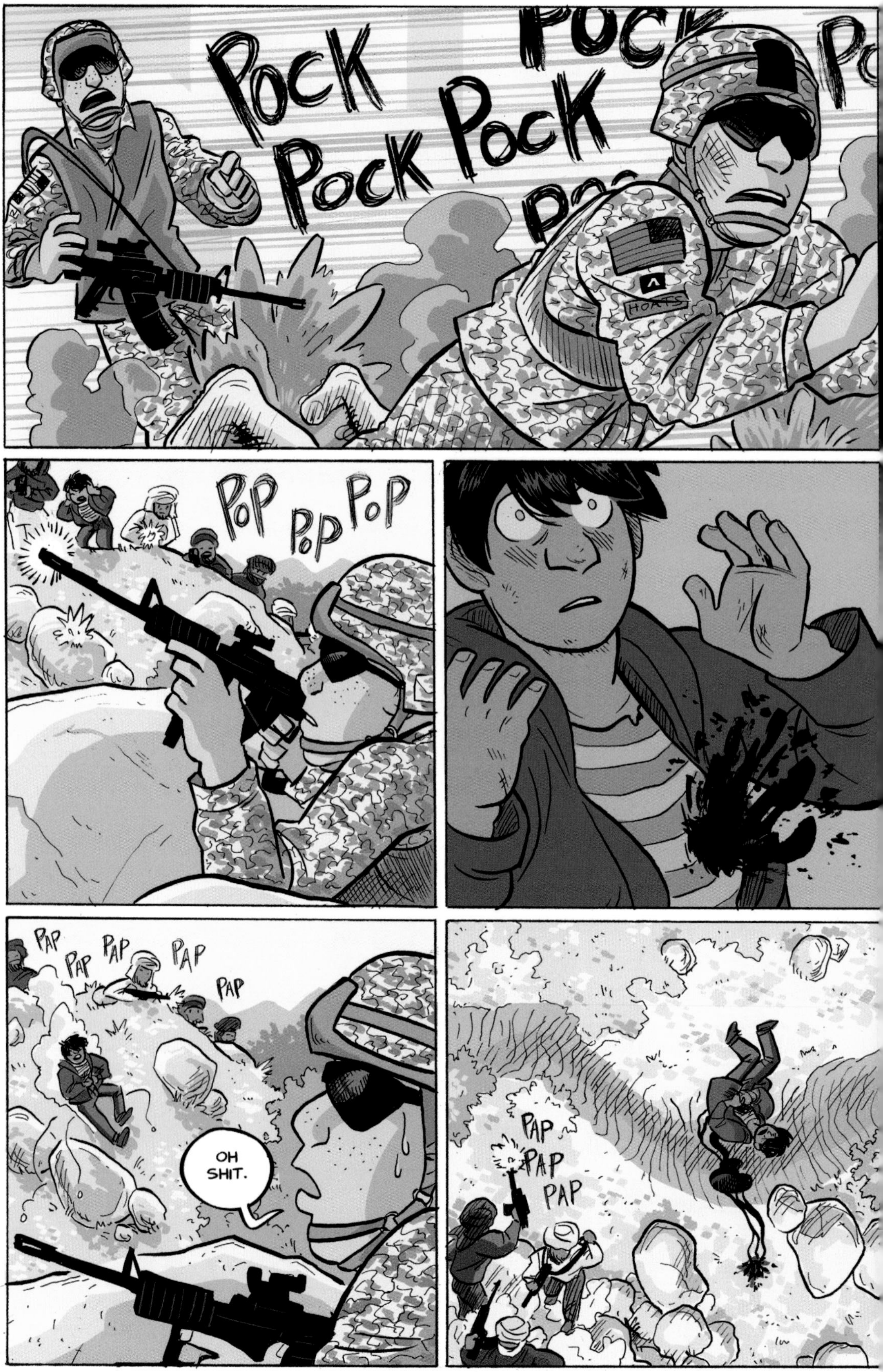
POCK
POCK
POCK POCK POCK
HOATS
POP POP POP
PAP PAP PAP PAP
PAP
OH SHIT.
PAP PAP PAP

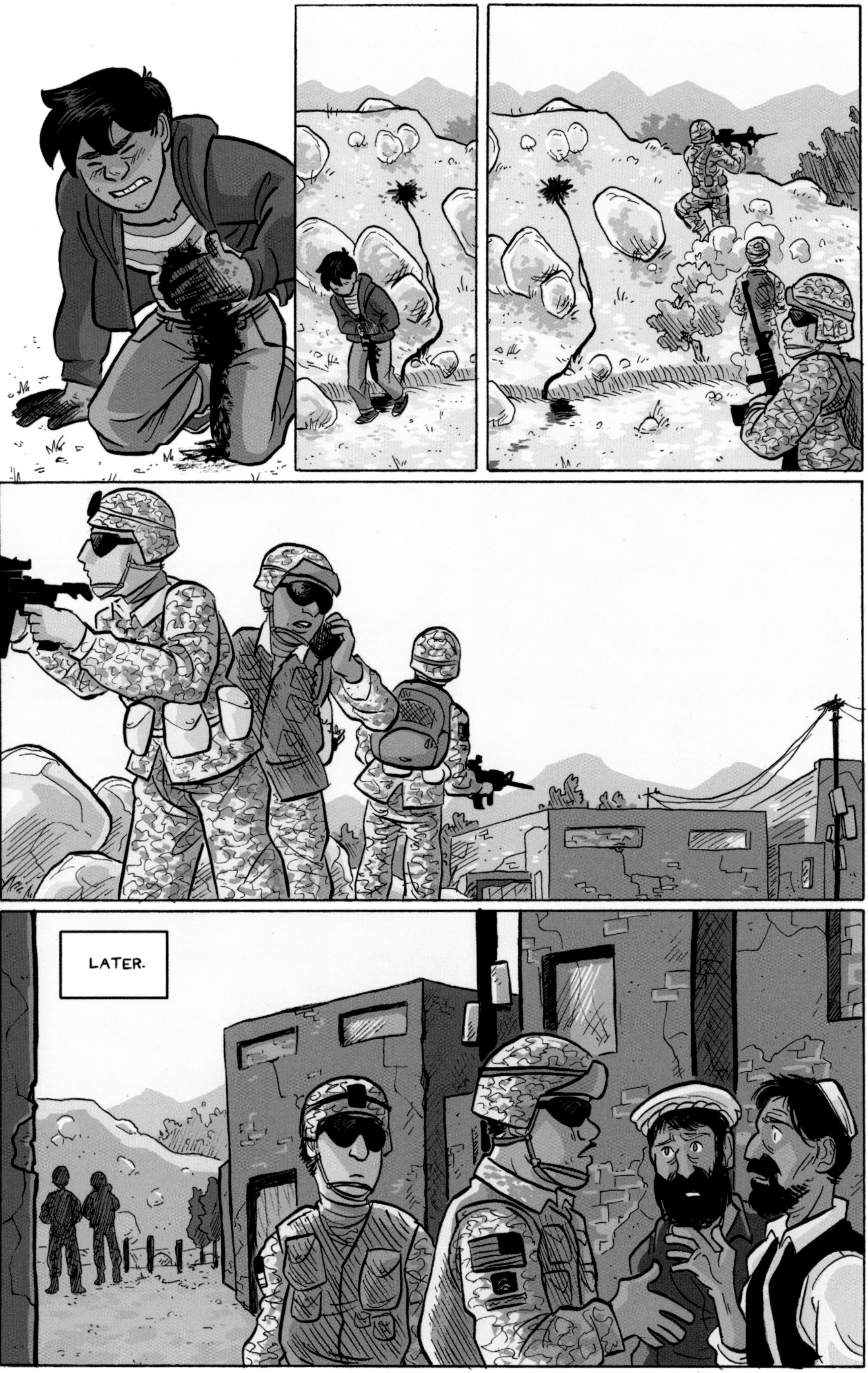
LATER.

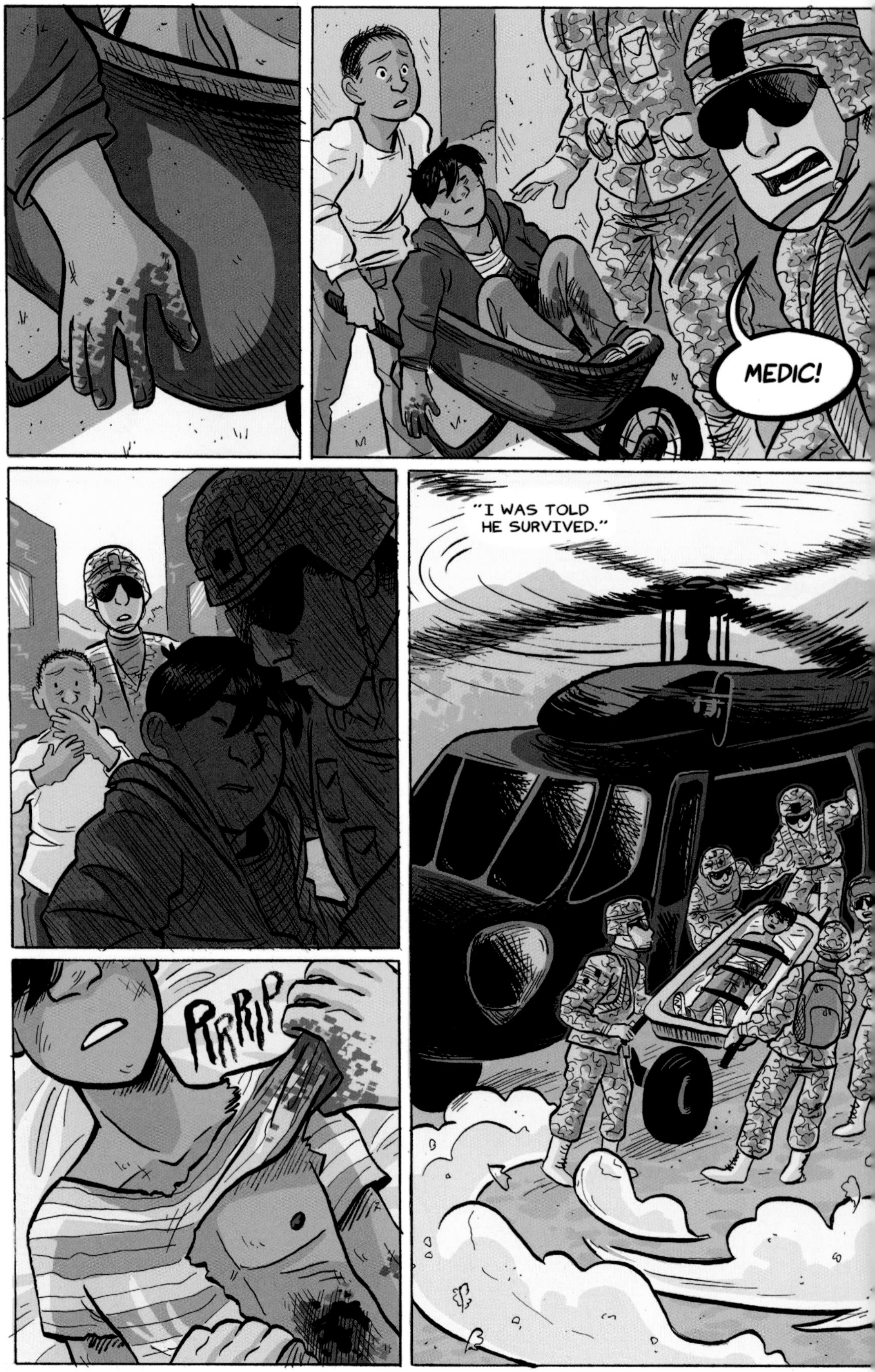
MEDIC!
"I WAS TOLD HE SURVIVED."
RRRIP

5 "OPERATION DONKEY HAUL"

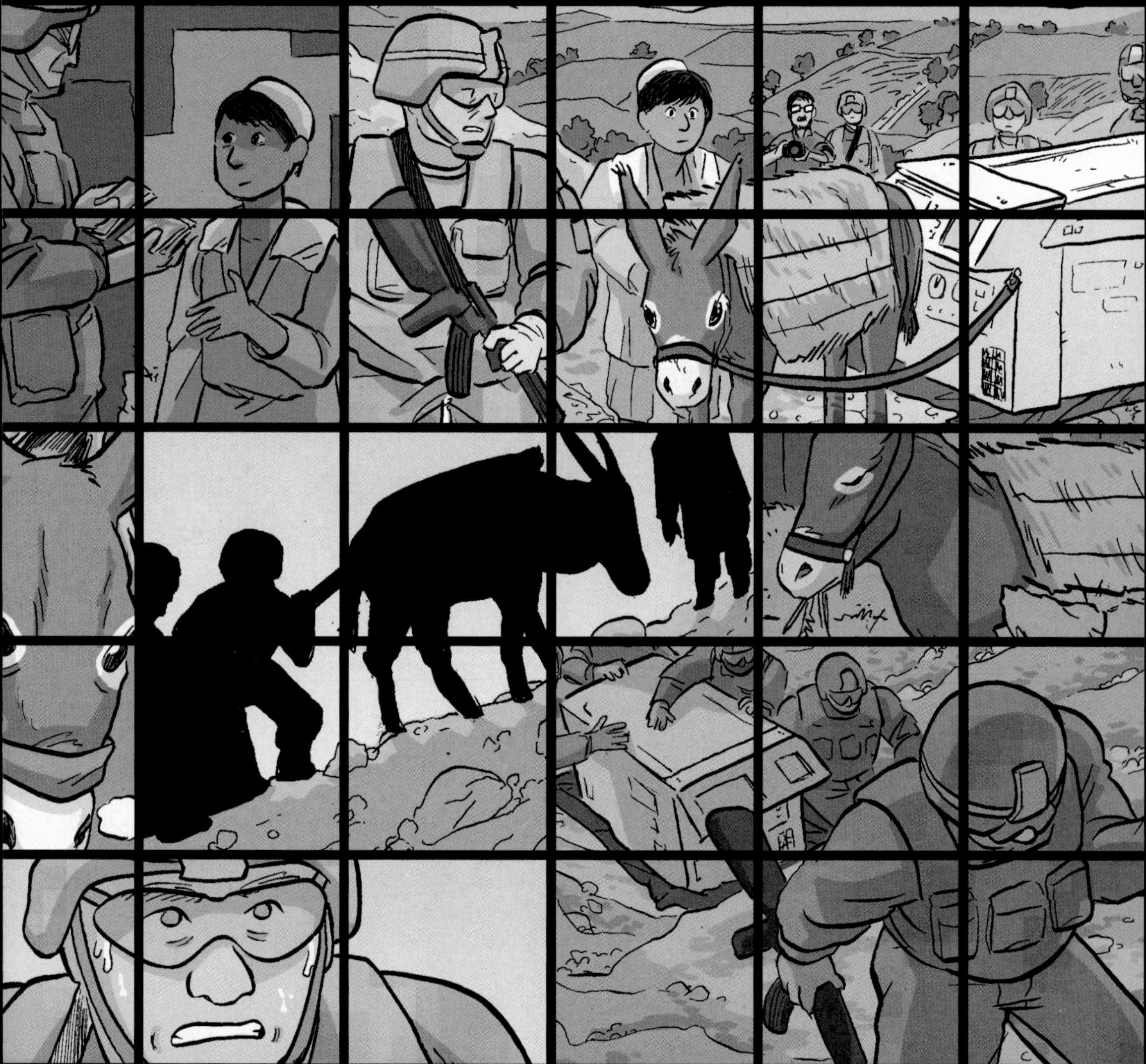

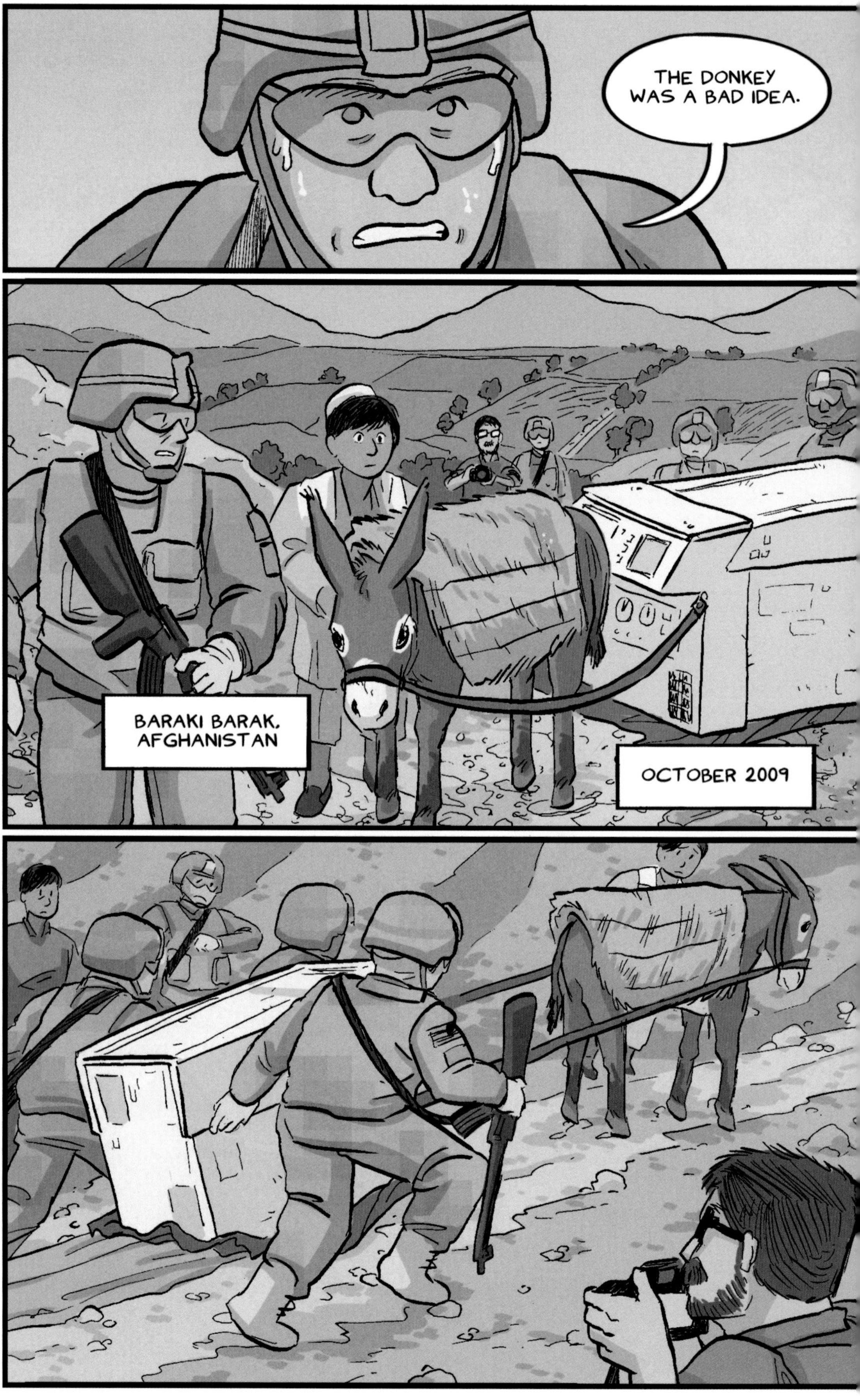
THE DONKEY WAS A BAD IDEA.
BARAKI BARAK, AFGHANISTAN
OCTOBER 2009

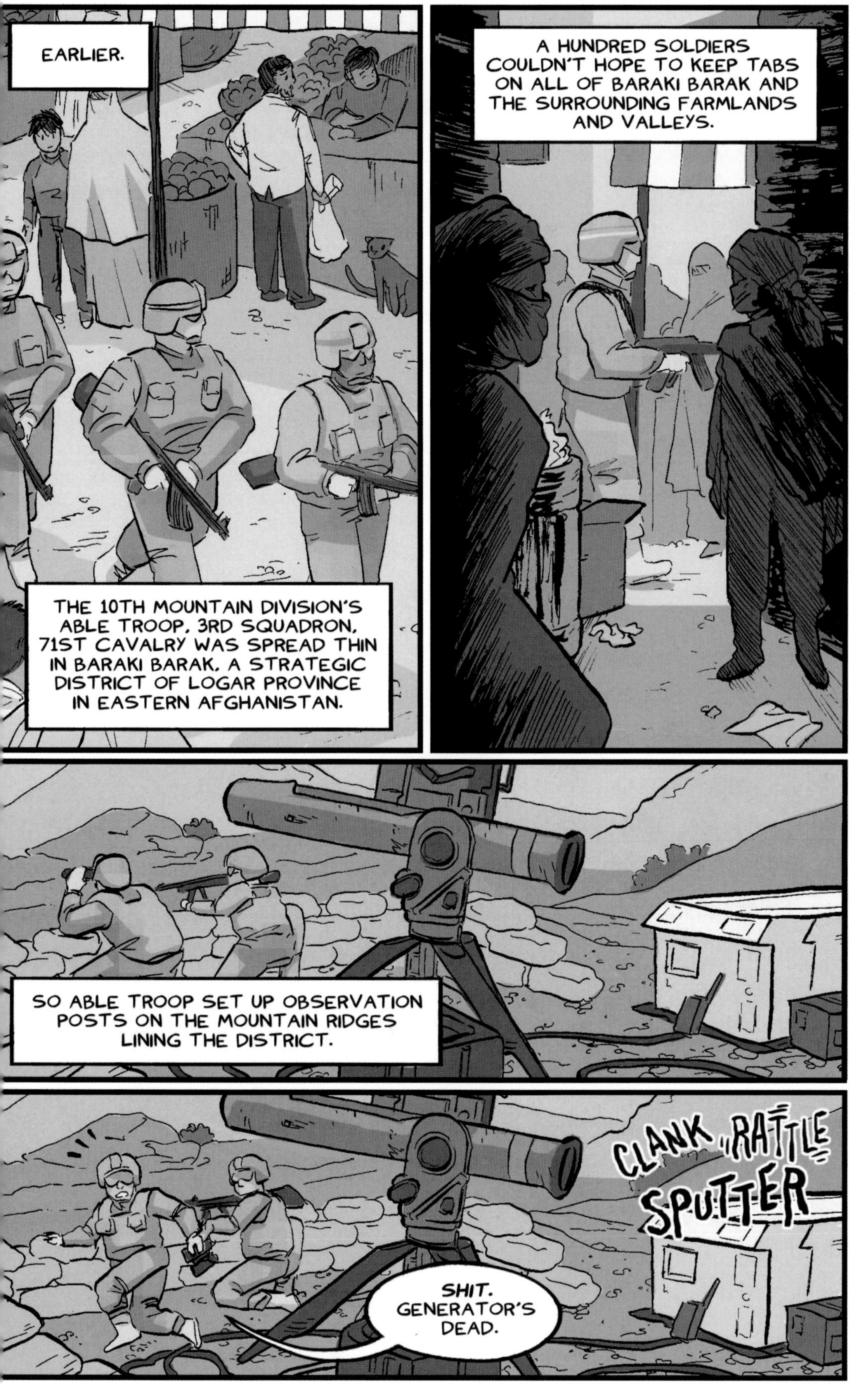
EARLIER.
THE 10TH MOUNTAIN DIVISION'S ABLE TROOP, 3RD SQUADRON, 71ST CAVALRY WAS SPREAD THIN IN BARAKI BARAK, A STRATEGIC DISTRICT OF LOGAR PROVINCE IN EASTERN AFGHANISTAN.
A HUNDRED SOLDIERS COULDN'T HOPE TO KEEP TABS ON ALL OF BARAKI BARAK AND THE SURROUNDING FARMLANDS AND VALLEYS.
SO ABLE TROOP SET UP OBSERVATION POSTS ON THE MOUNTAIN RIDGES LINING THE DISTRICT.
CLANK RATTLE
SPUTTER
SHIT. GENERATOR'S DEAD.

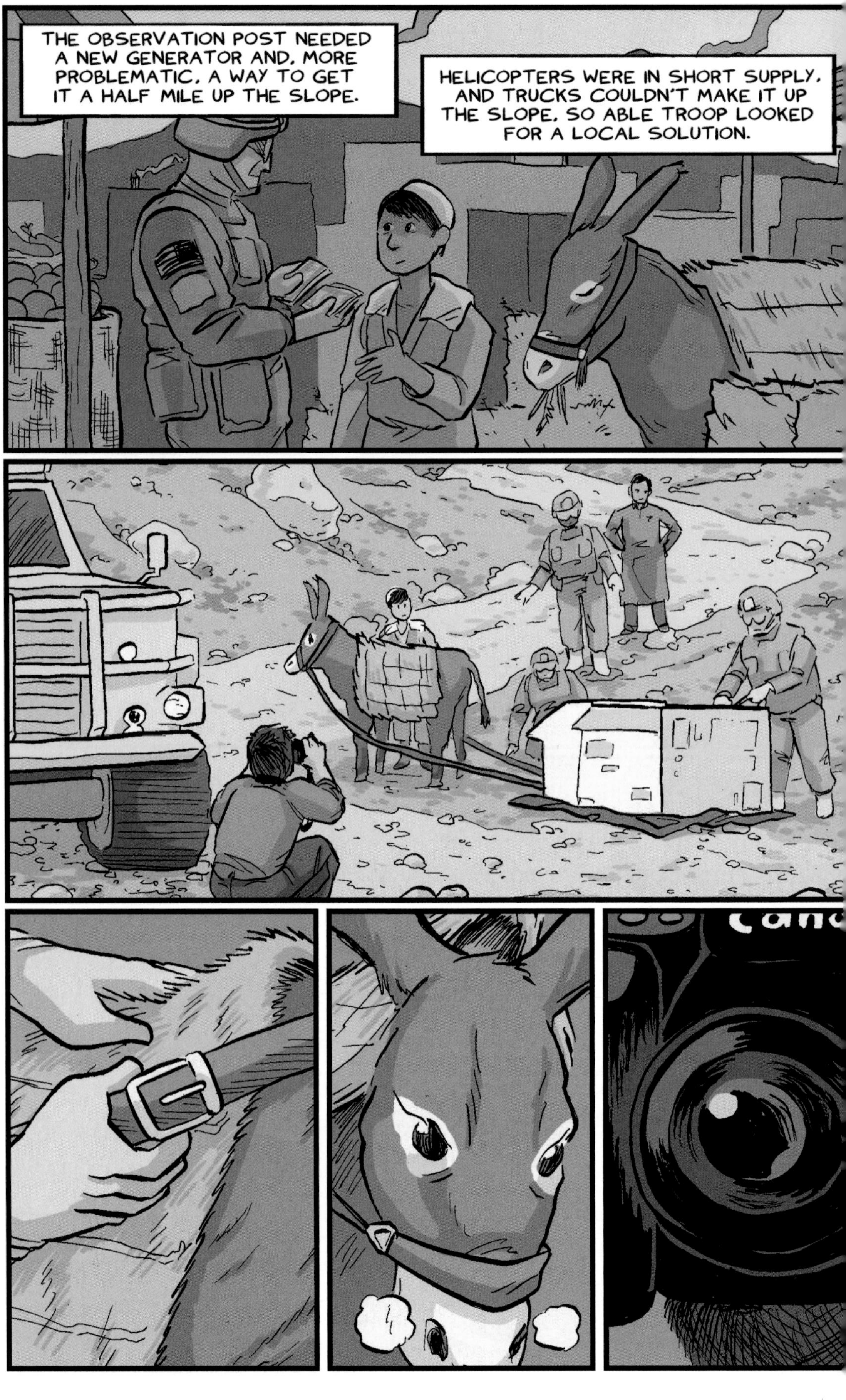
THE OBSERVATION POST NEEDED A NEW GENERATOR AND, MORE PROBLEMATIC, A WAY TO GET IT A HALF MILE UP THE SLOPE.
HELICOPTERS WERE IN SHORT SUPPLY, AND TRUCKS COULDN'T MAKE IT UP THE SLOPE, SO ABLE TROOP LOOKED FOR A LOCAL SOLUTION.

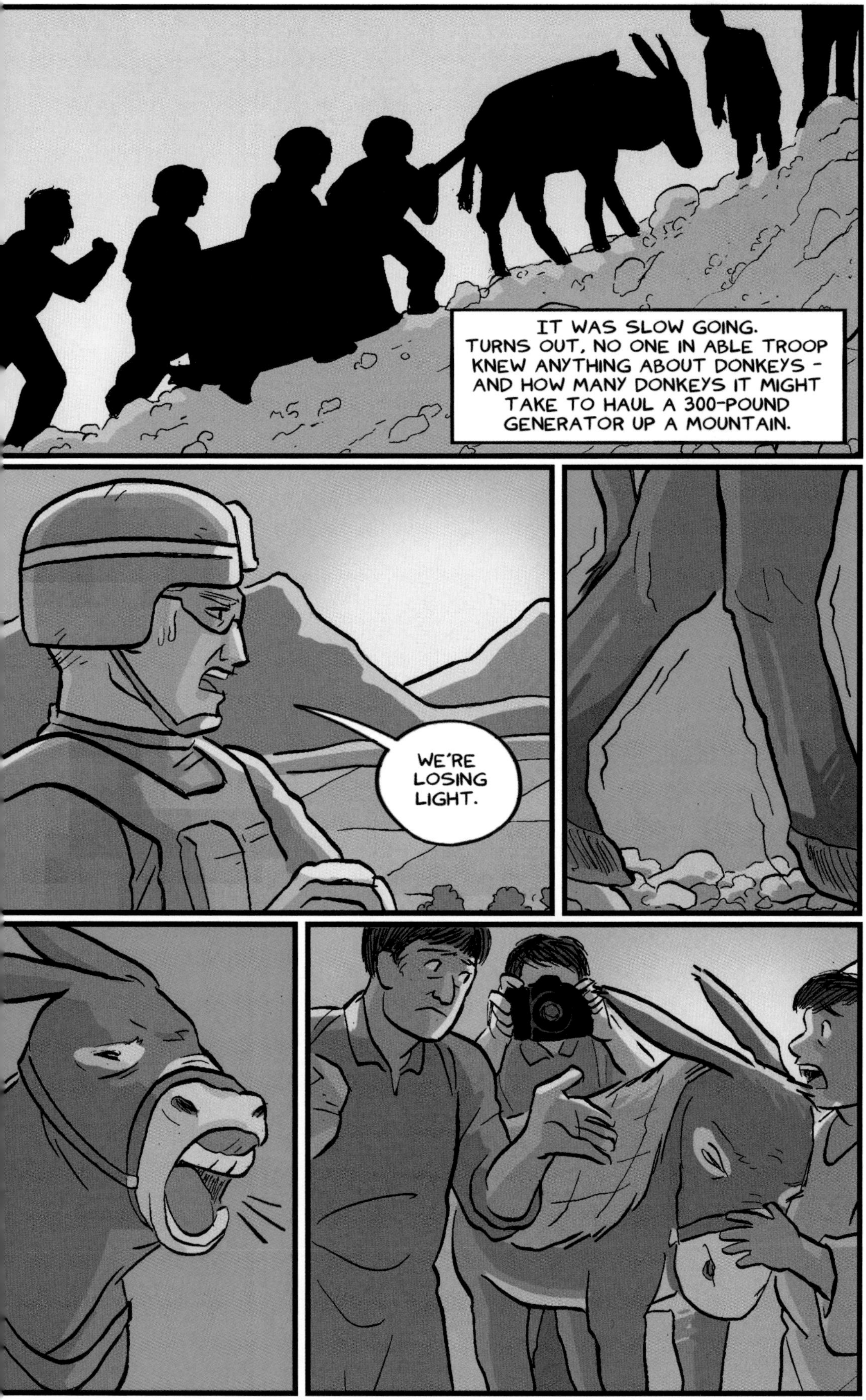
IT WAS SLOW GOING.
TURNS OUT, NO ONE IN ABLE TROOP KNEW ANYTHING ABOUT DONKEYS - AND HOW MANY DONKEYS IT MIGHT TAKE TO HAUL A 300-POUND GENERATOR UP A MOUNTAIN.
WE'RE LOSING LIGHT.

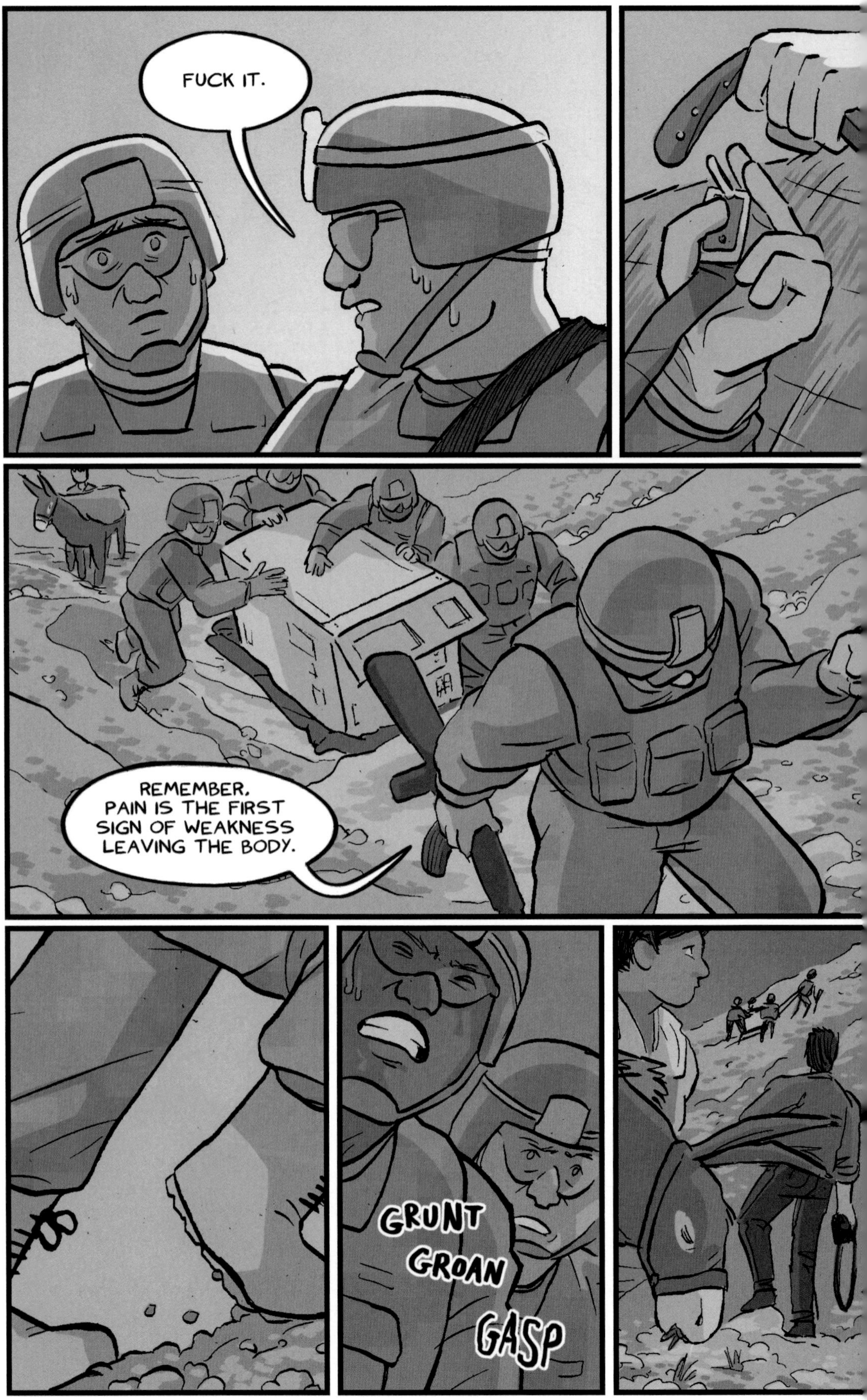
FUCK IT.
REMEMBER, PAIN IS THE FIRST SIGN OF WEAKNESS LEAVING THE BODY.
GRUNT
GROAN
GASP

6 "I CAN NEVER GO HOME"

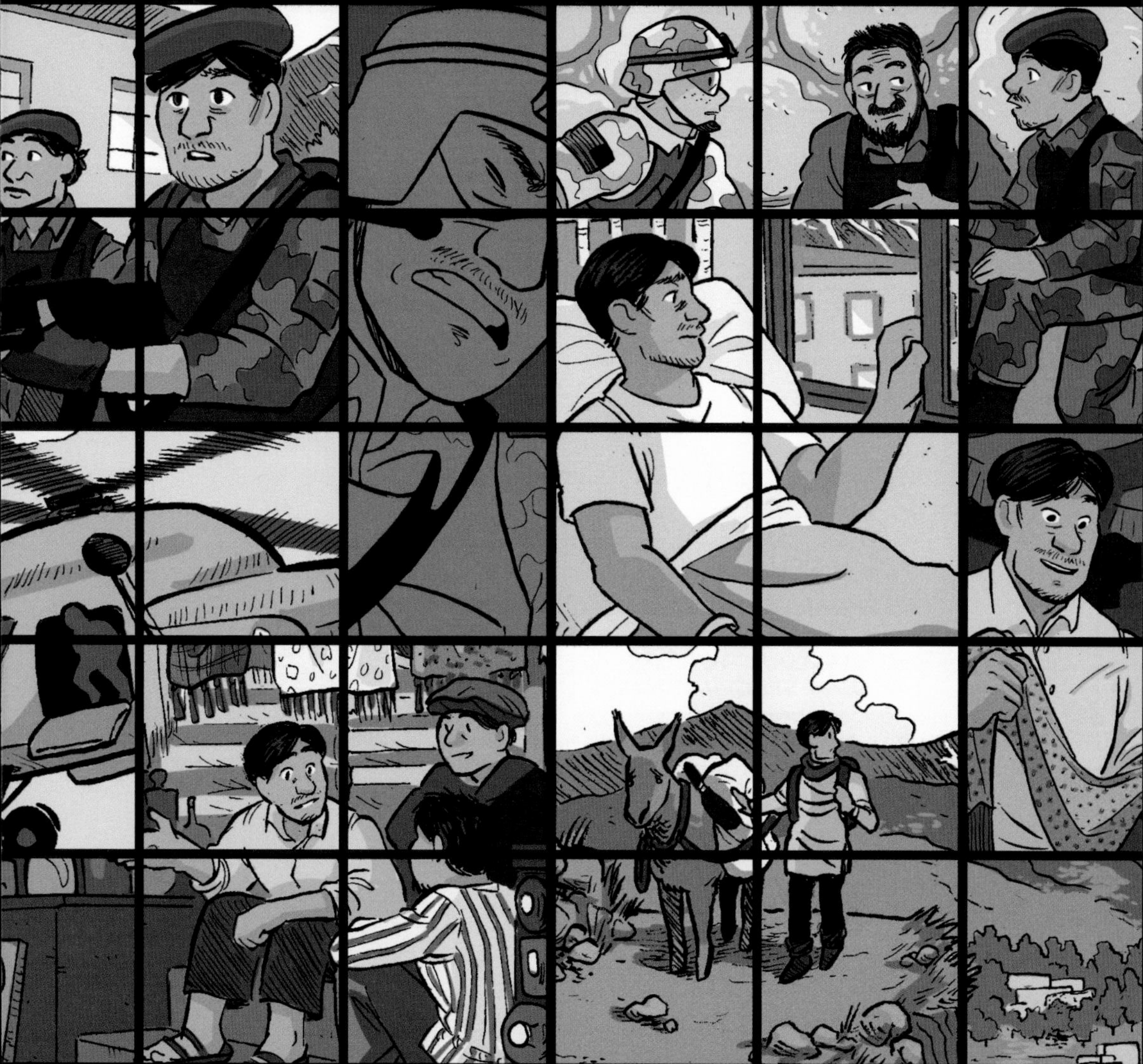

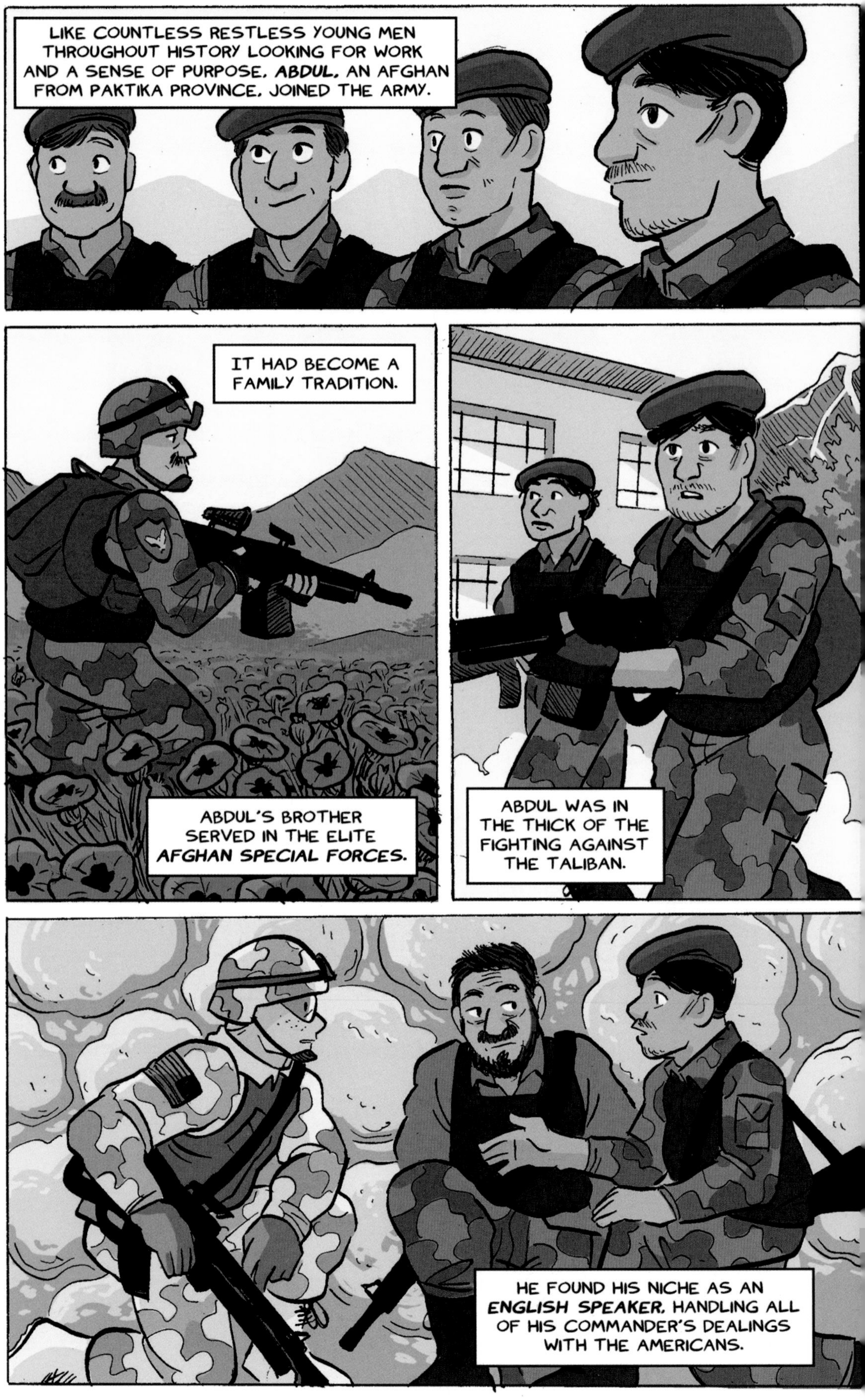
LIKE COUNTLESS RESTLESS YOUNG MEN THROUGHOUT HISTORY LOOKING FOR WORK AND A SENSE OF PURPOSE, ABDUL, AN AFGHAN FROM PAKTIKA PROVINCE, JOINED THE ARMY.
IT HAD BECOME A FAMILY TRADITION.
ABDUL'S BROTHER SERVED IN THE ELITE AFGHAN SPECIAL FORCES.
ABDUL WAS IN THE THICK OF THE FIGHTING AGAINST THE TALIBAN.
HE FOUND HIS NICHE AS AN ENGLISH SPEAKER, HANDLING ALL OF HIS COMMANDER'S DEALINGS WITH THE AMERICANS.

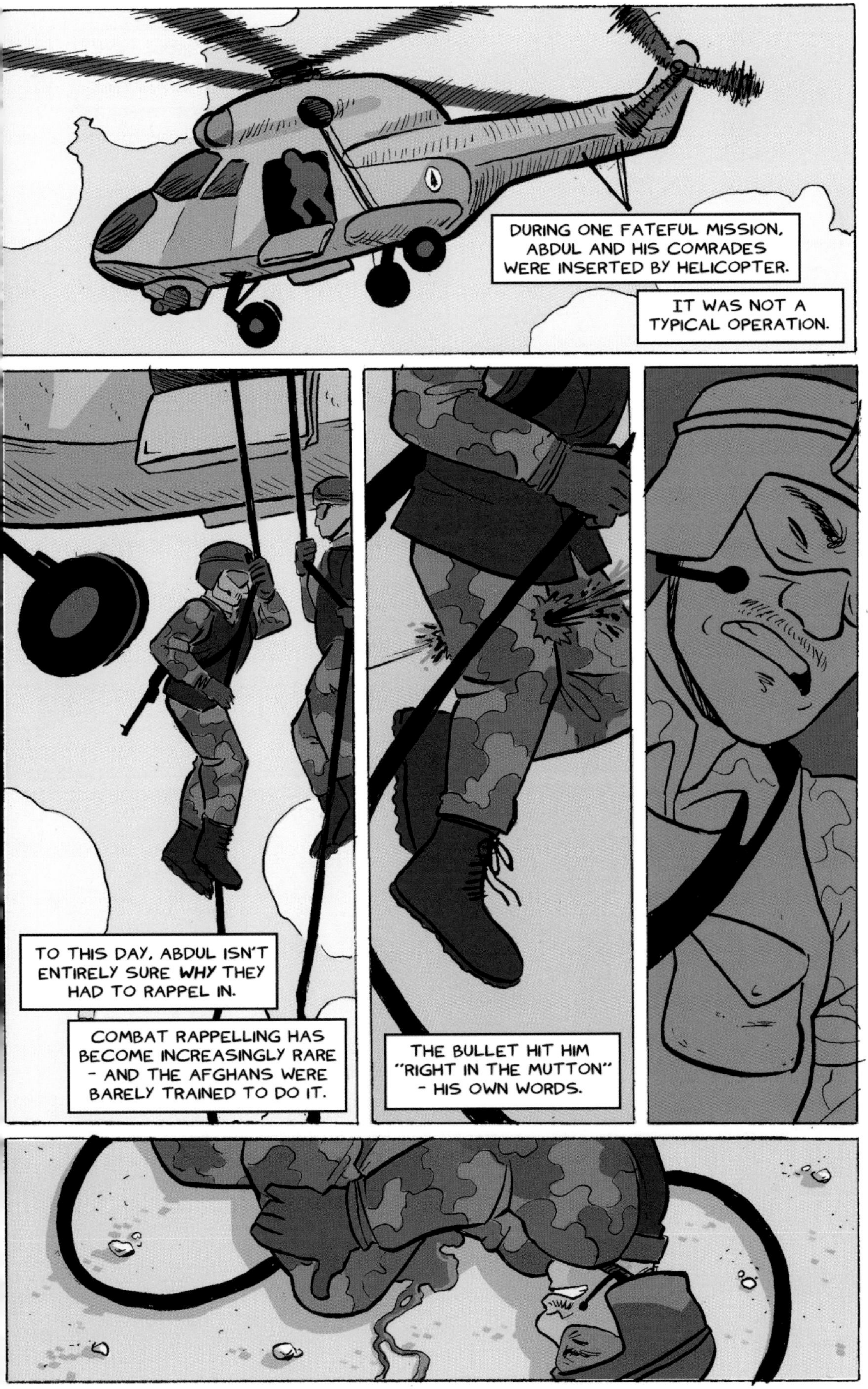
DURING ONE FATEFUL MISSION, ABDUL AND HIS COMRADES WERE INSERTED BY HELICOPTER.
IT WAS NOT A TYPICAL OPERATION.
TO THIS DAY, ABDUL ISN'T ENTIRELY SURE **WHY** THEY HAD TO RAPPEL IN.
COMBAT RAPPELLING HAS BECOME INCREASINGLY RARE - AND THE AFGHANS WERE BARELY TRAINED TO DO IT.
THE BULLET HIT HIM "RIGHT IN THE MUTTON" - HIS OWN WORDS.

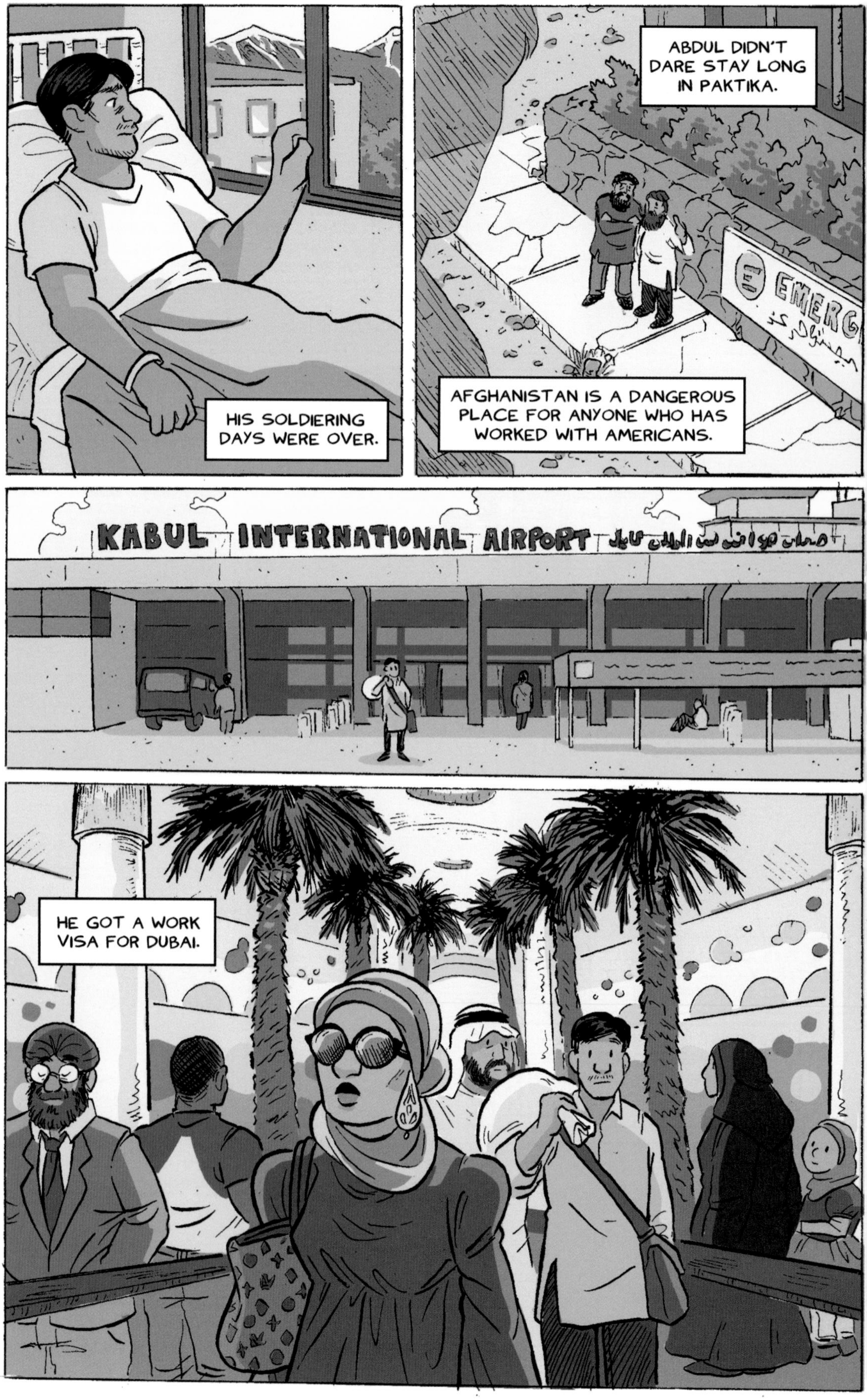
HIS SOLDIERING DAYS WERE OVER.
ABDUL DIDN'T DARE STAY LONG IN PAKTIKA.
AFGHANISTAN IS A DANGEROUS PLACE FOR ANYONE WHO HAS WORKED WITH AMERICANS.
KABUL INTERNATIONAL AIRPORT
HE GOT A WORK VISA FOR DUBAI.

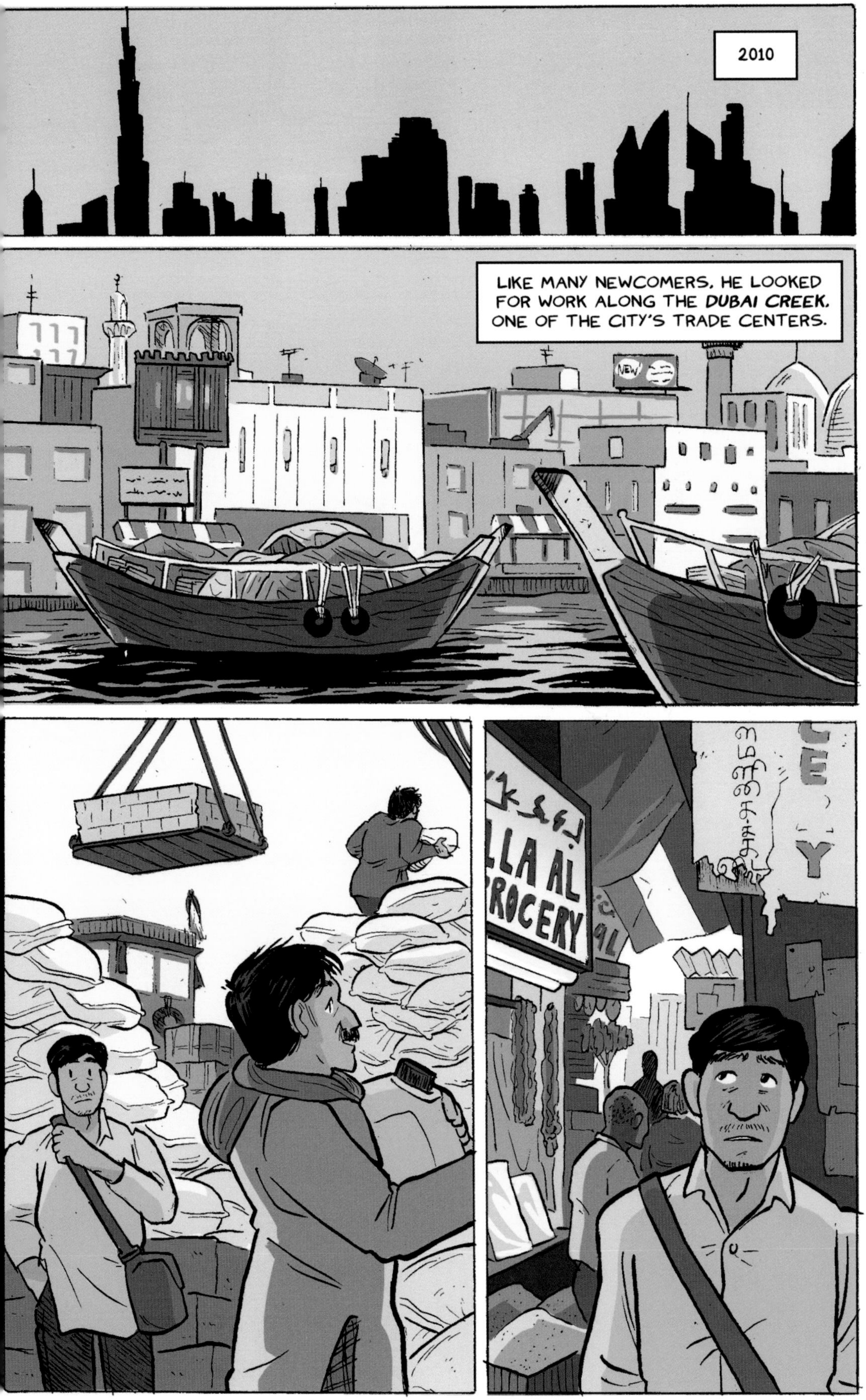
2010
LIKE MANY NEWCOMERS, HE LOOKED FOR WORK ALONG THE *DUBAI CREEK,* ONE OF THE CITY'S TRADE CENTERS.
NEW!

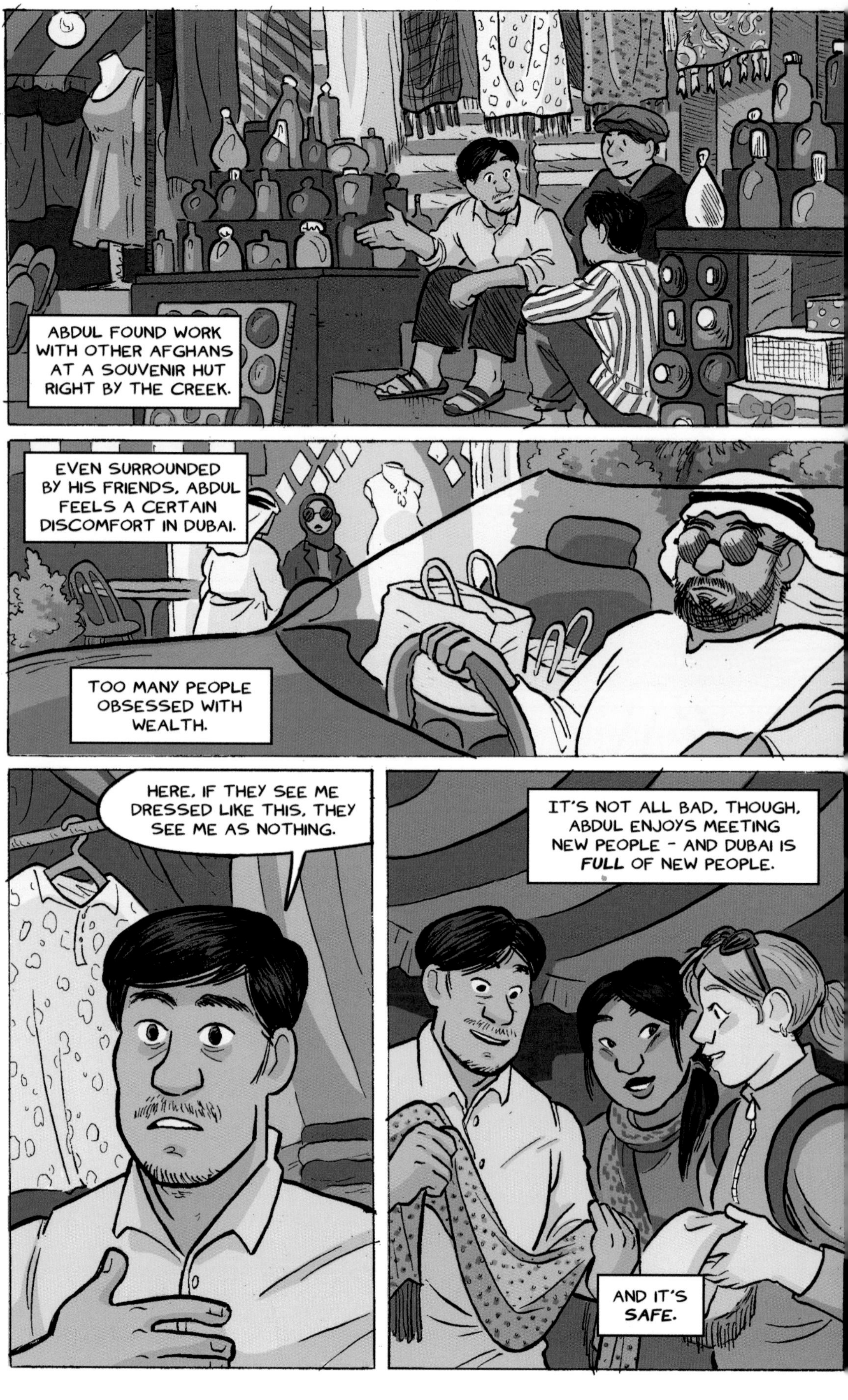
ABDUL FOUND WORK WITH OTHER AFGHANS AT A SOUVENIR HUT RIGHT BY THE CREEK.
EVEN SURROUNDED BY HIS FRIENDS, ABDUL FEELS A CERTAIN DISCOMFORT IN DUBAI.
TOO MANY PEOPLE OBSESSED WITH WEALTH.
HERE, IF THEY SEE ME DRESSED LIKE THIS, THEY SEE ME AS NOTHING.
IT'S NOT ALL BAD, THOUGH. ABDUL ENJOYS MEETING NEW PEOPLE - AND DUBAI IS *FULL* OF NEW PEOPLE.
AND IT'S SAFE.

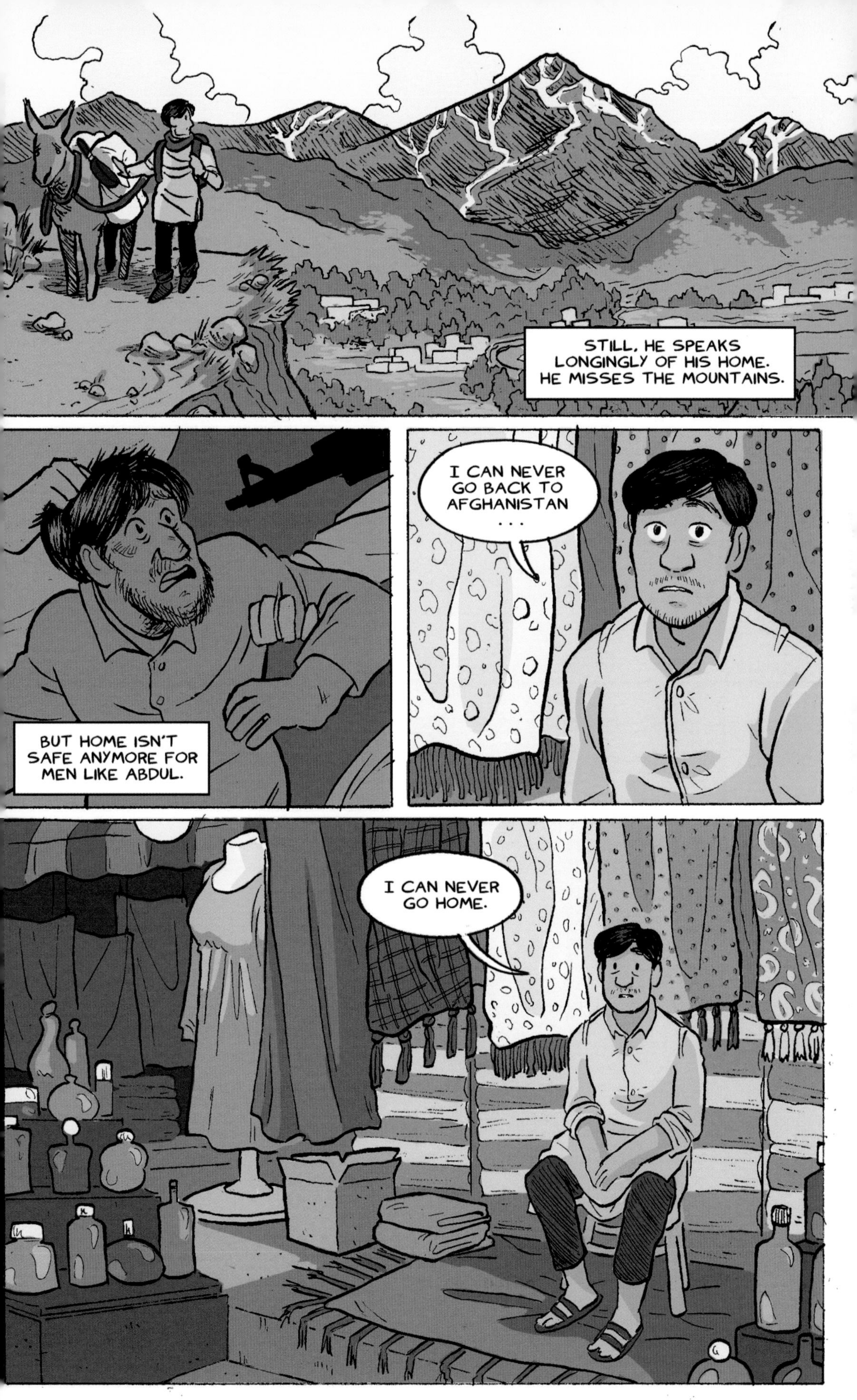
STILL, HE SPEAKS LONGINGLY OF HIS HOME. HE MISSES THE MOUNTAINS.
BUT HOME ISN'T SAFE ANYMORE FOR MEN LIKE ABDUL.
I CAN NEVER GO BACK TO AFGHANISTAN . . .
I CAN NEVER GO HOME.

7 "MARGAH"

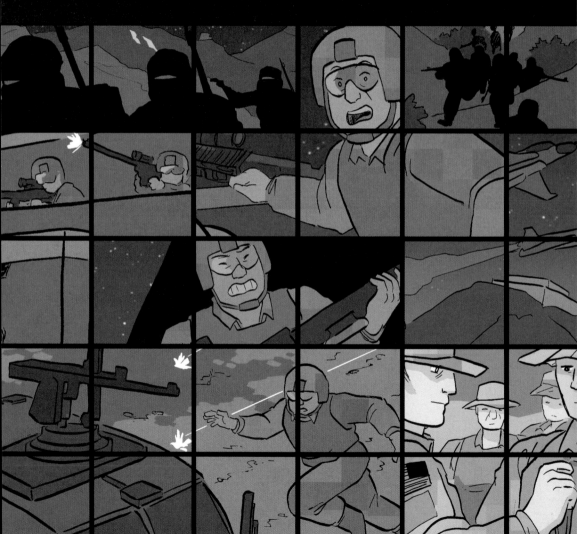

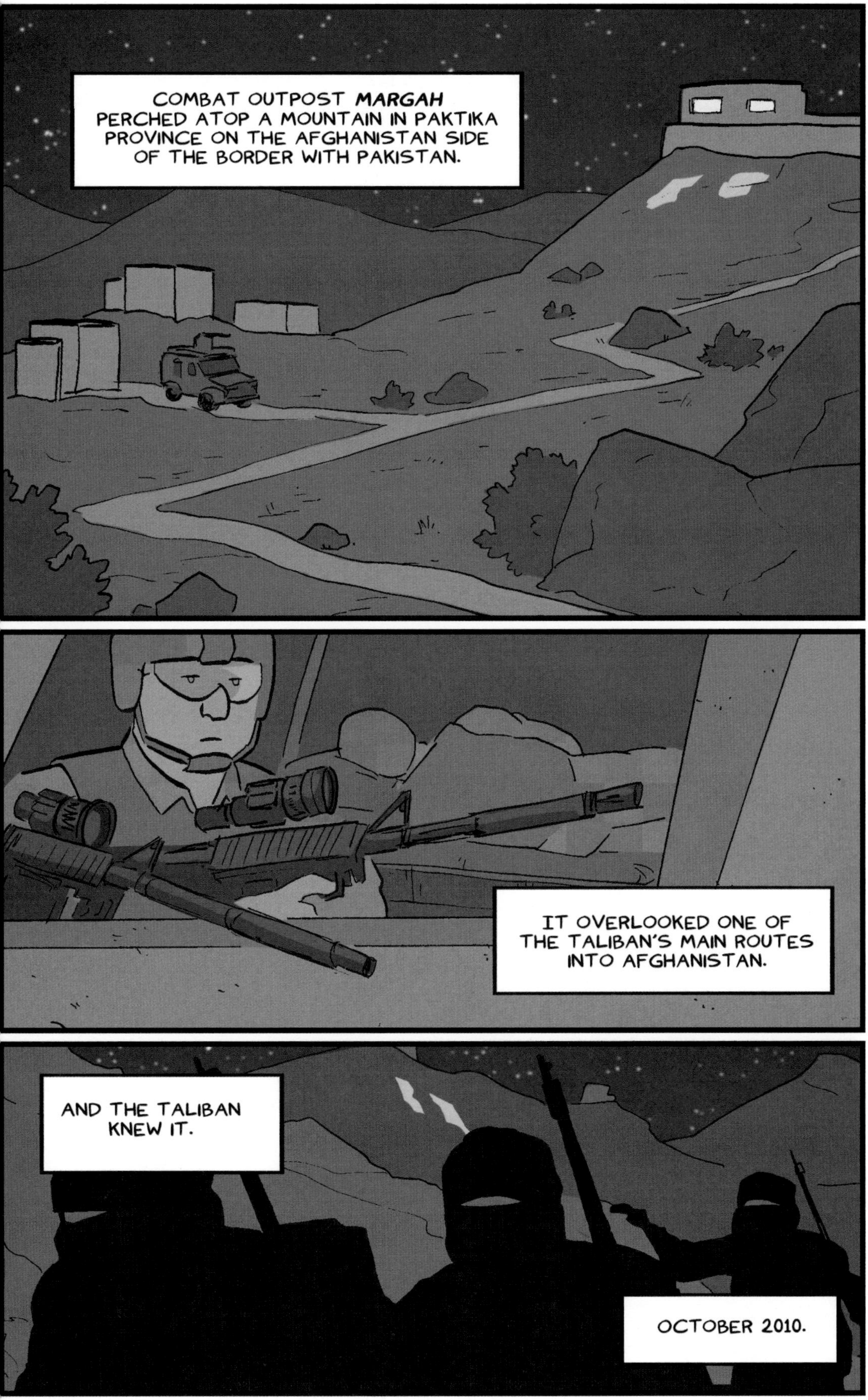
COMBAT OUTPOST **MARGAH** PERCHED ATOP A MOUNTAIN IN PAKTIKA PROVINCE ON THE AFGHANISTAN SIDE OF THE BORDER WITH PAKISTAN.
IT OVERLOOKED ONE OF THE TALIBAN'S MAIN ROUTES INTO AFGHANISTAN.
AND THE TALIBAN KNEW IT.
OCTOBER 2010.

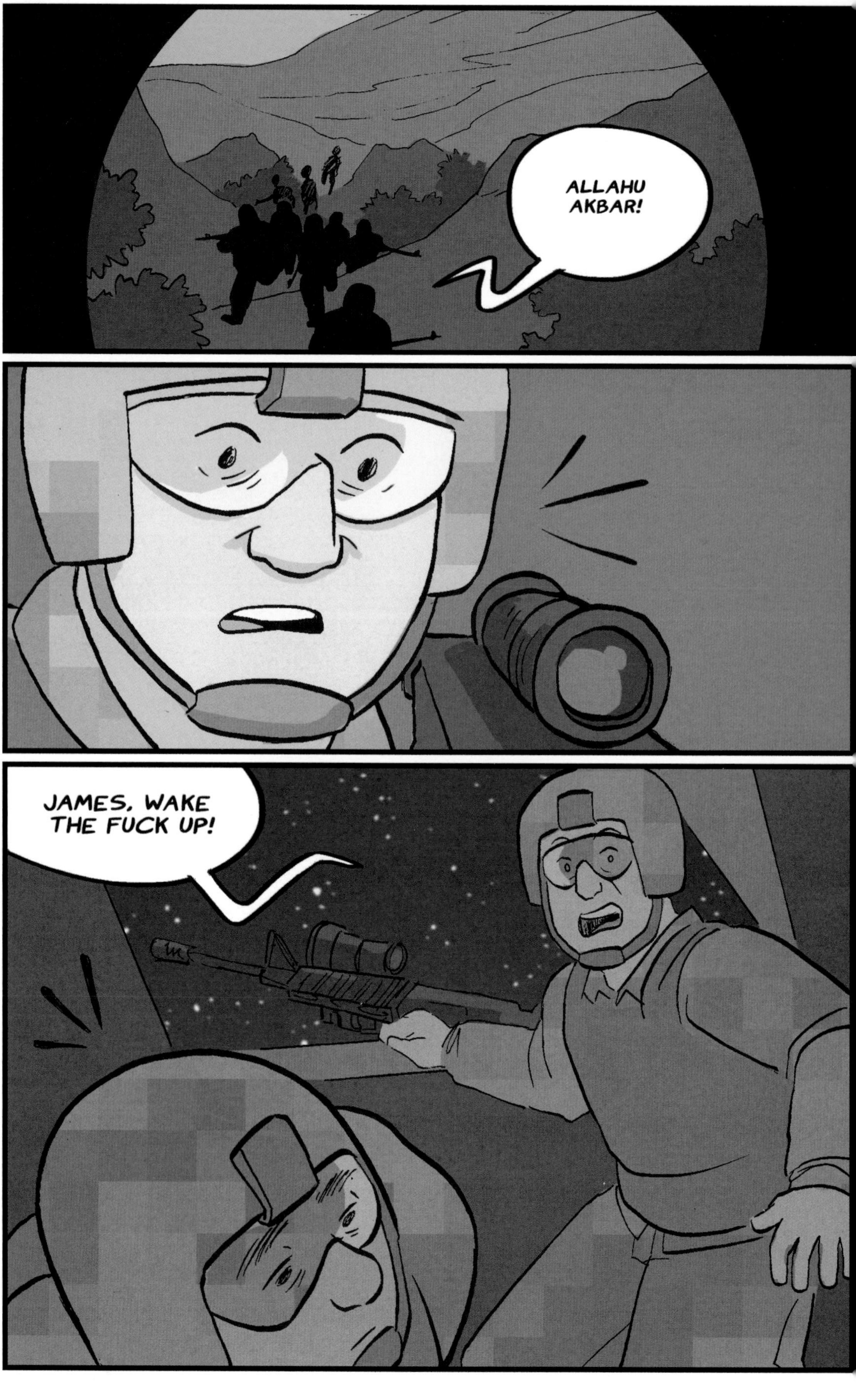
ALLAHU AKBAR!
JAMES, WAKE THE FUCK UP!

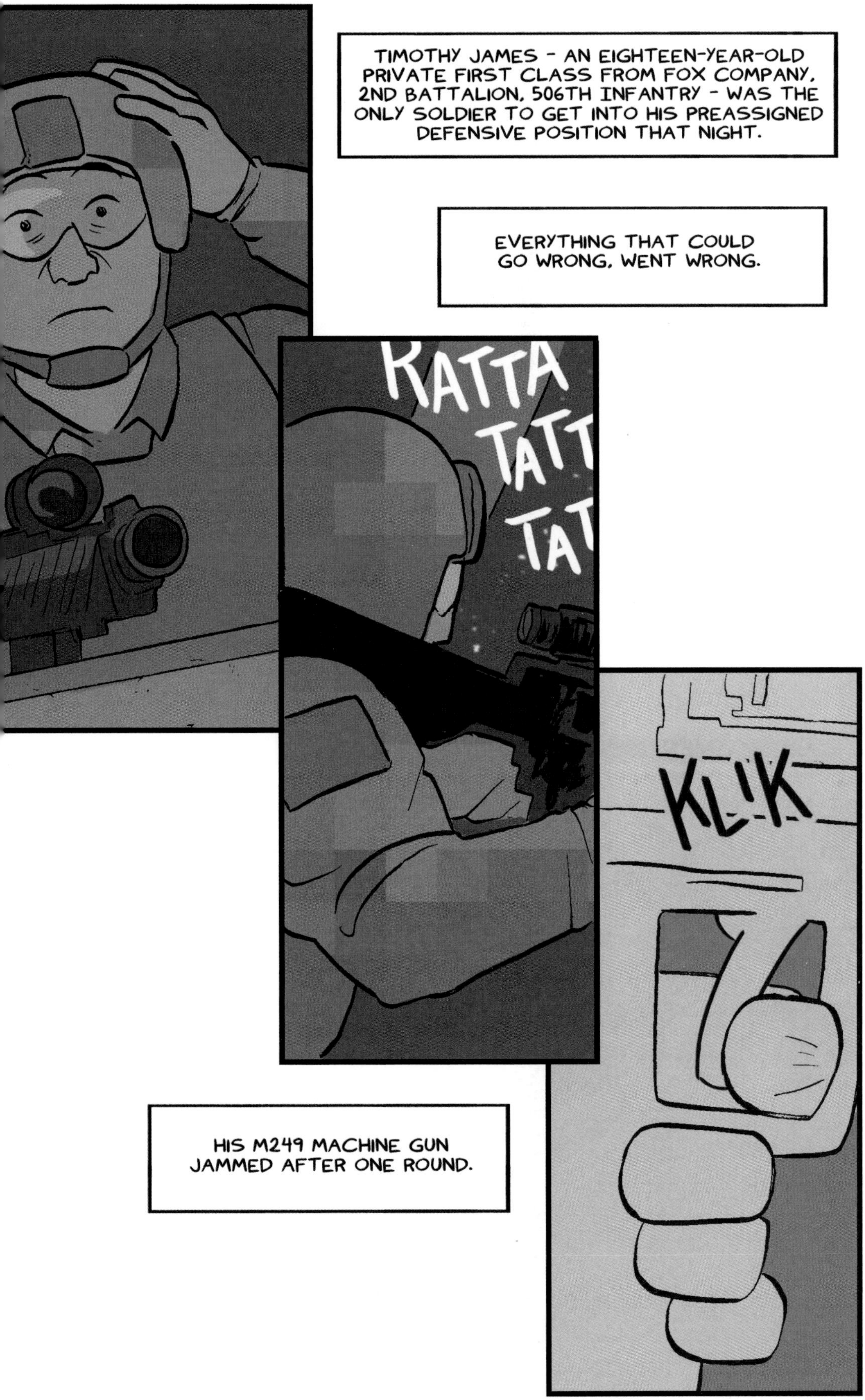
TIMOTHY JAMES - AN EIGHTEEN-YEAR-OLD PRIVATE FIRST CLASS FROM FOX COMPANY, 2ND BATTALION, 506TH INFANTRY - WAS THE ONLY SOLDIER TO GET INTO HIS PREASSIGNED DEFENSIVE POSITION THAT NIGHT.
EVERYTHING THAT COULD GO WRONG, WENT WRONG.
RATTA
TATT
TAT
KLIK
HIS M249 MACHINE GUN JAMMED AFTER ONE ROUND.

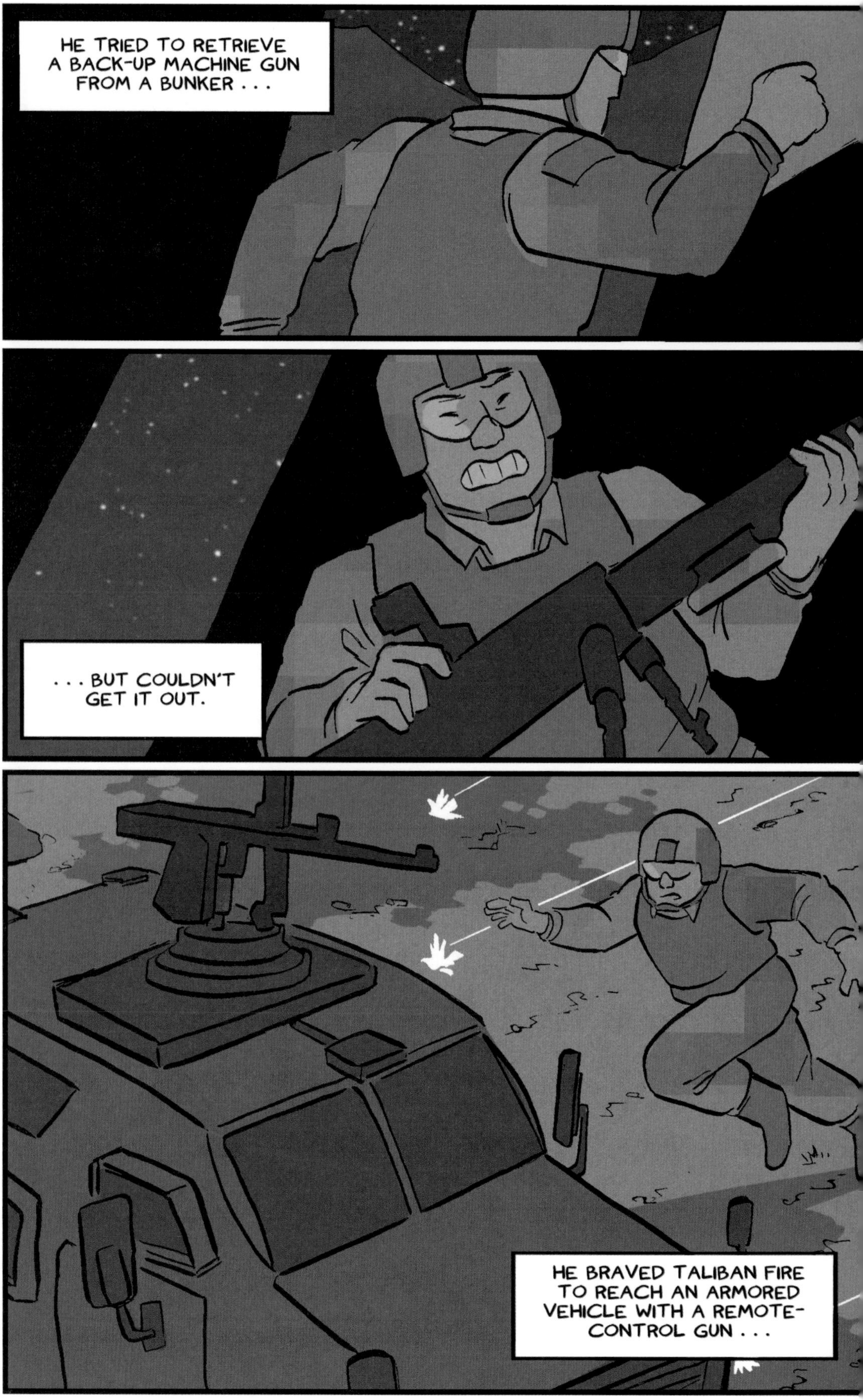
HE TRIED TO RETRIEVE A BACK-UP MACHINE GUN FROM A BUNKER . . .
. . . BUT COULDN'T GET IT OUT.
HE BRAVED TALIBAN FIRE TO REACH AN ARMORED VEHICLE WITH A REMOTE-CONTROL GUN . . .

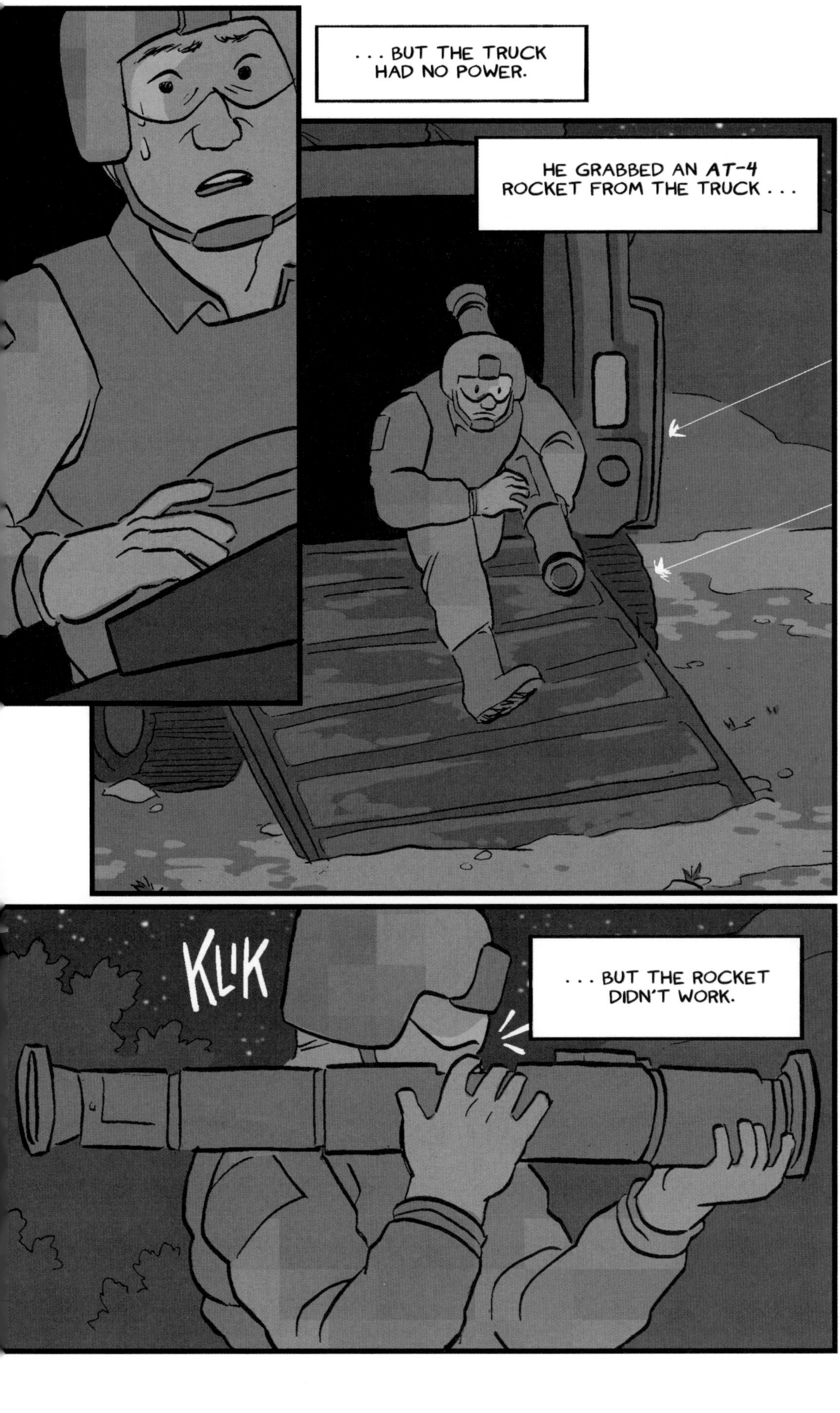
. . . BUT THE TRUCK HAD NO POWER.
HE GRABBED AN AT-4 ROCKET FROM THE TRUCK . . .
KLIK
. . . BUT THE ROCKET DIDN'T WORK.

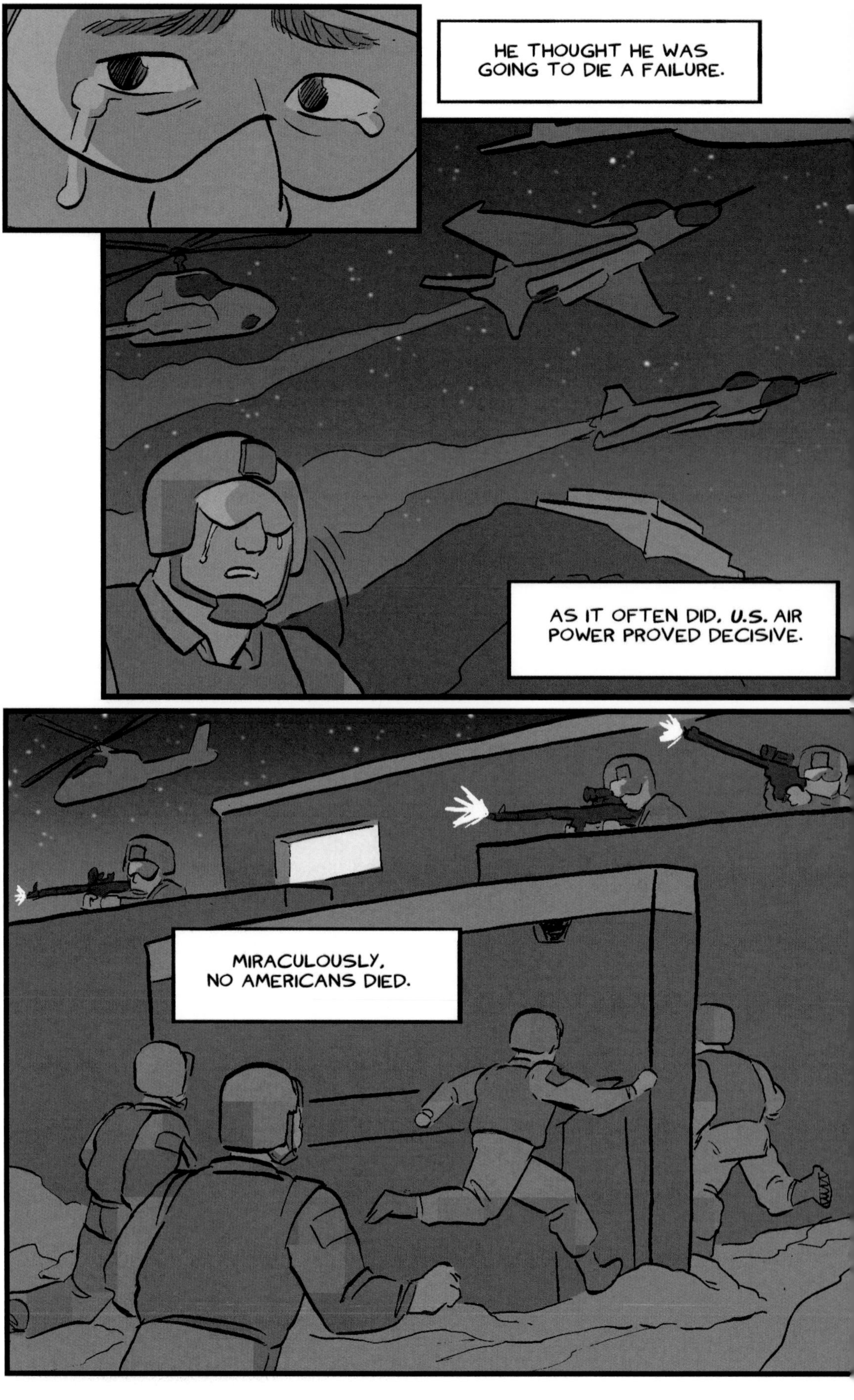
HE THOUGHT HE WAS GOING TO DIE A FAILURE.
AS IT OFTEN DID, U.S. AIR POWER PROVED DECISIVE.
MIRACULOUSLY, NO AMERICANS DIED.

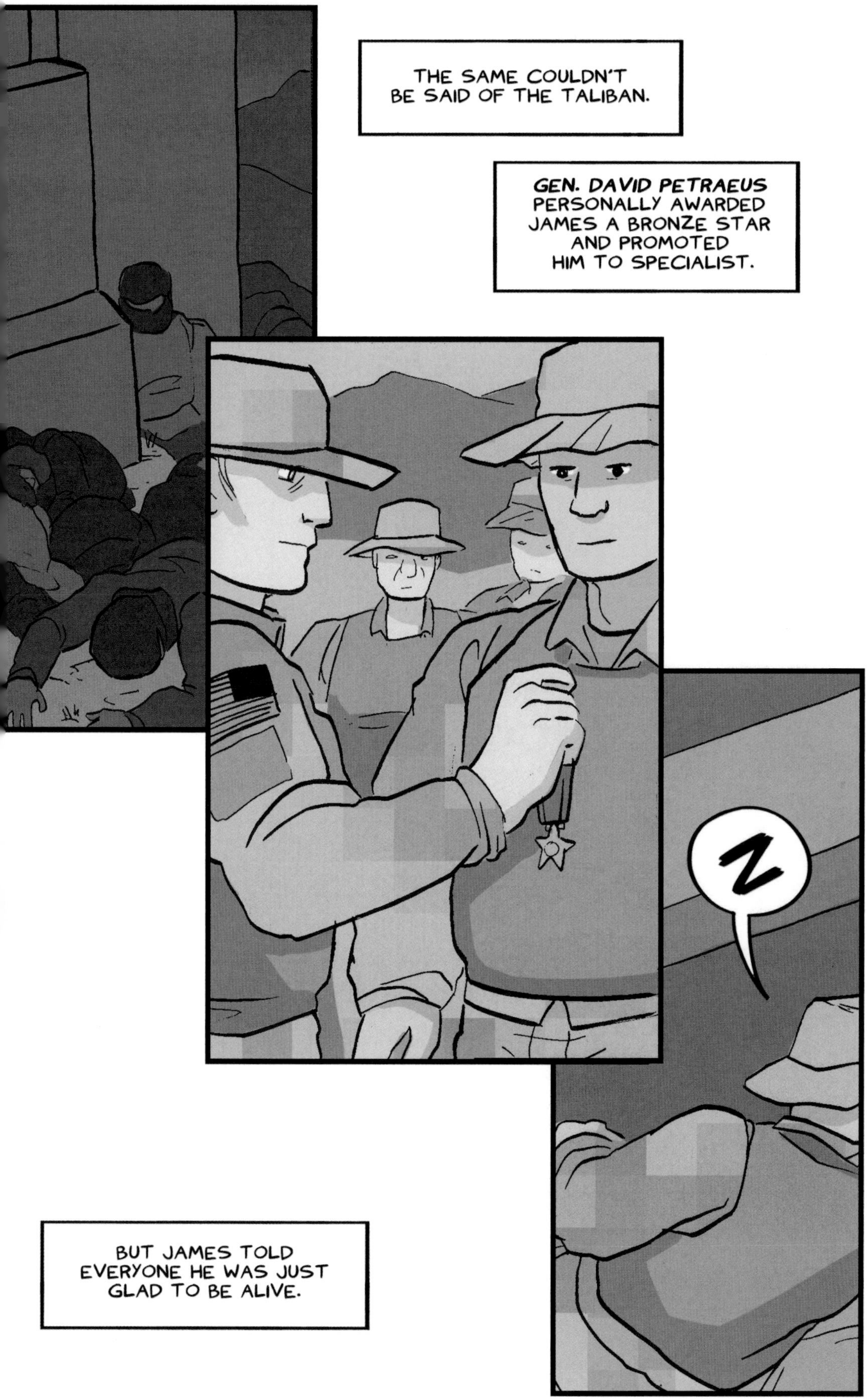
THE SAME COULDN'T BE SAID OF THE TALIBAN.
GEN. DAVID PETRAEUS PERSONALLY AWARDED JAMES A BRONZE STAR AND PROMOTED HIM TO SPECIALIST.
Z
BUT JAMES TOLD EVERYONE HE WAS JUST GLAD TO BE ALIVE.

8 "FROM HOOTERS WAITRESS TO SOLDIER"

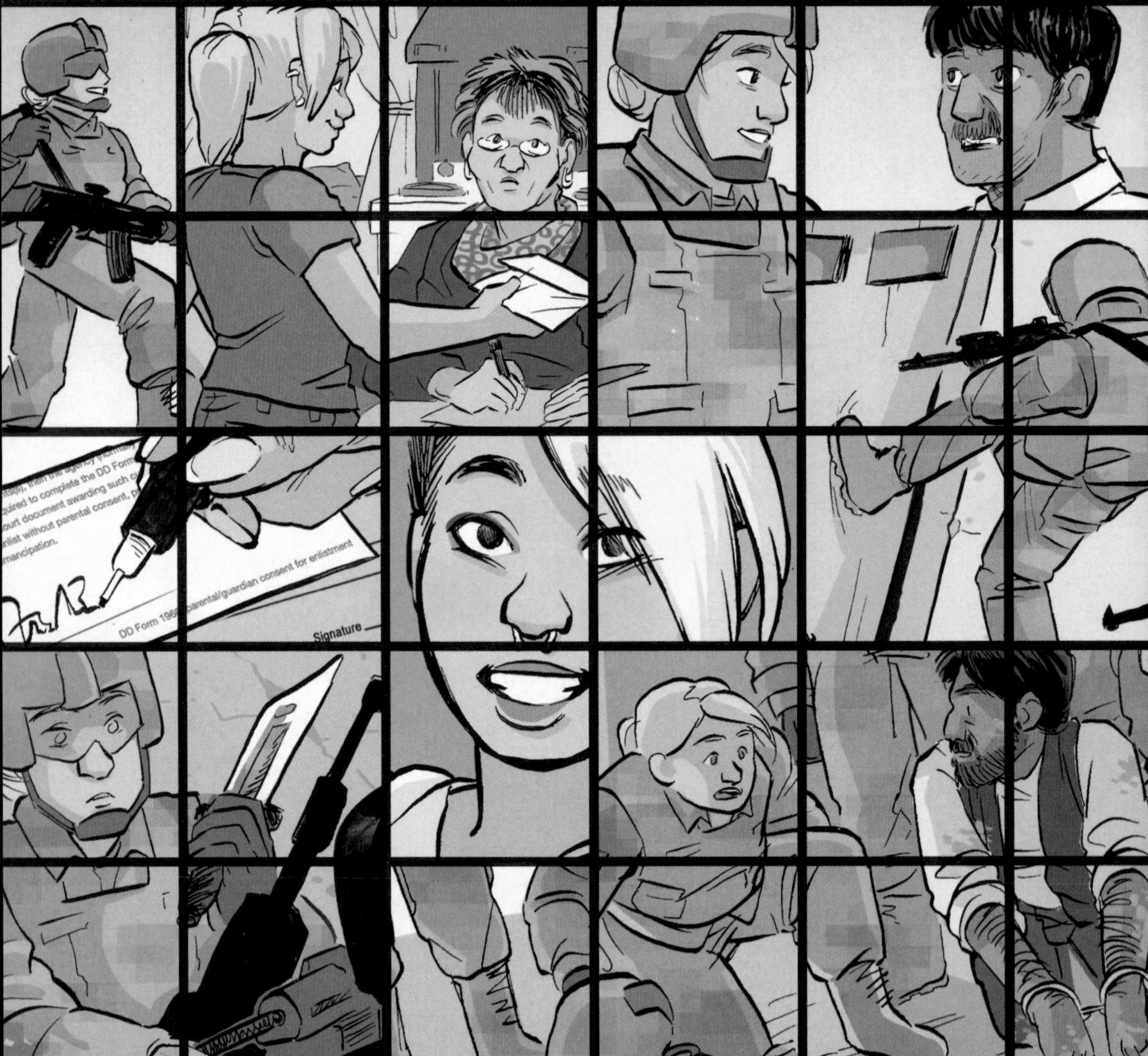
parental/guardian consent for enlistment
Signature

**Spec. Alison Parton, USA,
somewhere in Afghanistan**

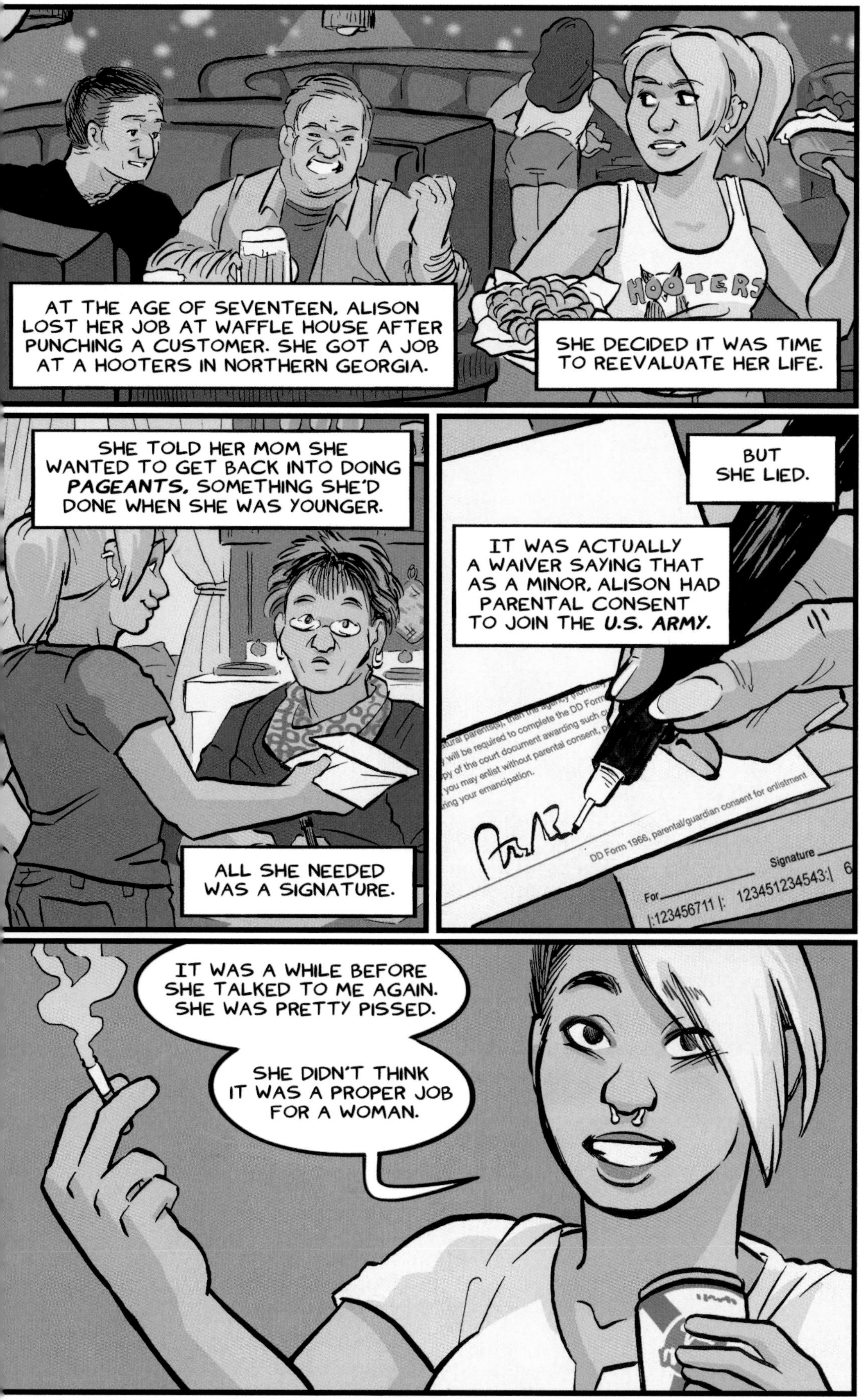
AT THE AGE OF SEVENTEEN, ALISON LOST HER JOB AT WAFFLE HOUSE AFTER PUNCHING A CUSTOMER. SHE GOT A JOB AT A HOOTERS IN NORTHERN GEORGIA.
HOOTERS
SHE DECIDED IT WAS TIME TO REEVALUATE HER LIFE.
SHE TOLD HER MOM SHE WANTED TO GET BACK INTO DOING *PAGEANTS*, SOMETHING SHE'D DONE WHEN SHE WAS YOUNGER.
ALL SHE NEEDED WAS A SIGNATURE.
BUT SHE LIED.
IT WAS ACTUALLY A WAIVER SAYING THAT AS A MINOR, ALISON HAD PARENTAL CONSENT TO JOIN THE *U.S. ARMY*.
DD Form 1966, parental/guardian consent for enlistment
Signature
For
IT WAS A WHILE BEFORE SHE TALKED TO ME AGAIN. SHE WAS PRETTY PISSED.
SHE DIDN'T THINK IT WAS A PROPER JOB FOR A WOMAN.

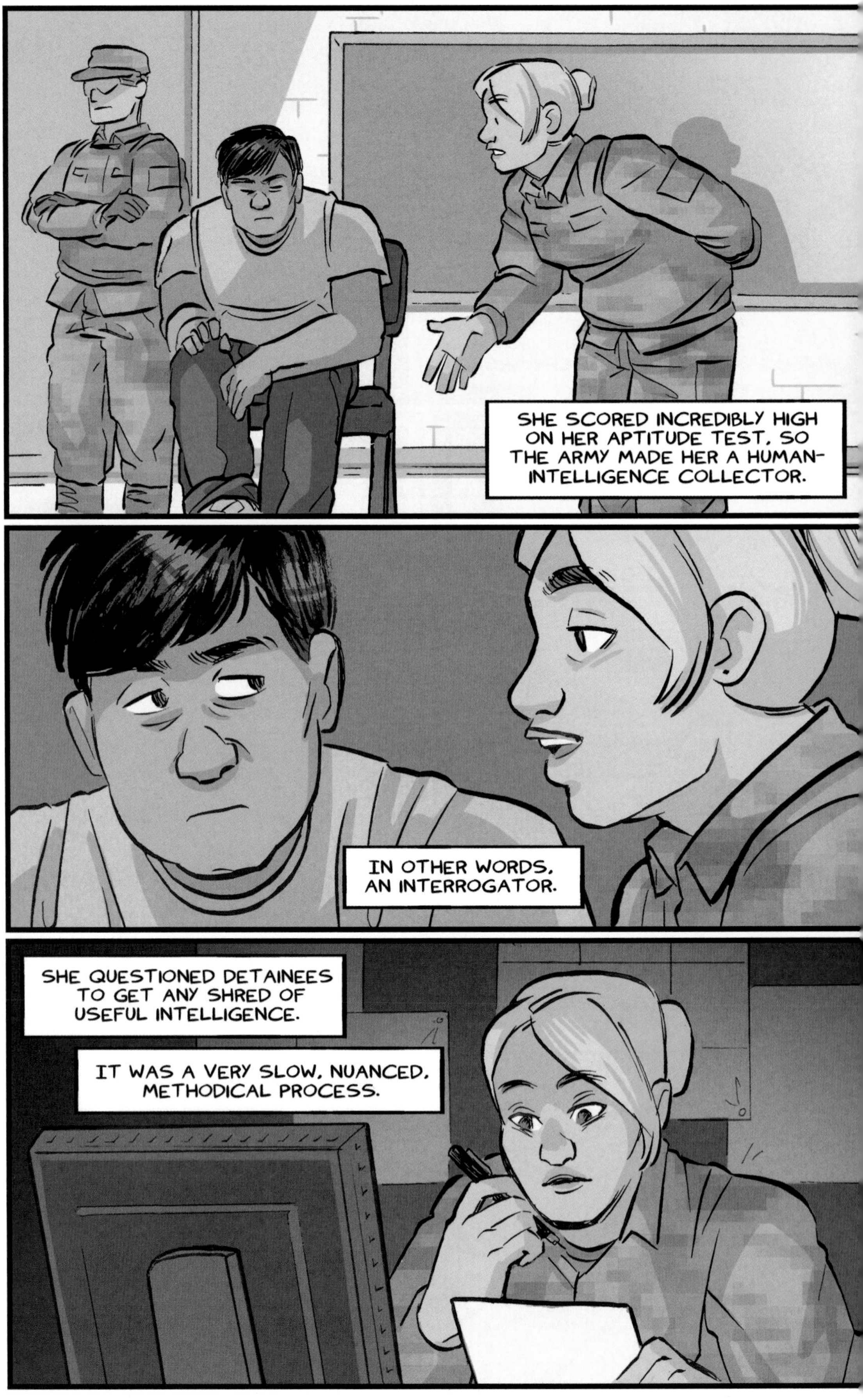
SHE SCORED INCREDIBLY HIGH ON HER APTITUDE TEST, SO THE ARMY MADE HER A HUMAN-INTELLIGENCE COLLECTOR.
IN OTHER WORDS, AN INTERROGATOR.
SHE QUESTIONED DETAINEES TO GET ANY SHRED OF USEFUL INTELLIGENCE.
IT WAS A VERY SLOW, NUANCED, METHODICAL PROCESS.

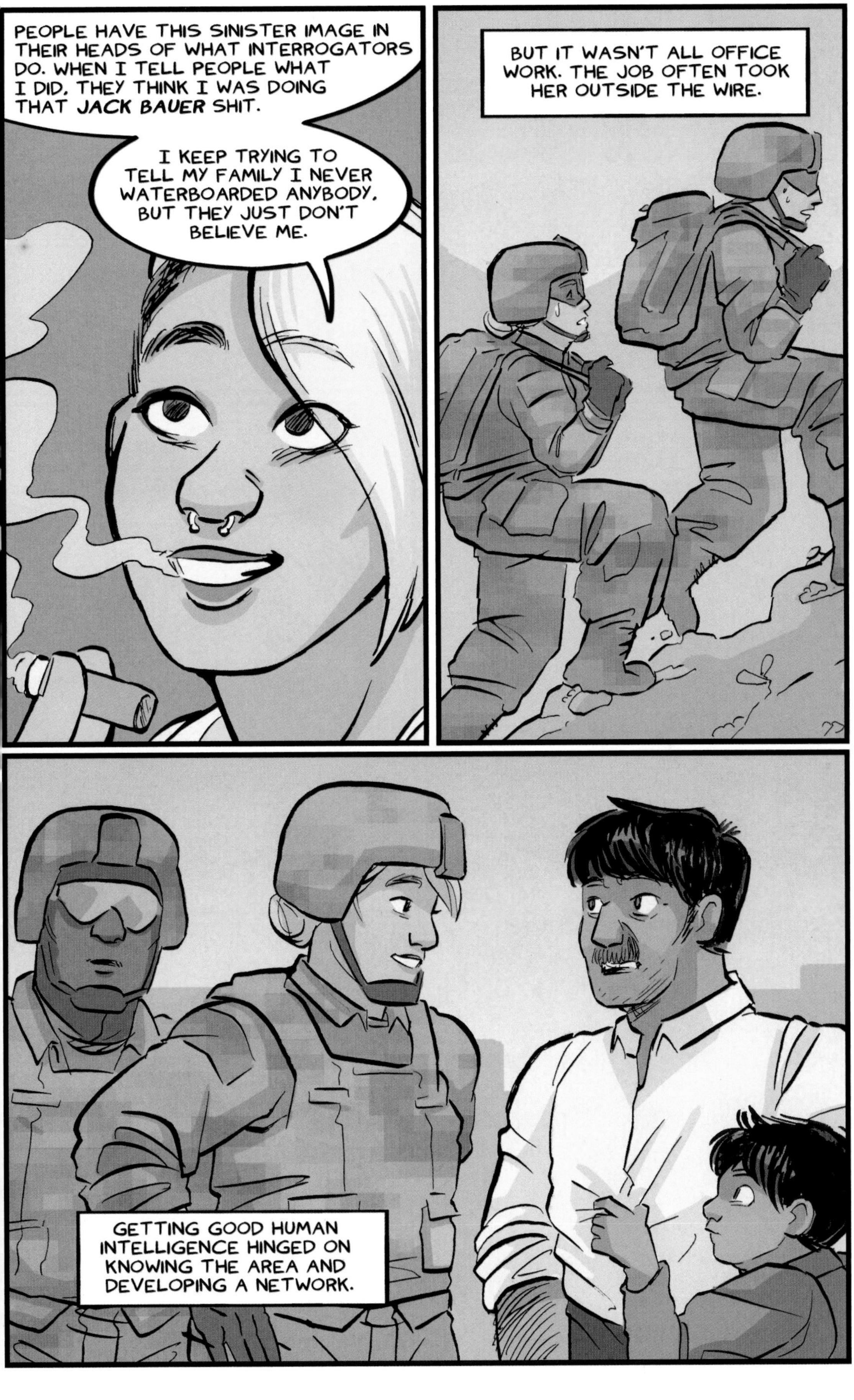

PEOPLE HAVE THIS SINISTER IMAGE IN THEIR HEADS OF WHAT INTERROGATORS DO. WHEN I TELL PEOPLE WHAT I DID, THEY THINK I WAS DOING THAT JACK BAUER SHIT.
I KEEP TRYING TO TELL MY FAMILY I NEVER WATERBOARDED ANYBODY, BUT THEY JUST DON'T BELIEVE ME.
BUT IT WASN'T ALL OFFICE WORK. THE JOB OFTEN TOOK HER OUTSIDE THE WIRE.
GETTING GOOD HUMAN INTELLIGENCE HINGED ON KNOWING THE AREA AND DEVELOPING A NETWORK.

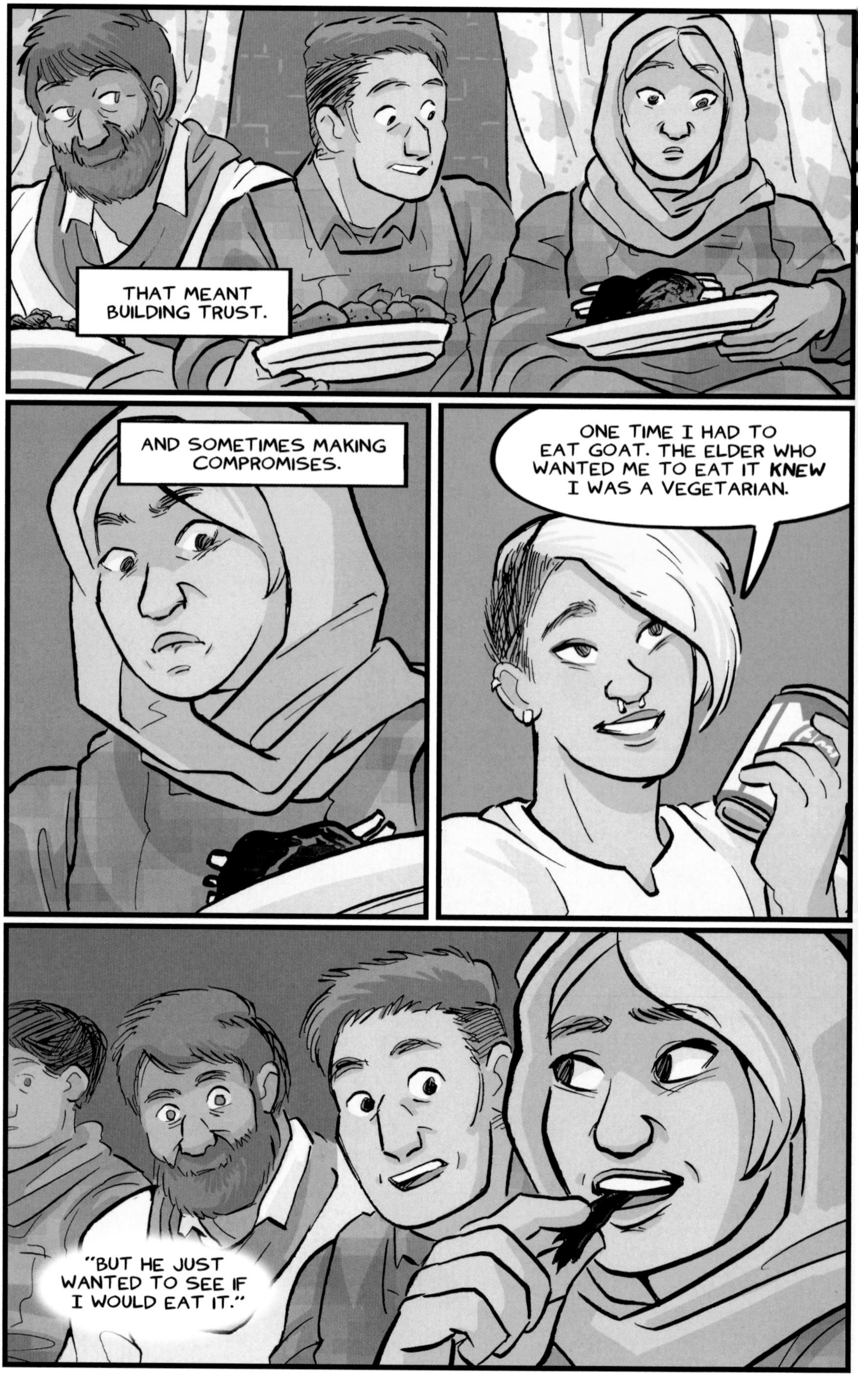
THAT MEANT BUILDING TRUST.
AND SOMETIMES MAKING COMPROMISES.
ONE TIME I HAD TO EAT GOAT. THE ELDER WHO WANTED ME TO EAT IT **KNEW** I WAS A VEGETARIAN.
"BUT HE JUST WANTED TO SEE IF I WOULD EAT IT."

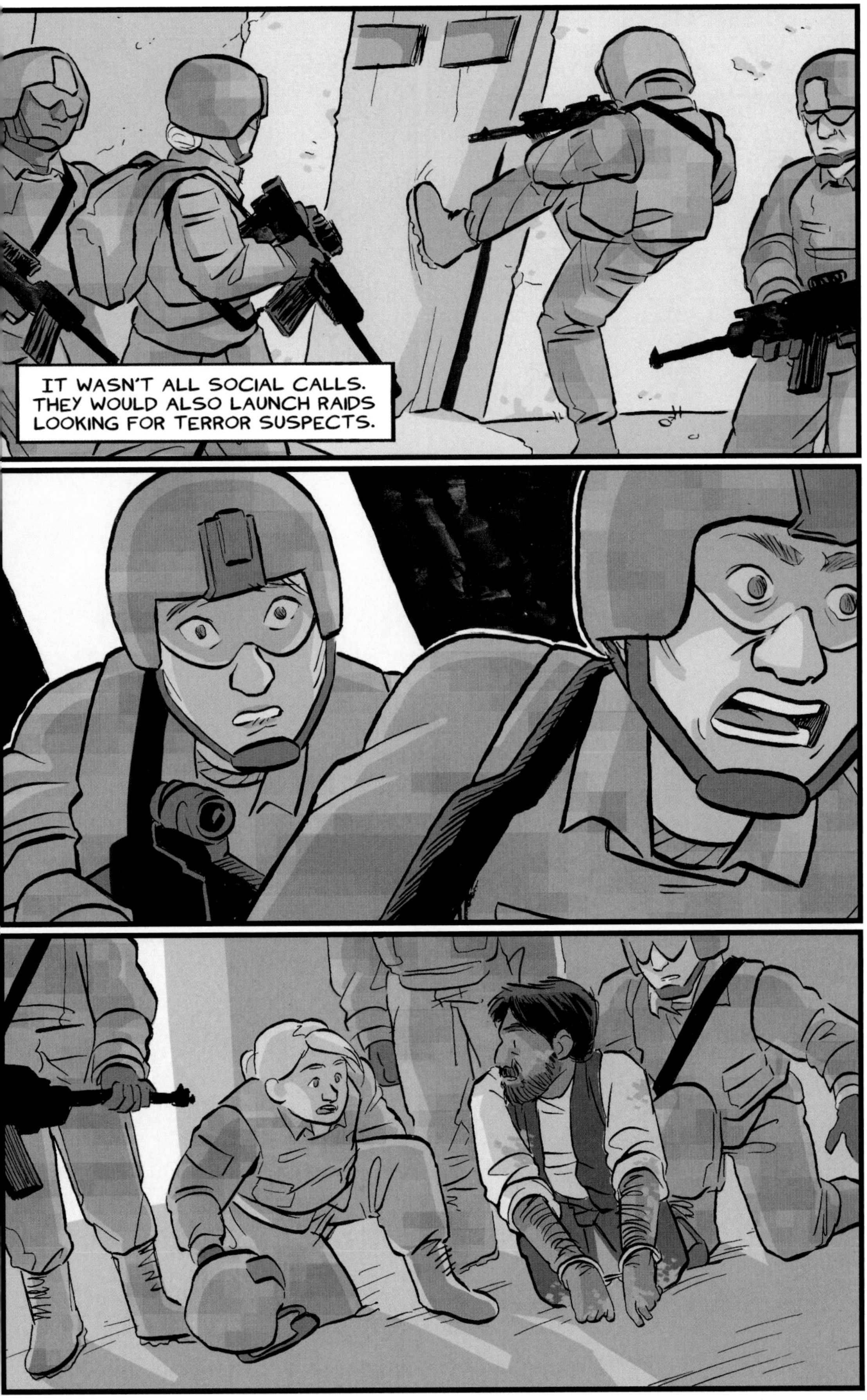
IT WASN'T ALL SOCIAL CALLS. THEY WOULD ALSO LAUNCH RAIDS LOOKING FOR TERROR SUSPECTS.

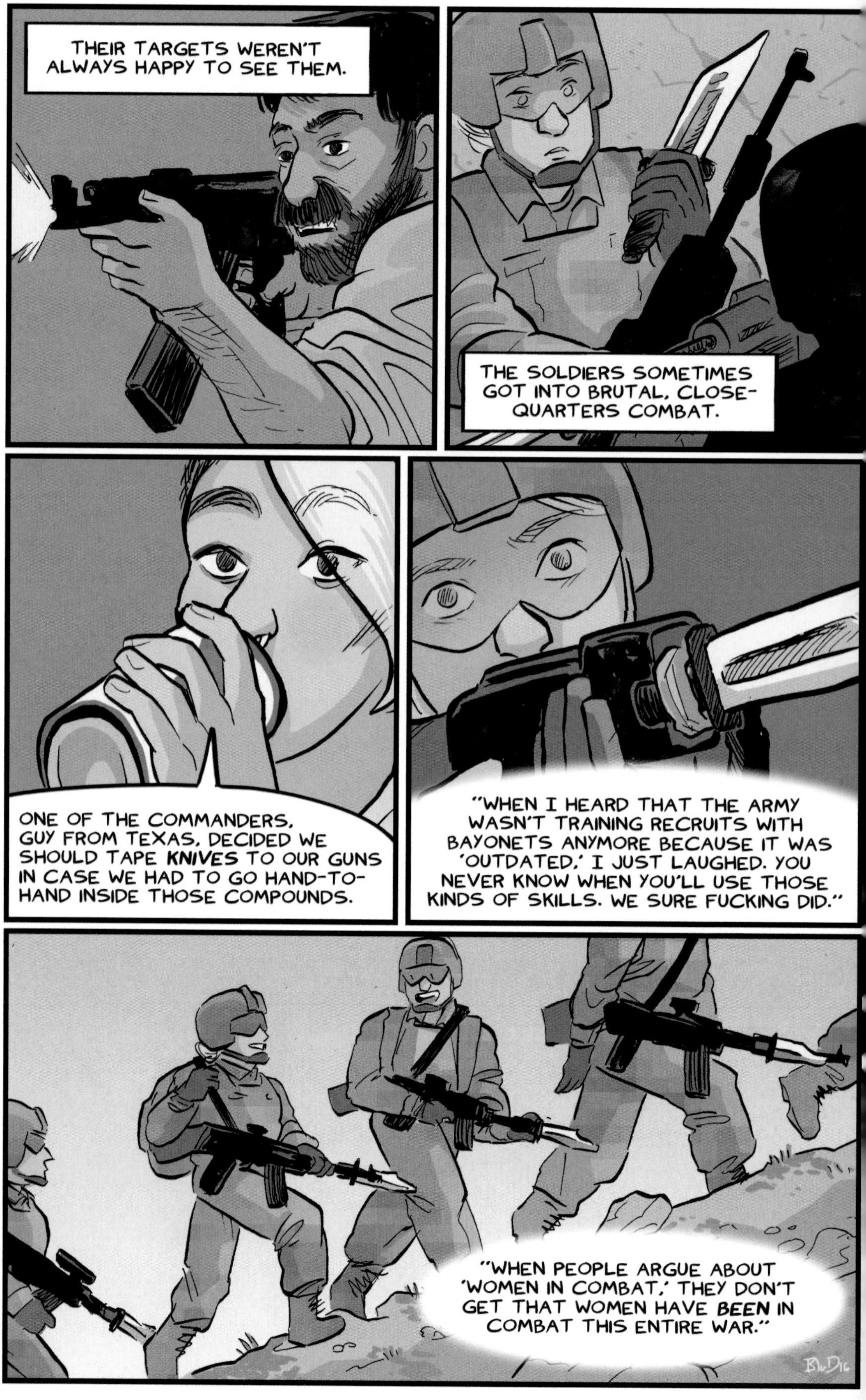
THEIR TARGETS WEREN'T ALWAYS HAPPY TO SEE THEM.
THE SOLDIERS SOMETIMES GOT INTO BRUTAL, CLOSE-QUARTERS COMBAT.
ONE OF THE COMMANDERS, GUY FROM TEXAS, DECIDED WE SHOULD TAPE **KNIVES** TO OUR GUNS IN CASE WE HAD TO GO HAND-TO-HAND INSIDE THOSE COMPOUNDS.
"WHEN I HEARD THAT THE ARMY WASN'T TRAINING RECRUITS WITH BAYONETS ANYMORE BECAUSE IT WAS 'OUTDATED,' I JUST LAUGHED. YOU NEVER KNOW WHEN YOU'LL USE THOSE KINDS OF SKILLS. WE SURE FUCKING DID."
"WHEN PEOPLE ARGUE ABOUT 'WOMEN IN COMBAT,' THEY DON'T GET THAT WOMEN HAVE **BEEN** IN COMBAT THIS ENTIRE WAR."

9 "ORDNANCE DISPOSAL"

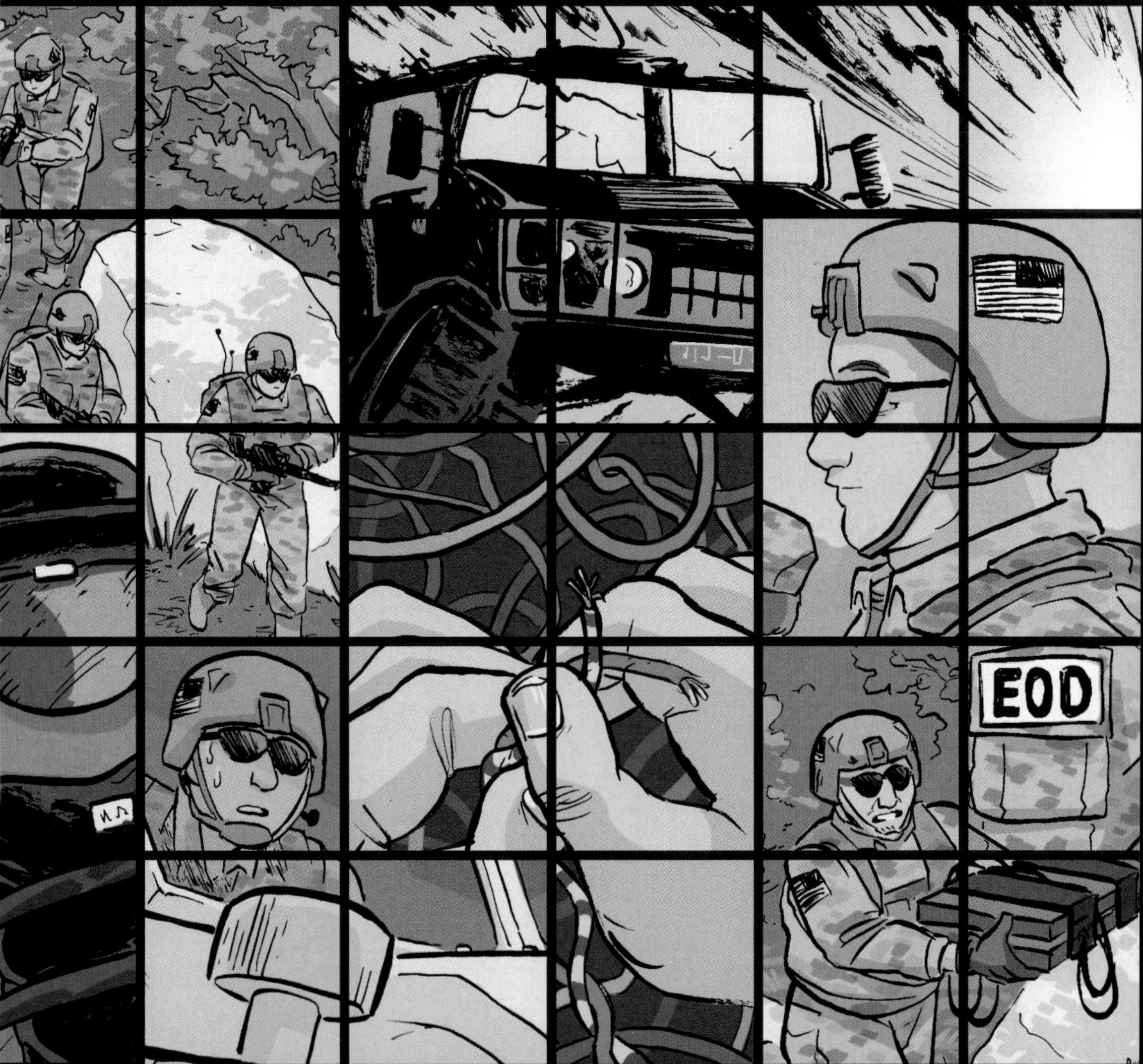
EOD

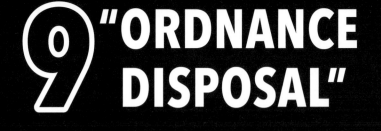

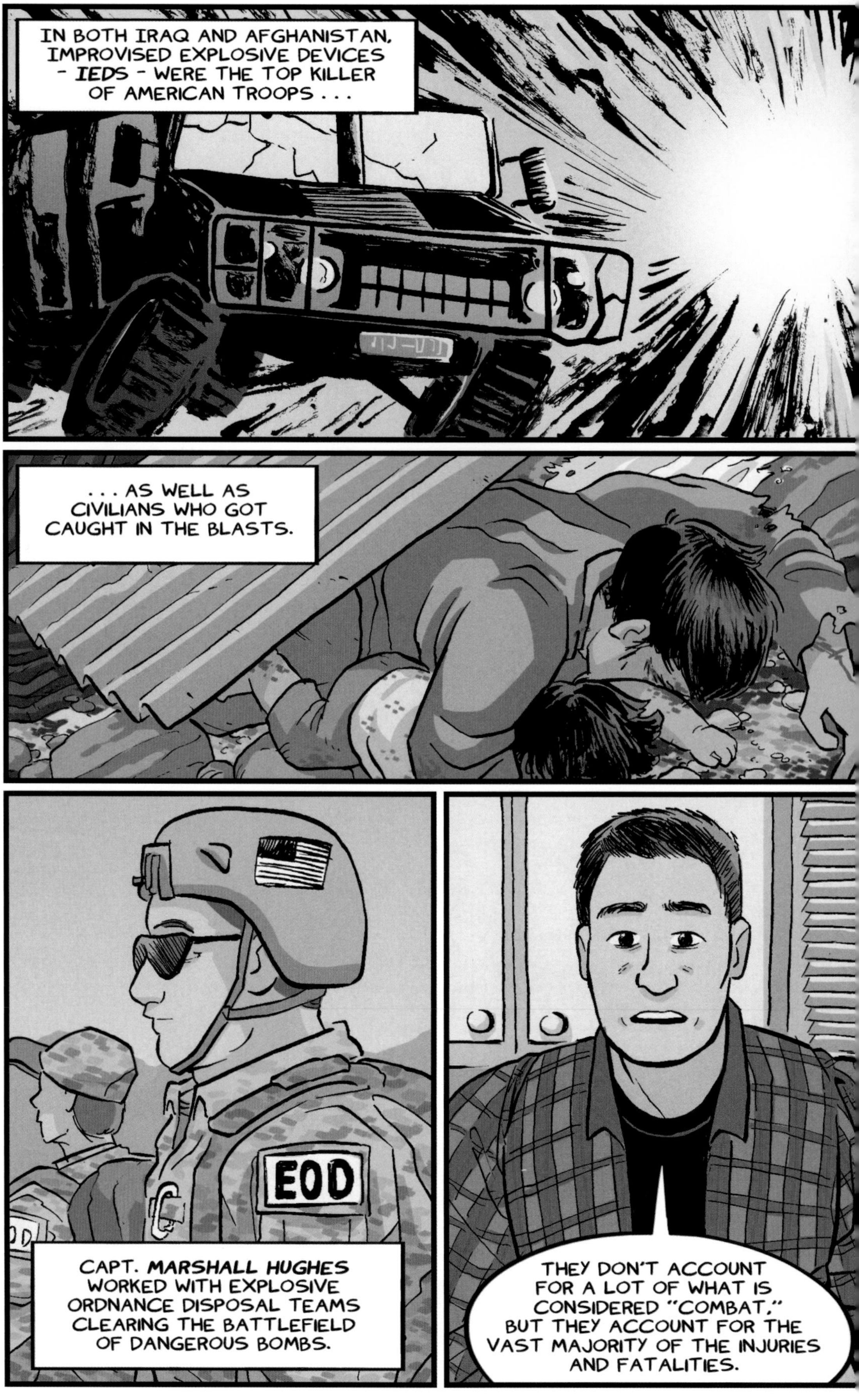
IN BOTH IRAQ AND AFGHANISTAN, IMPROVISED EXPLOSIVE DEVICES - IEDS - WERE THE TOP KILLER OF AMERICAN TROOPS . . .
. . . AS WELL AS CIVILIANS WHO GOT CAUGHT IN THE BLASTS.
EOD
CAPT. MARSHALL HUGHES WORKED WITH EXPLOSIVE ORDNANCE DISPOSAL TEAMS CLEARING THE BATTLEFIELD OF DANGEROUS BOMBS.
THEY DON'T ACCOUNT FOR A LOT OF WHAT IS CONSIDERED "COMBAT," BUT THEY ACCOUNT FOR THE VAST MAJORITY OF THE INJURIES AND FATALITIES.

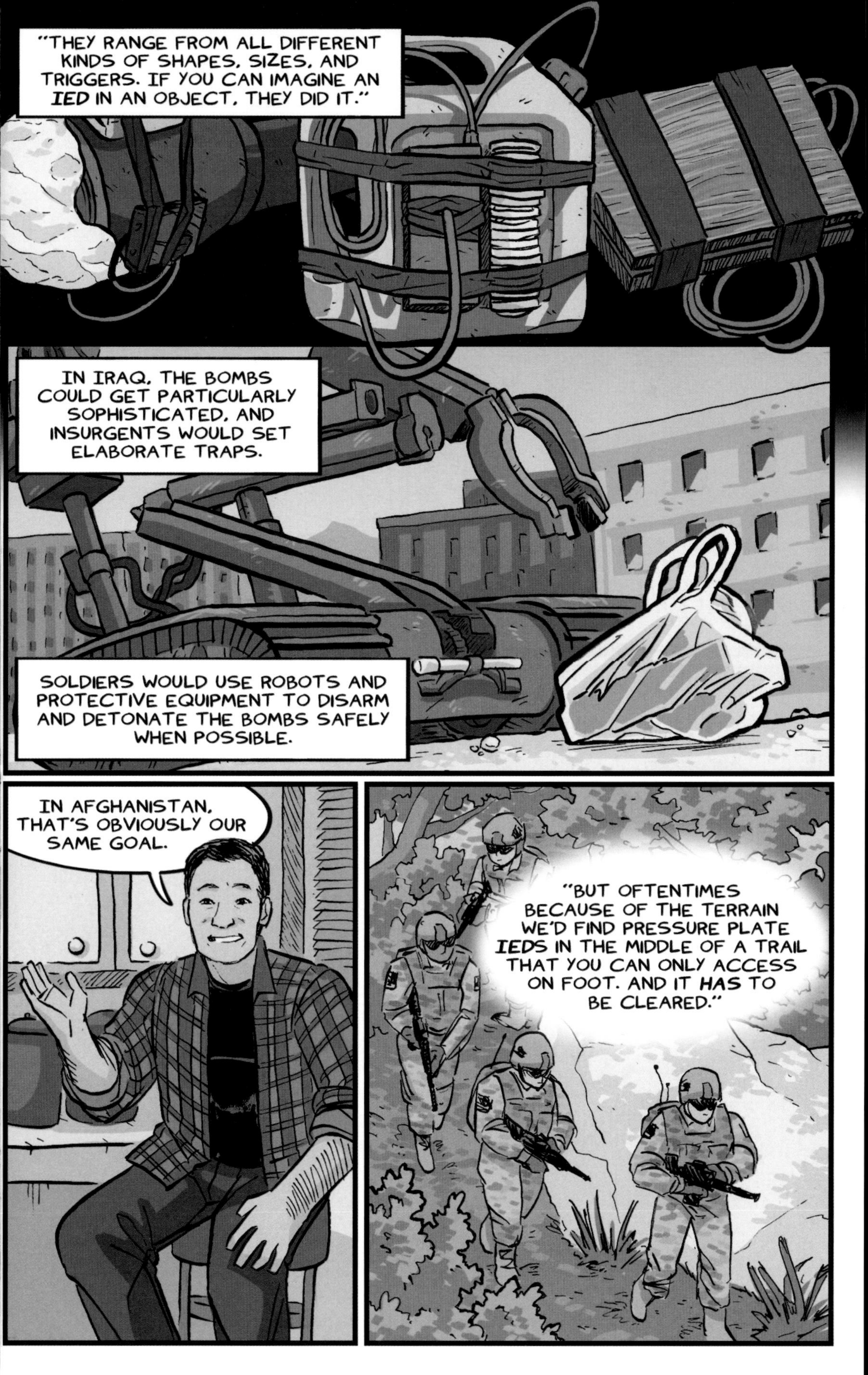
"THEY RANGE FROM ALL DIFFERENT KINDS OF SHAPES, SIZES, AND TRIGGERS. IF YOU CAN IMAGINE AN *IED* IN AN OBJECT, THEY DID IT."
IN IRAQ, THE BOMBS COULD GET PARTICULARLY SOPHISTICATED, AND INSURGENTS WOULD SET ELABORATE TRAPS.
SOLDIERS WOULD USE ROBOTS AND PROTECTIVE EQUIPMENT TO DISARM AND DETONATE THE BOMBS SAFELY WHEN POSSIBLE.
IN AFGHANISTAN, THAT'S OBVIOUSLY OUR SAME GOAL.
"BUT OFTENTIMES BECAUSE OF THE TERRAIN WE'D FIND PRESSURE PLATE *IEDS* IN THE MIDDLE OF A TRAIL THAT YOU CAN ONLY ACCESS ON FOOT. AND IT **HAS** TO BE CLEARED."

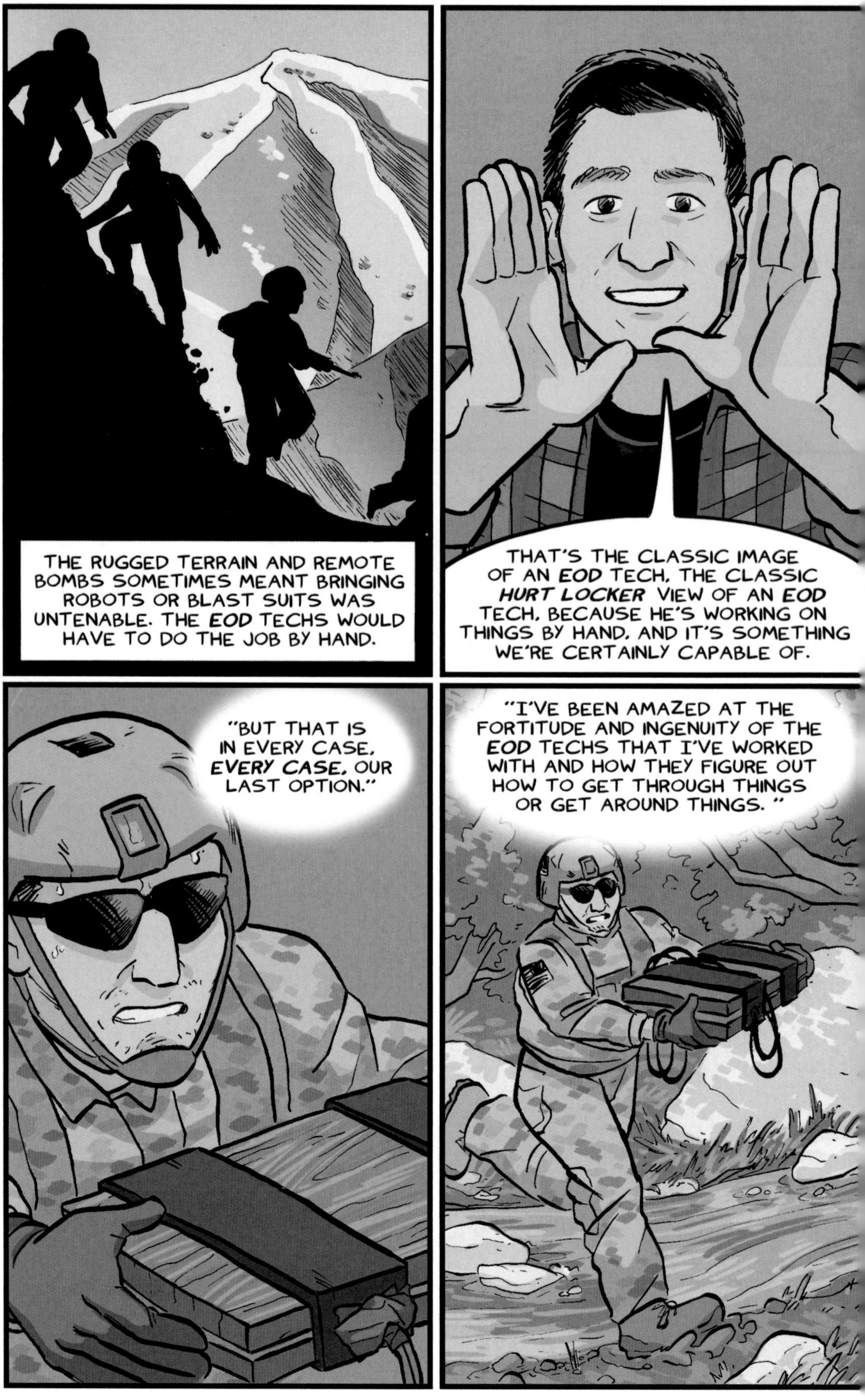
THE RUGGED TERRAIN AND REMOTE BOMBS SOMETIMES MEANT BRINGING ROBOTS OR BLAST SUITS WAS UNTENABLE. THE *EOD* TECHS WOULD HAVE TO DO THE JOB BY HAND.
THAT'S THE CLASSIC IMAGE OF AN *EOD* TECH, THE CLASSIC ***HURT LOCKER*** VIEW OF AN *EOD* TECH, BECAUSE HE'S WORKING ON THINGS BY HAND, AND IT'S SOMETHING WE'RE CERTAINLY CAPABLE OF.
"BUT THAT IS IN EVERY CASE, ***EVERY CASE,*** OUR LAST OPTION."
"I'VE BEEN AMAZED AT THE FORTITUDE AND INGENUITY OF THE *EOD* TECHS THAT I'VE WORKED WITH AND HOW THEY FIGURE OUT HOW TO GET THROUGH THINGS OR GET AROUND THINGS."

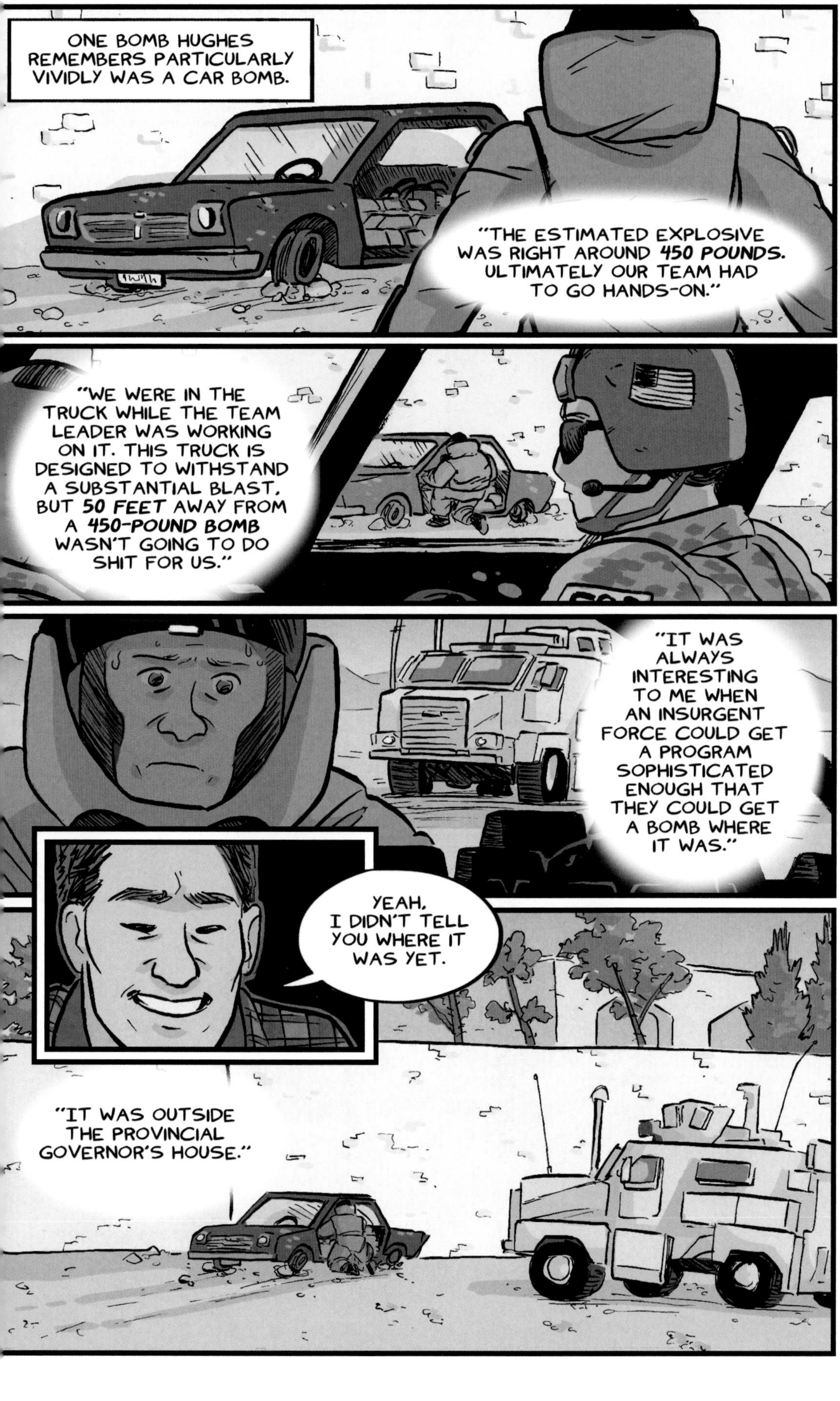
ONE BOMB HUGHES REMEMBERS PARTICULARLY VIVIDLY WAS A CAR BOMB.
"THE ESTIMATED EXPLOSIVE WAS RIGHT AROUND **450 POUNDS.** ULTIMATELY OUR TEAM HAD TO GO HANDS-ON."
"WE WERE IN THE TRUCK WHILE THE TEAM LEADER WAS WORKING ON IT. THIS TRUCK IS DESIGNED TO WITHSTAND A SUBSTANTIAL BLAST, BUT **50 FEET** AWAY FROM A **450-POUND BOMB** WASN'T GOING TO DO SHIT FOR US."
"IT WAS ALWAYS INTERESTING TO ME WHEN AN INSURGENT FORCE COULD GET A PROGRAM SOPHISTICATED ENOUGH THAT THEY COULD GET A BOMB WHERE IT WAS."
YEAH, I DIDN'T TELL YOU WHERE IT WAS YET.
"IT WAS OUTSIDE THE PROVINCIAL GOVERNOR'S HOUSE."

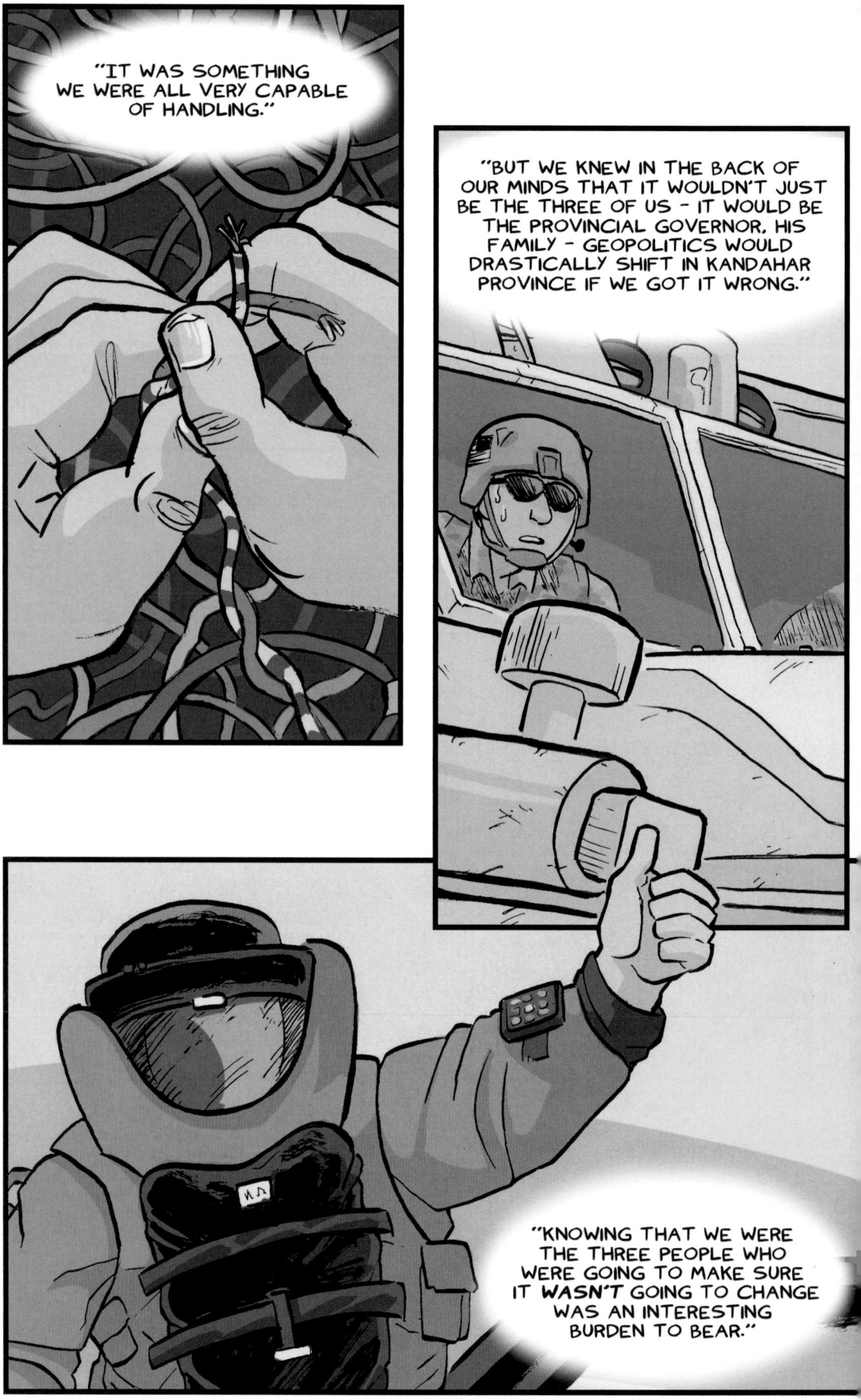
"IT WAS SOMETHING WE WERE ALL VERY CAPABLE OF HANDLING."
"BUT WE KNEW IN THE BACK OF OUR MINDS THAT IT WOULDN'T JUST BE THE THREE OF US - IT WOULD BE THE PROVINCIAL GOVERNOR, HIS FAMILY - GEOPOLITICS WOULD DRASTICALLY SHIFT IN KANDAHAR PROVINCE IF WE GOT IT WRONG."
"KNOWING THAT WE WERE THE THREE PEOPLE WHO WERE GOING TO MAKE SURE IT **WASN'T** GOING TO CHANGE WAS AN INTERESTING BURDEN TO BEAR."

10 "GOING ROGUE"

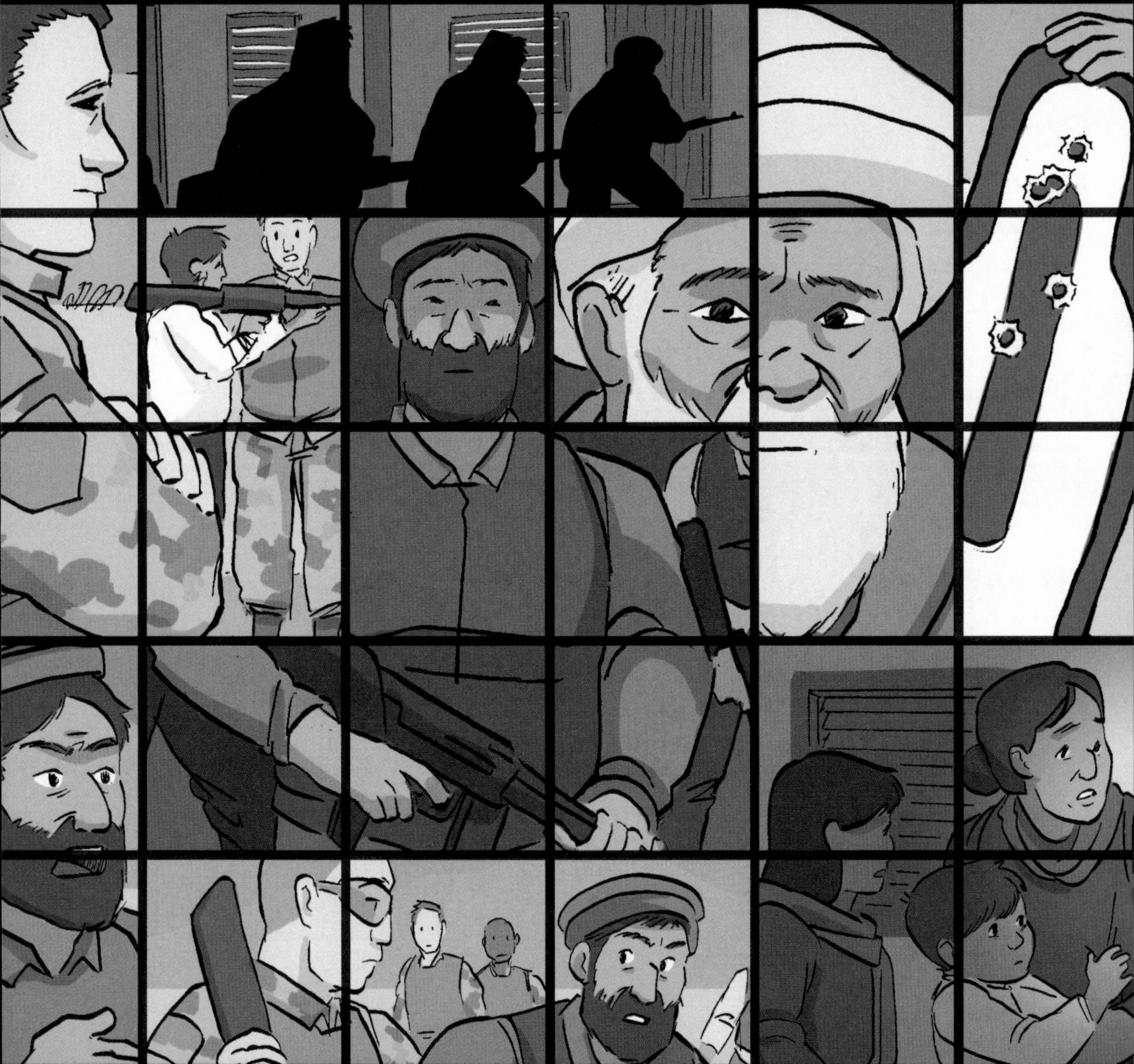

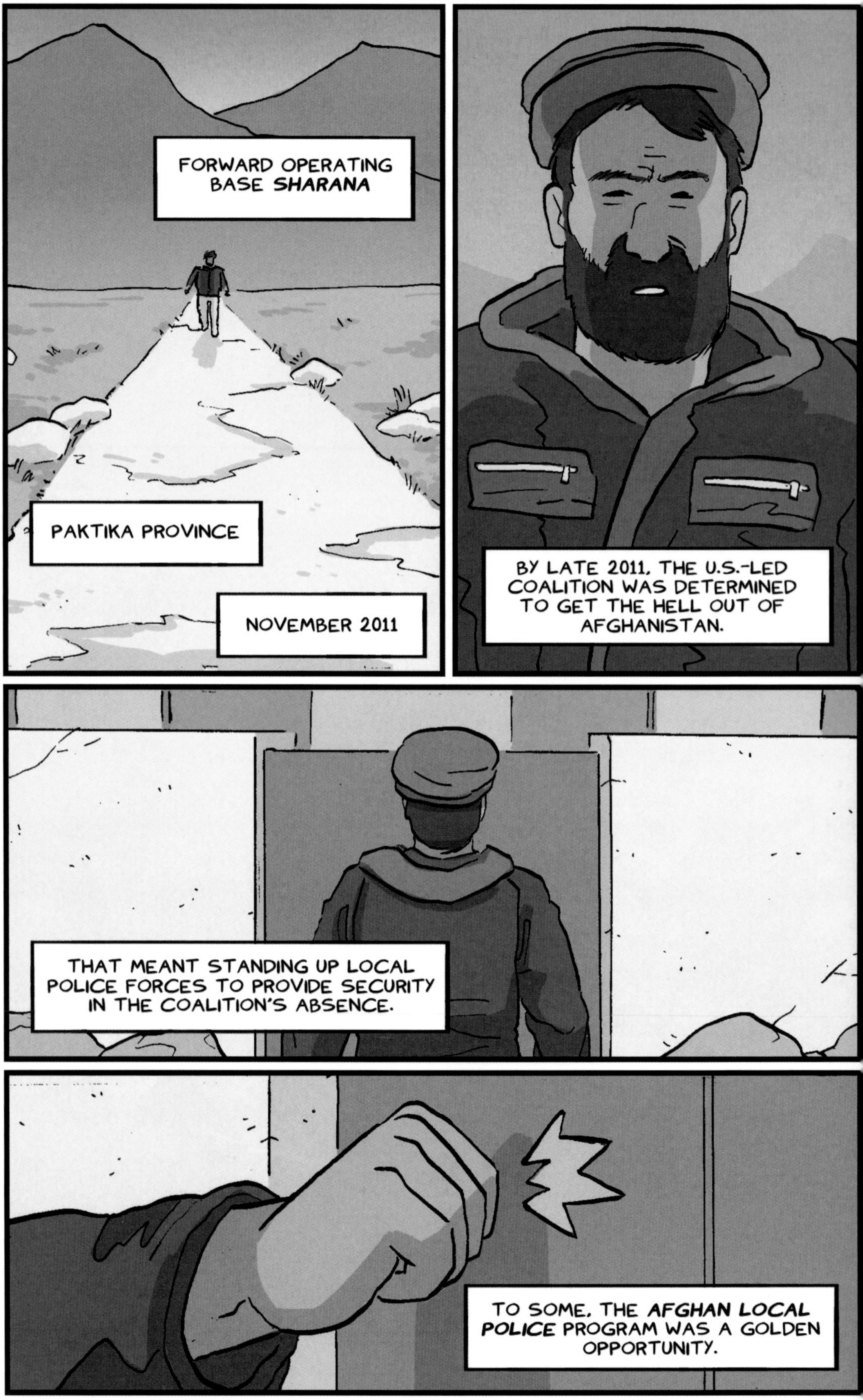

FORWARD OPERATING BASE SHARANA
PAKTIKA PROVINCE
NOVEMBER 2011
BY LATE 2011, THE U.S.-LED COALITION WAS DETERMINED TO GET THE HELL OUT OF AFGHANISTAN.
THAT MEANT STANDING UP LOCAL POLICE FORCES TO PROVIDE SECURITY IN THE COALITION'S ABSENCE.
TO SOME, THE AFGHAN LOCAL POLICE PROGRAM WAS A GOLDEN OPPORTUNITY.

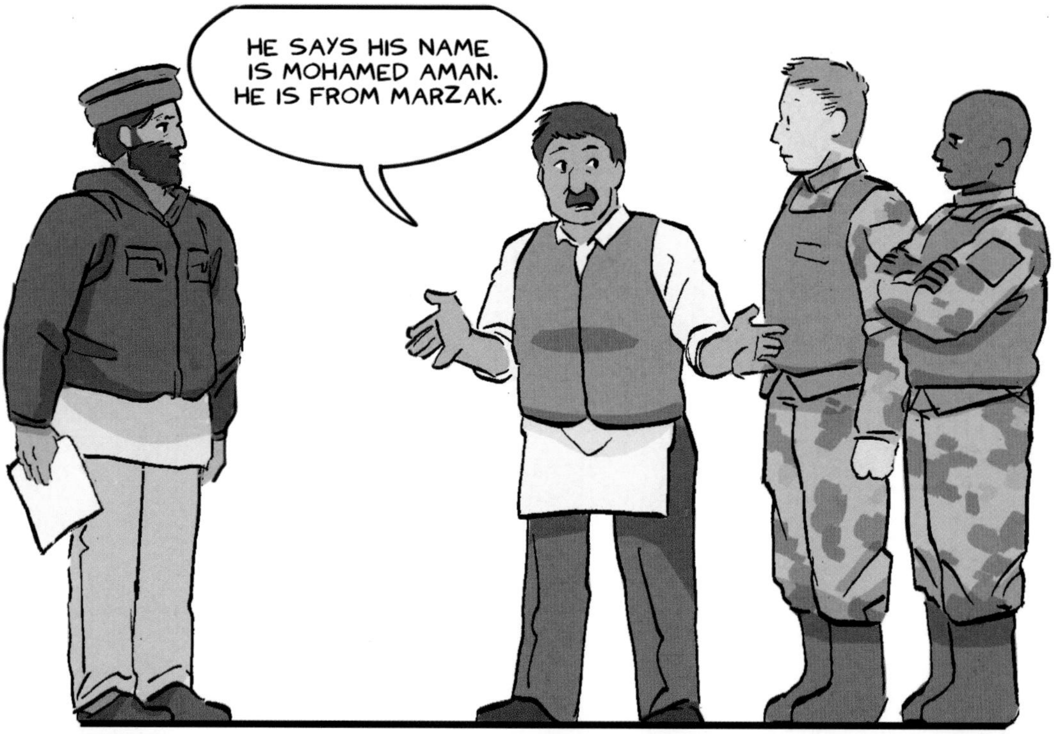
HE SAYS HIS NAME IS MOHAMED AMAN. HE IS FROM MARZAK.

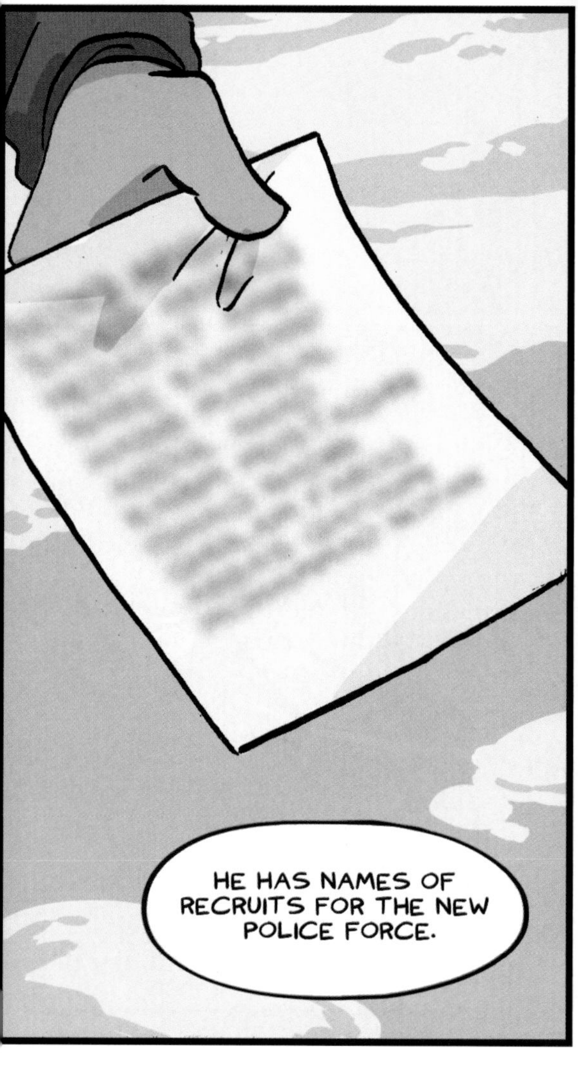
HE HAS NAMES OF RECRUITS FOR THE NEW POLICE FORCE.

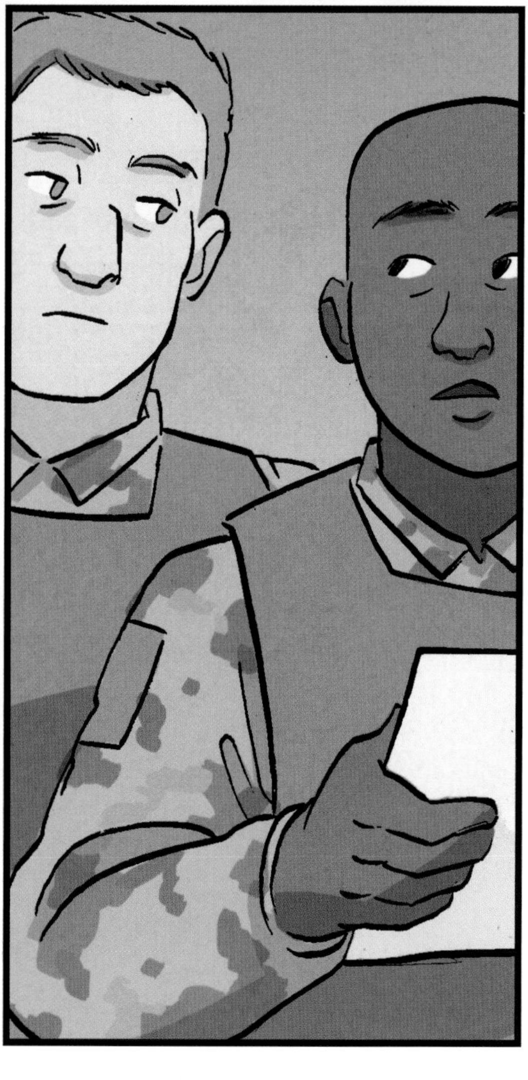

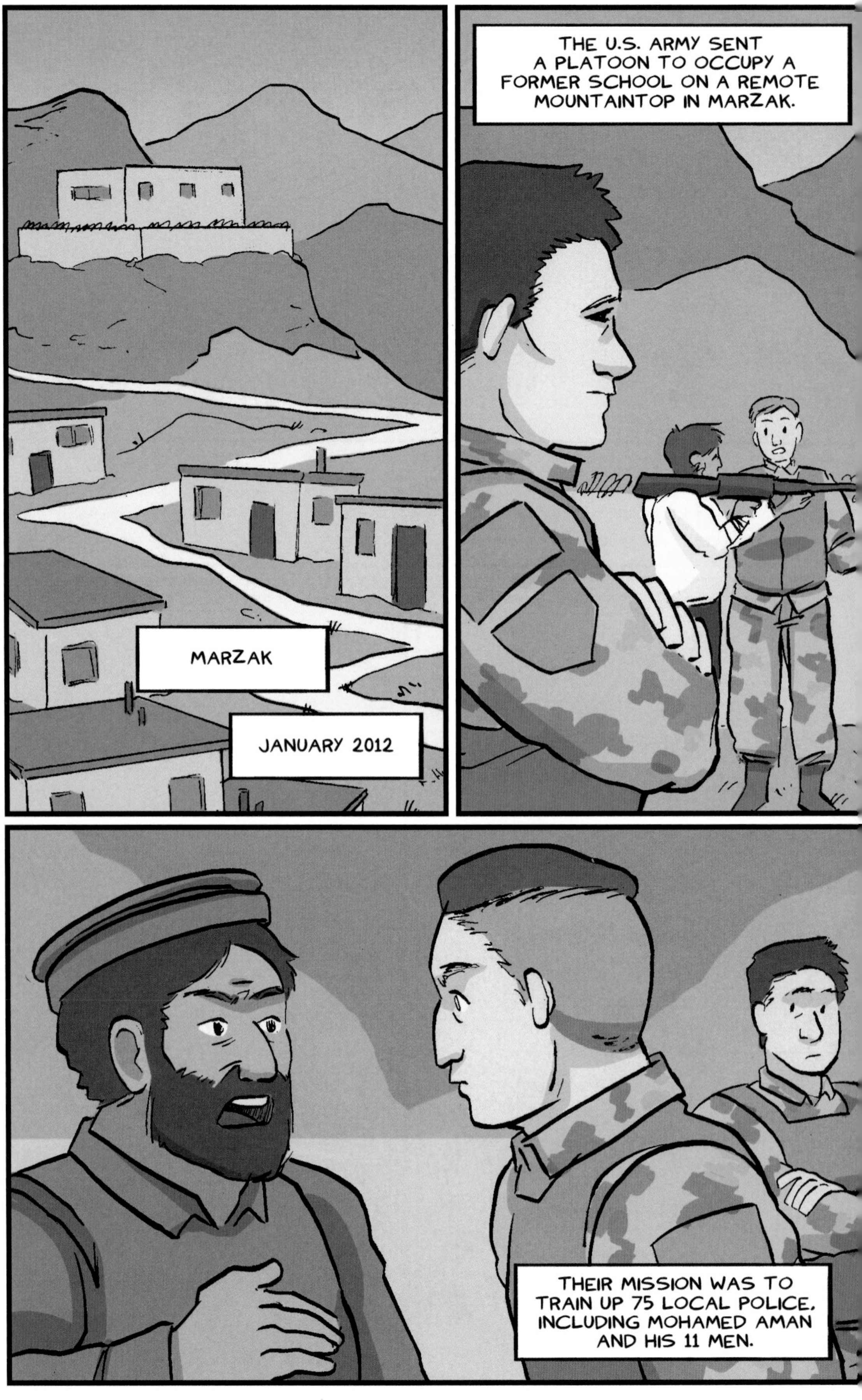
MARZAK
JANUARY 2012
THE U.S. ARMY SENT A PLATOON TO OCCUPY A FORMER SCHOOL ON A REMOTE MOUNTAINTOP IN MARZAK.
THEIR MISSION WAS TO TRAIN UP 75 LOCAL POLICE, INCLUDING MOHAMED AMAN AND HIS 11 MEN.

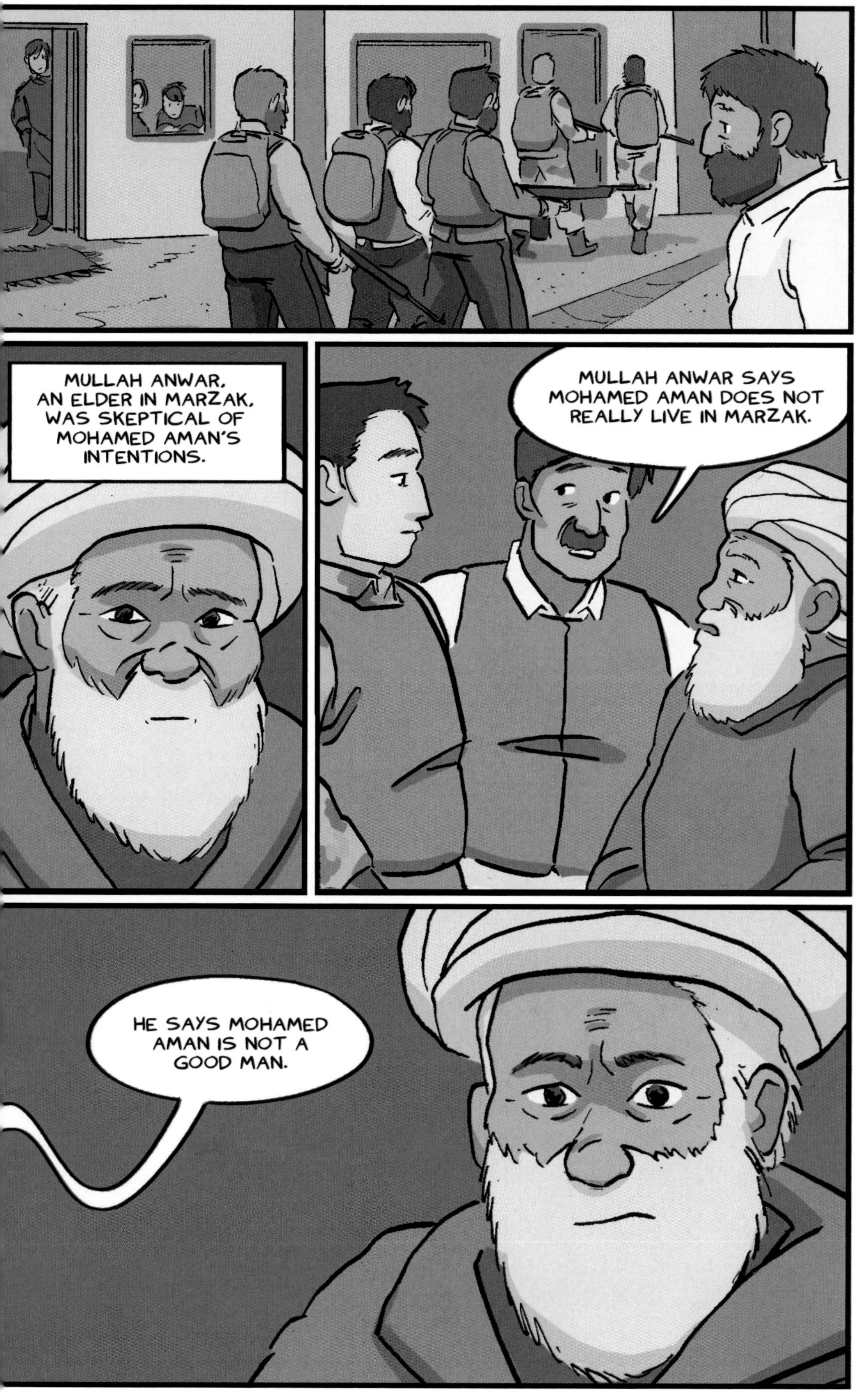
MULLAH ANWAR, AN ELDER IN MARZAK, WAS SKEPTICAL OF MOHAMED AMAN'S INTENTIONS.
MULLAH ANWAR SAYS MOHAMED AMAN DOES NOT REALLY LIVE IN MARZAK.
HE SAYS MOHAMED AMAN IS NOT A GOOD MAN.

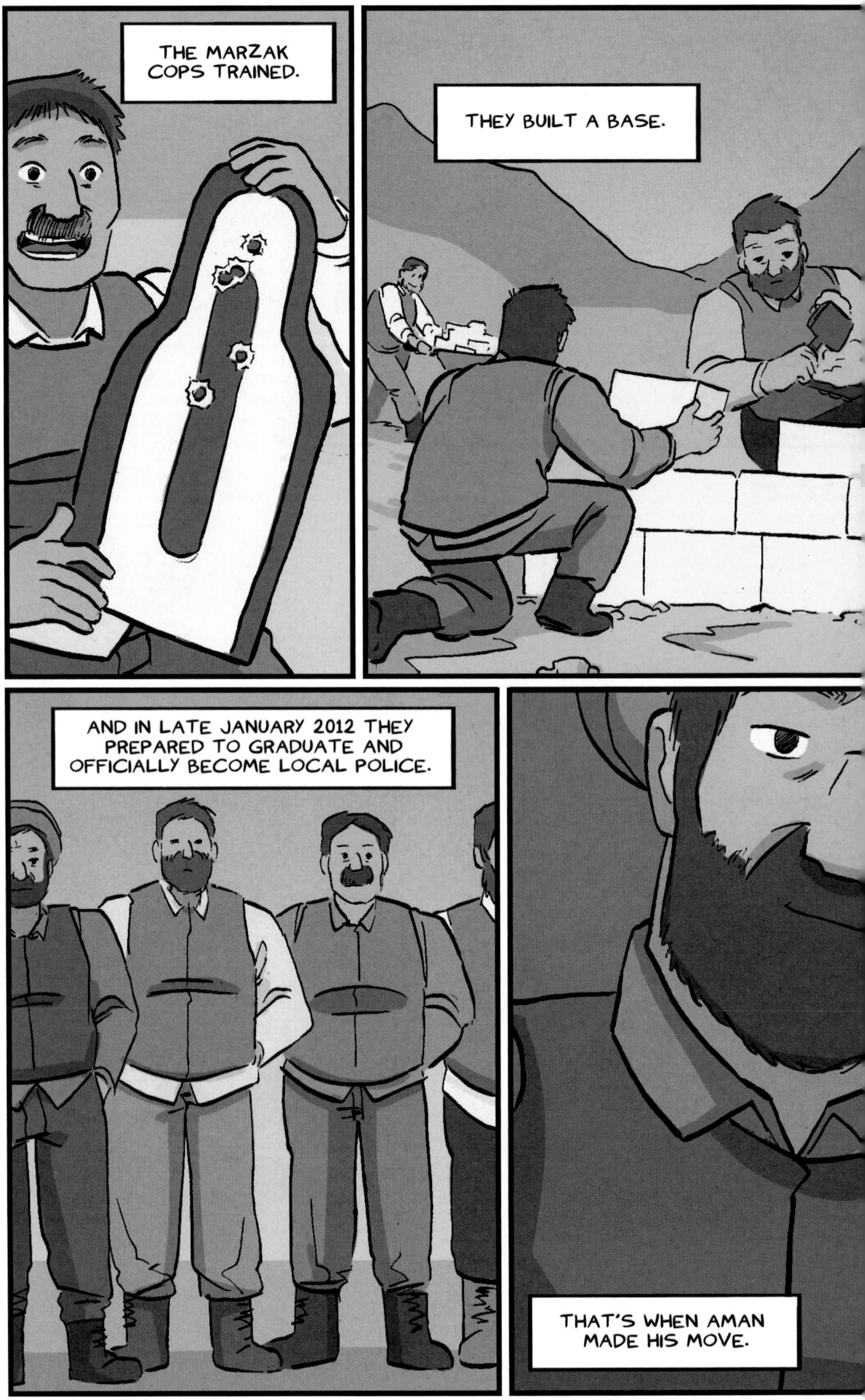
THE MARZAK COPS TRAINED.
THEY BUILT A BASE.
AND IN LATE JANUARY 2012 THEY PREPARED TO GRADUATE AND OFFICIALLY BECOME LOCAL POLICE.
THAT'S WHEN AMAN MADE HIS MOVE.

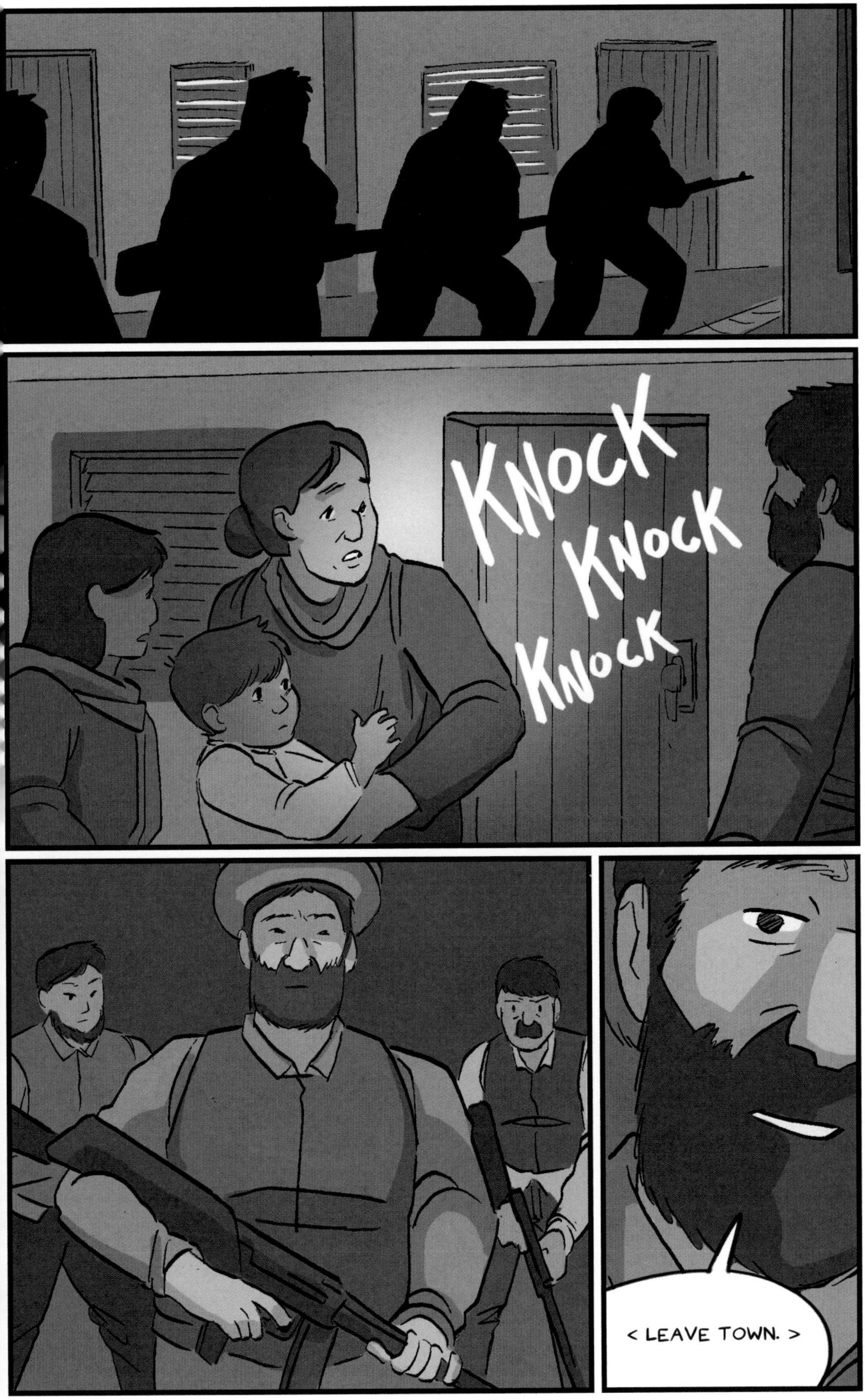
KNOCK
KNOCK
KNOCK
< LEAVE TOWN. >

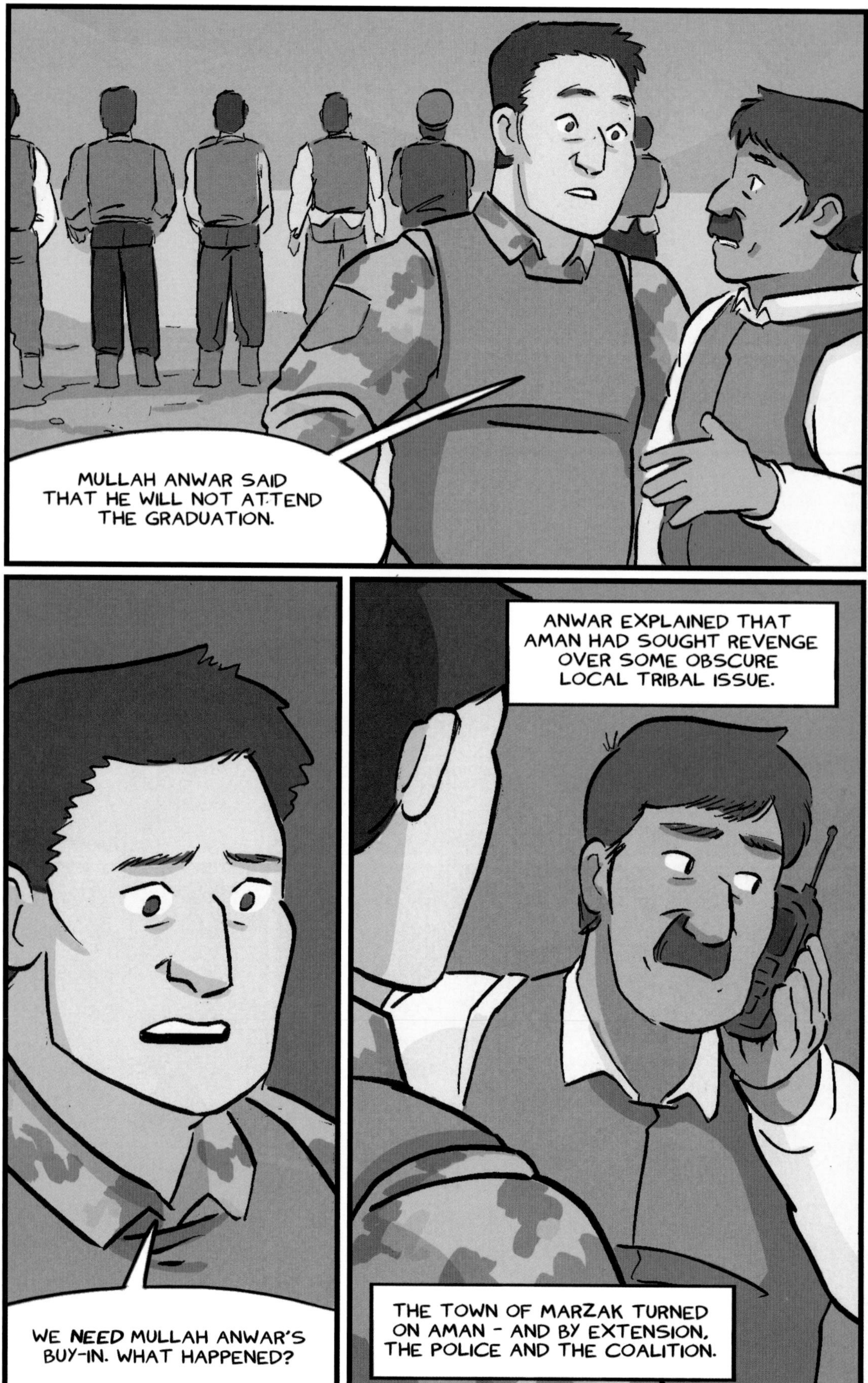
MULLAH ANWAR SAID THAT HE WILL NOT ATTEND THE GRADUATION.
WE NEED MULLAH ANWAR'S BUY-IN. WHAT HAPPENED?
ANWAR EXPLAINED THAT AMAN HAD SOUGHT REVENGE OVER SOME OBSCURE LOCAL TRIBAL ISSUE.
THE TOWN OF MARZAK TURNED ON AMAN - AND BY EXTENSION, THE POLICE AND THE COALITION.

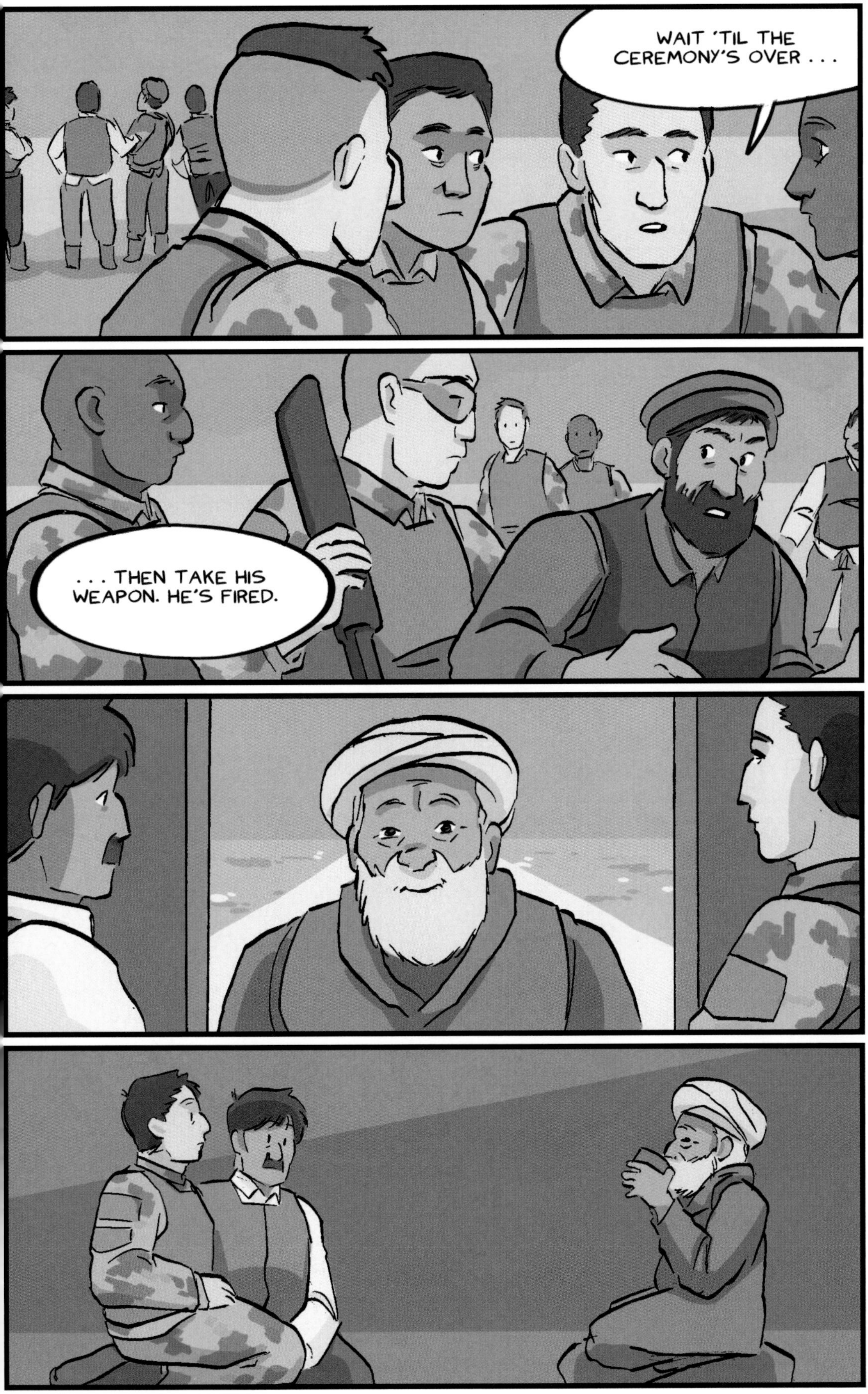
WAIT 'TIL THE CEREMONY'S OVER . . .
. . . THEN TAKE HIS WEAPON. HE'S FIRED.

11 "ALWAYS BE PREPARED"

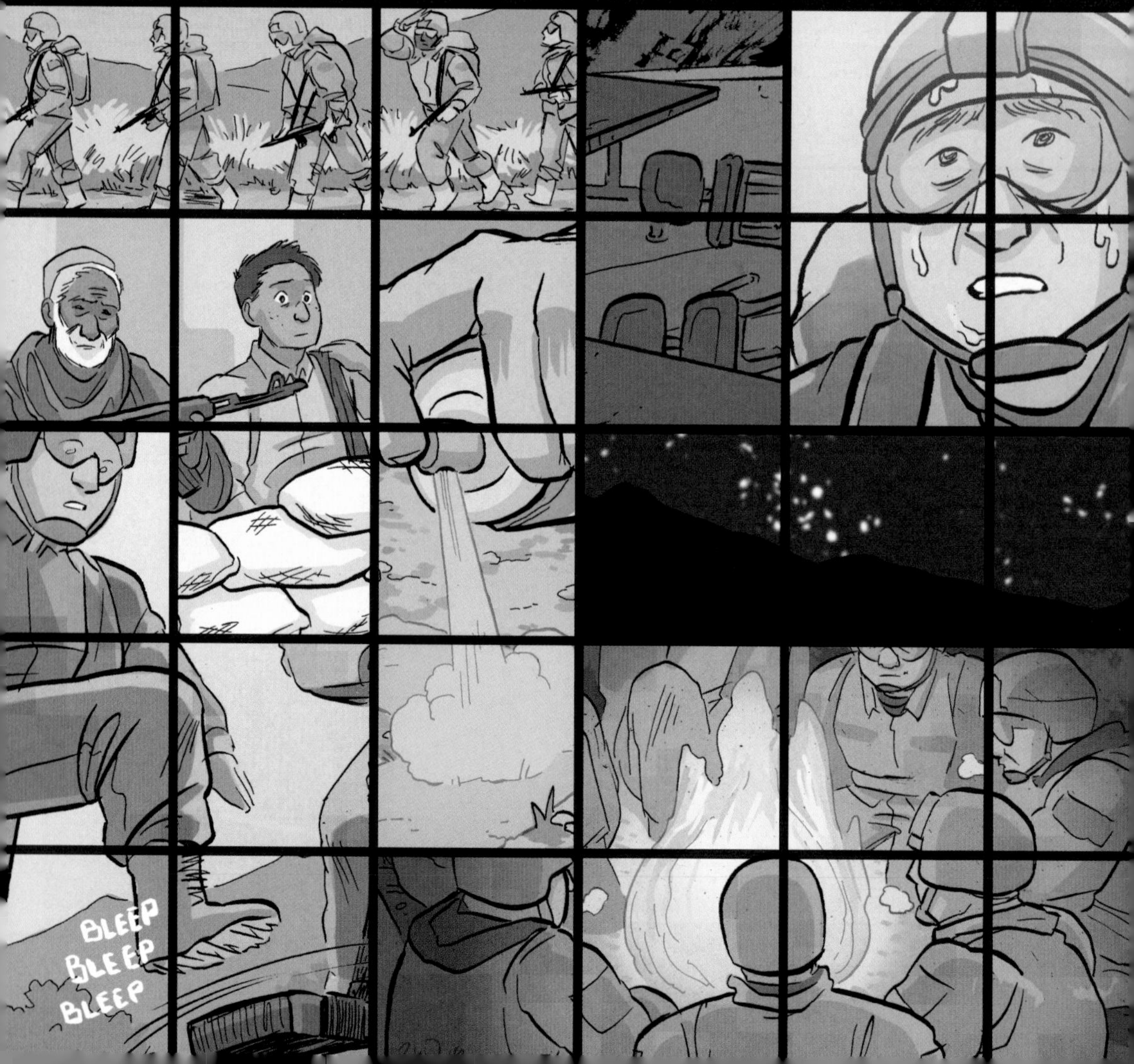
BLEEP
BLEEP
BLEEP

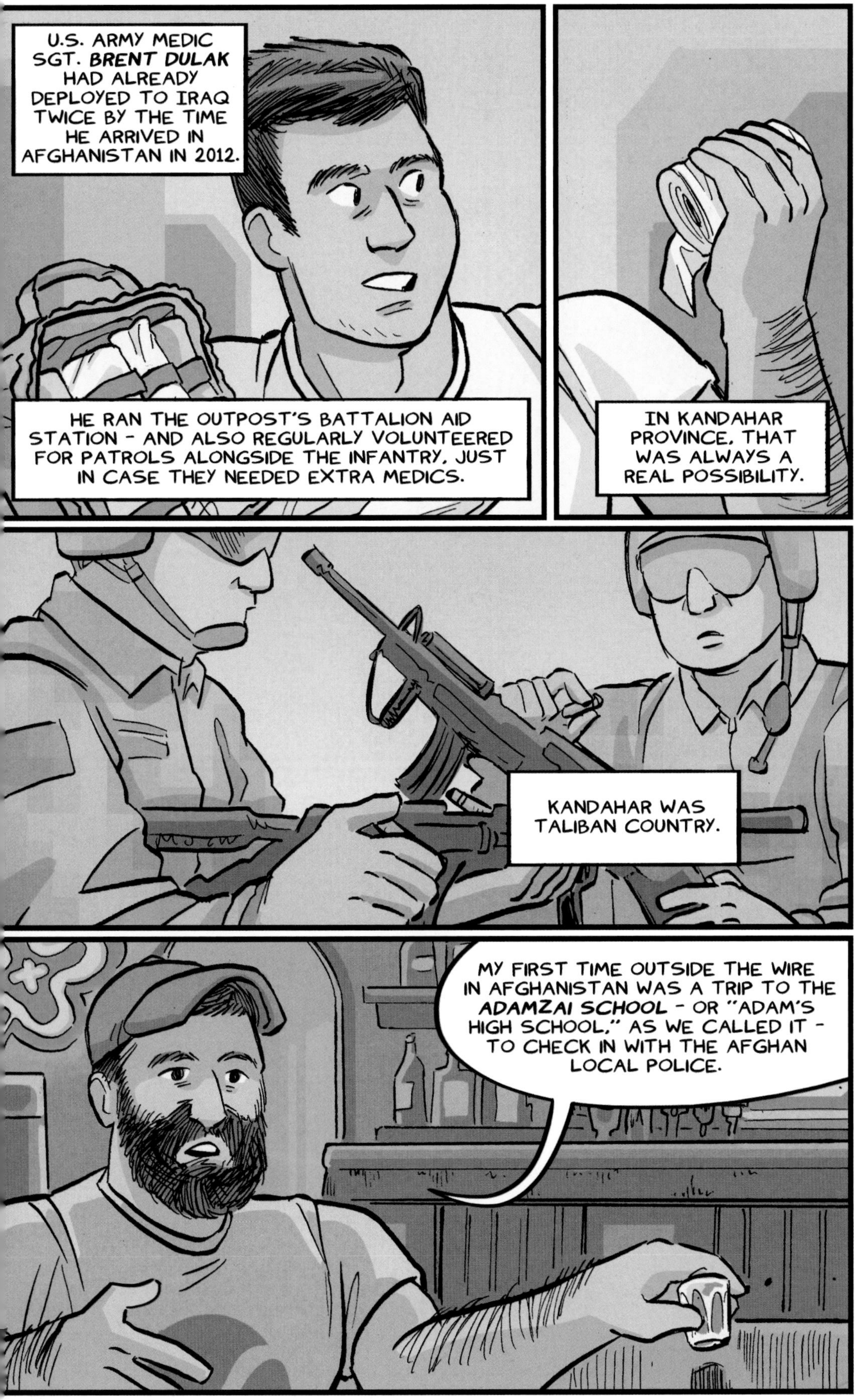
U.S. ARMY MEDIC SGT. **BRENT DULAK** HAD ALREADY DEPLOYED TO IRAQ TWICE BY THE TIME HE ARRIVED IN AFGHANISTAN IN 2012.
HE RAN THE OUTPOST'S BATTALION AID STATION - AND ALSO REGULARLY VOLUNTEERED FOR PATROLS ALONGSIDE THE INFANTRY, JUST IN CASE THEY NEEDED EXTRA MEDICS.
IN KANDAHAR PROVINCE, THAT WAS ALWAYS A REAL POSSIBILITY.
KANDAHAR WAS TALIBAN COUNTRY.
MY FIRST TIME OUTSIDE THE WIRE IN AFGHANISTAN WAS A TRIP TO THE **ADAMZAI SCHOOL** - OR "ADAM'S HIGH SCHOOL," AS WE CALLED IT - TO CHECK IN WITH THE AFGHAN LOCAL POLICE.

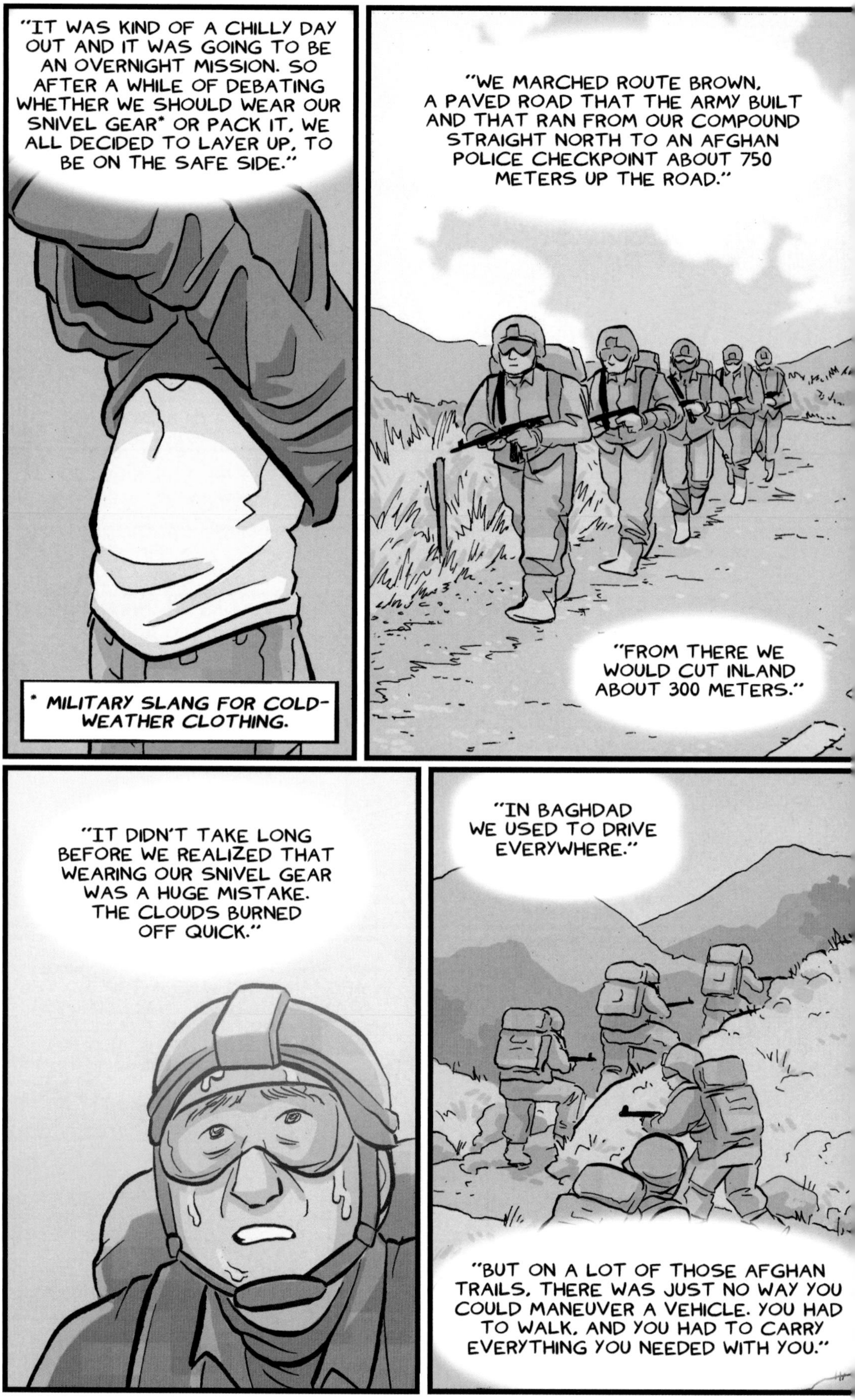
"IT WAS KIND OF A CHILLY DAY OUT AND IT WAS GOING TO BE AN OVERNIGHT MISSION. SO AFTER A WHILE OF DEBATING WHETHER WE SHOULD WEAR OUR SNIVEL GEAR* OR PACK IT, WE ALL DECIDED TO LAYER UP, TO BE ON THE SAFE SIDE."
* MILITARY SLANG FOR COLD-WEATHER CLOTHING.
"WE MARCHED ROUTE BROWN, A PAVED ROAD THAT THE ARMY BUILT AND THAT RAN FROM OUR COMPOUND STRAIGHT NORTH TO AN AFGHAN POLICE CHECKPOINT ABOUT 750 METERS UP THE ROAD."
"FROM THERE WE WOULD CUT INLAND ABOUT 300 METERS."
"IT DIDN'T TAKE LONG BEFORE WE REALIZED THAT WEARING OUR SNIVEL GEAR WAS A HUGE MISTAKE. THE CLOUDS BURNED OFF QUICK."
"IN BAGHDAD WE USED TO DRIVE EVERYWHERE."
"BUT ON A LOT OF THOSE AFGHAN TRAILS, THERE WAS JUST NO WAY YOU COULD MANEUVER A VEHICLE. YOU HAD TO WALK, AND YOU HAD TO CARRY EVERYTHING YOU NEEDED WITH YOU."

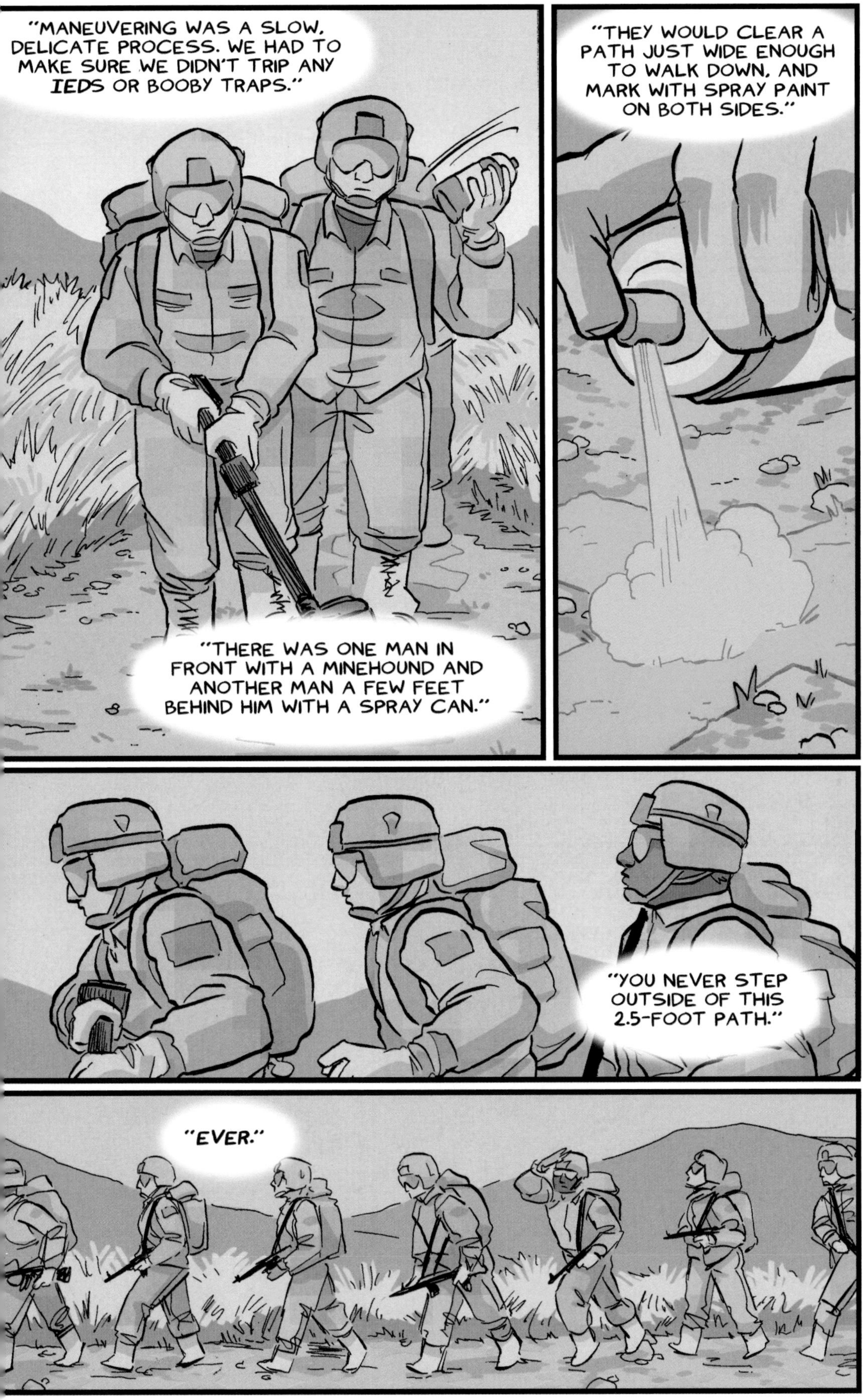
"MANEUVERING WAS A SLOW, DELICATE PROCESS. WE HAD TO MAKE SURE WE DIDN'T TRIP ANY IEDS OR BOOBY TRAPS."
"THERE WAS ONE MAN IN FRONT WITH A MINEHOUND AND ANOTHER MAN A FEW FEET BEHIND HIM WITH A SPRAY CAN."
"THEY WOULD CLEAR A PATH JUST WIDE ENOUGH TO WALK DOWN, AND MARK WITH SPRAY PAINT ON BOTH SIDES."
"YOU NEVER STEP OUTSIDE OF THIS 2.5-FOOT PATH."
"EVER."

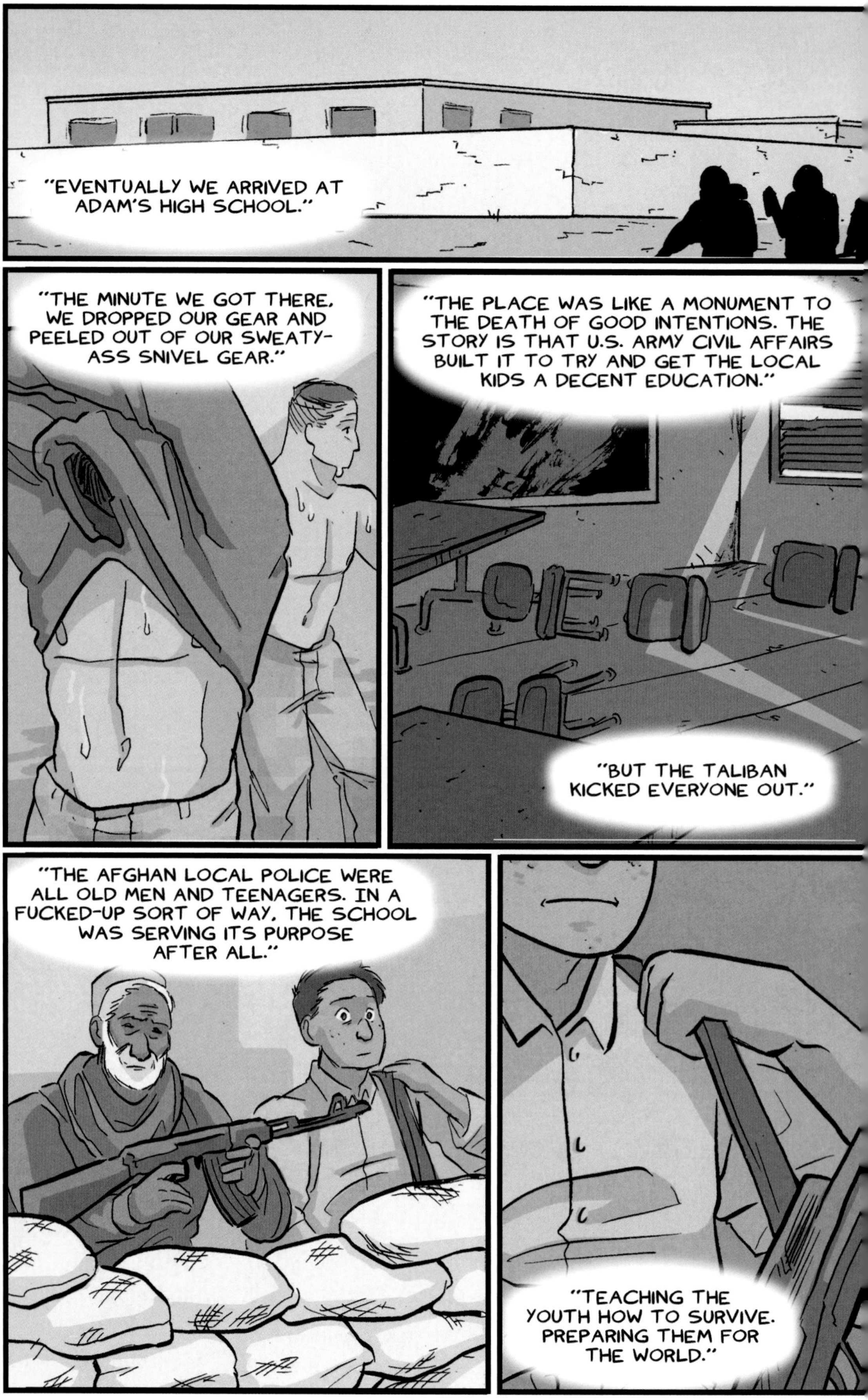
"EVENTUALLY WE ARRIVED AT ADAM'S HIGH SCHOOL."
"THE MINUTE WE GOT THERE, WE DROPPED OUR GEAR AND PEELED OUT OF OUR SWEATY-ASS SNIVEL GEAR."
"THE PLACE WAS LIKE A MONUMENT TO THE DEATH OF GOOD INTENTIONS. THE STORY IS THAT U.S. ARMY CIVIL AFFAIRS BUILT IT TO TRY AND GET THE LOCAL KIDS A DECENT EDUCATION."
"BUT THE TALIBAN KICKED EVERYONE OUT."
"THE AFGHAN LOCAL POLICE WERE ALL OLD MEN AND TEENAGERS. IN A FUCKED-UP SORT OF WAY, THE SCHOOL WAS SERVING ITS PURPOSE AFTER ALL."
"TEACHING THE YOUTH HOW TO SURVIVE. PREPARING THEM FOR THE WORLD."

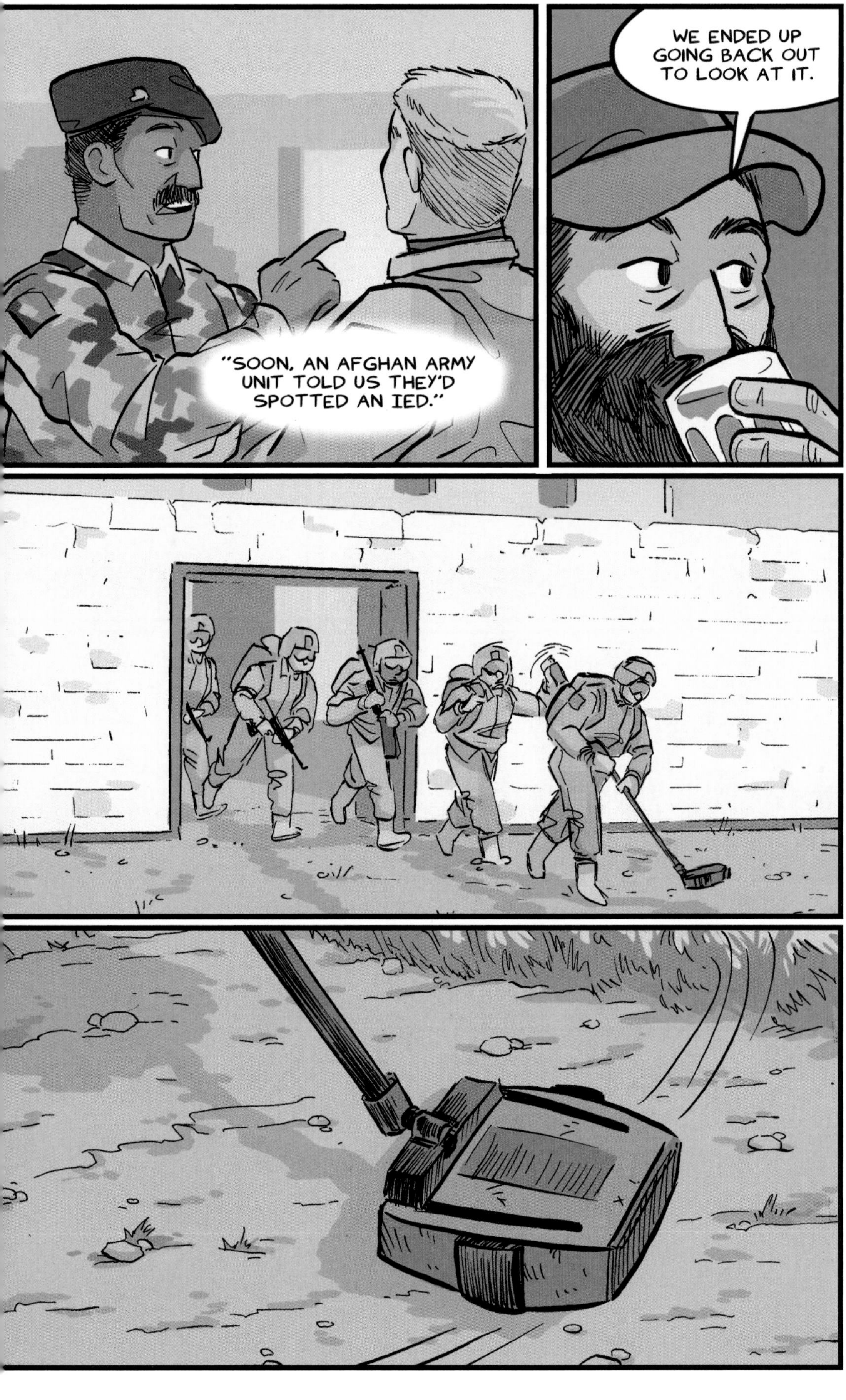
"SOON, AN AFGHAN ARMY UNIT TOLD US THEY'D SPOTTED AN IED."
WE ENDED UP GOING BACK OUT TO LOOK AT IT.

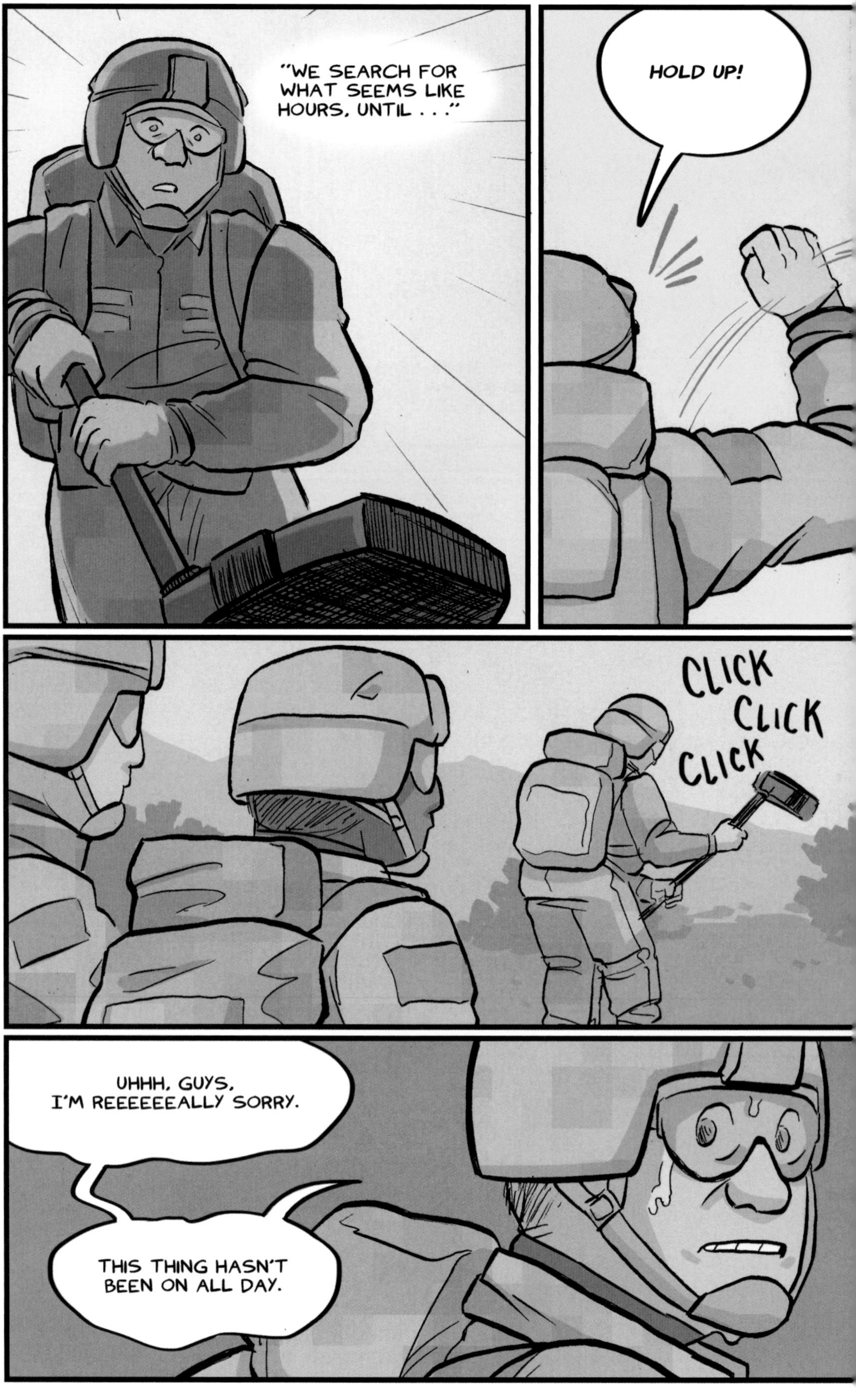
"WE SEARCH FOR WHAT SEEMS LIKE HOURS, UNTIL . . ."
HOLD UP!
CLICK
CLICK
CLICK
UHHH, GUYS, I'M REEEEEEALLY SORRY.
THIS THING HASN'T BEEN ON ALL DAY.

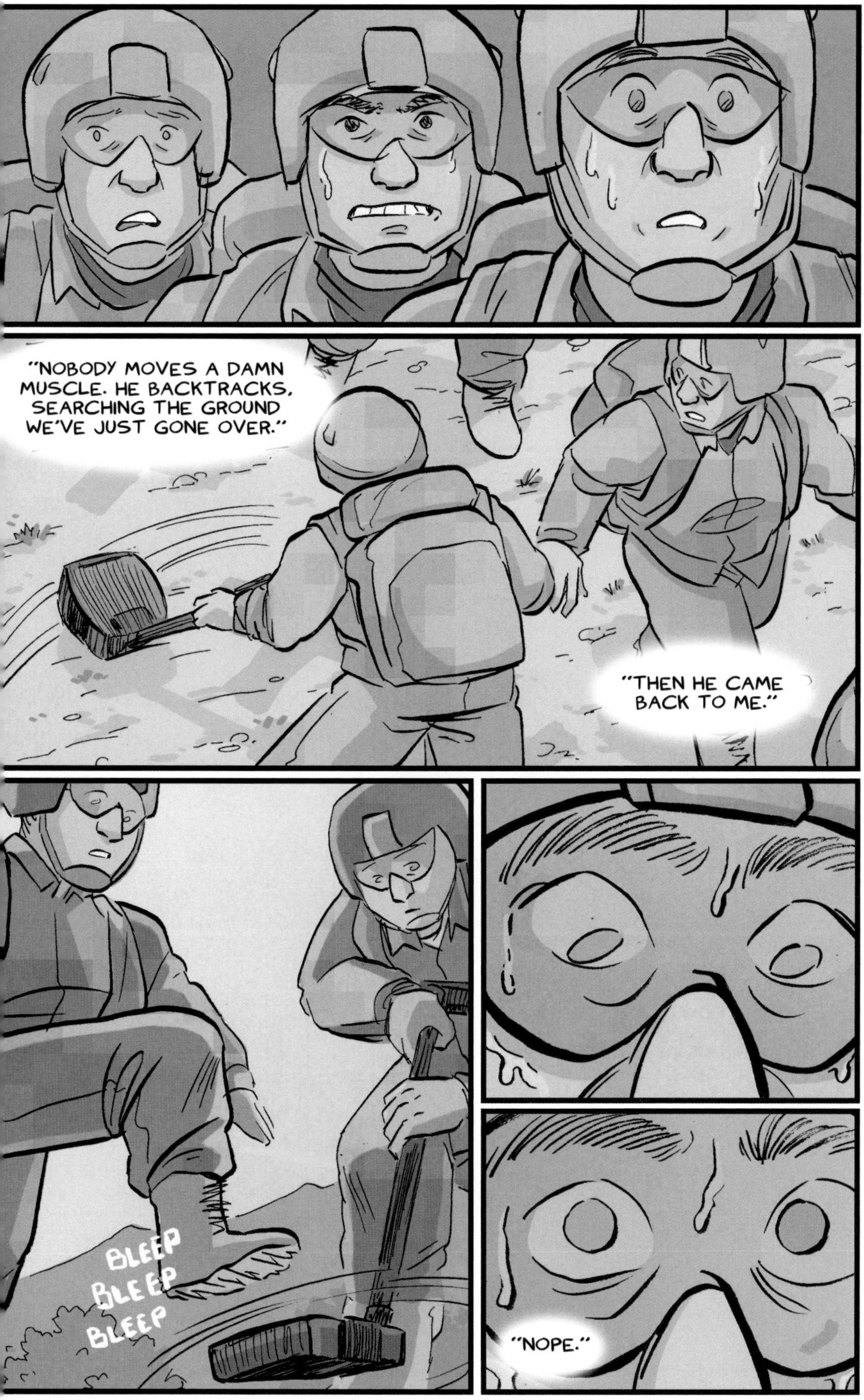
"NOBODY MOVES A DAMN MUSCLE. HE BACKTRACKS, SEARCHING THE GROUND WE'VE JUST GONE OVER."
"THEN HE CAME BACK TO ME."
BLEEP
BLEEP
BLEEP
"NOPE."

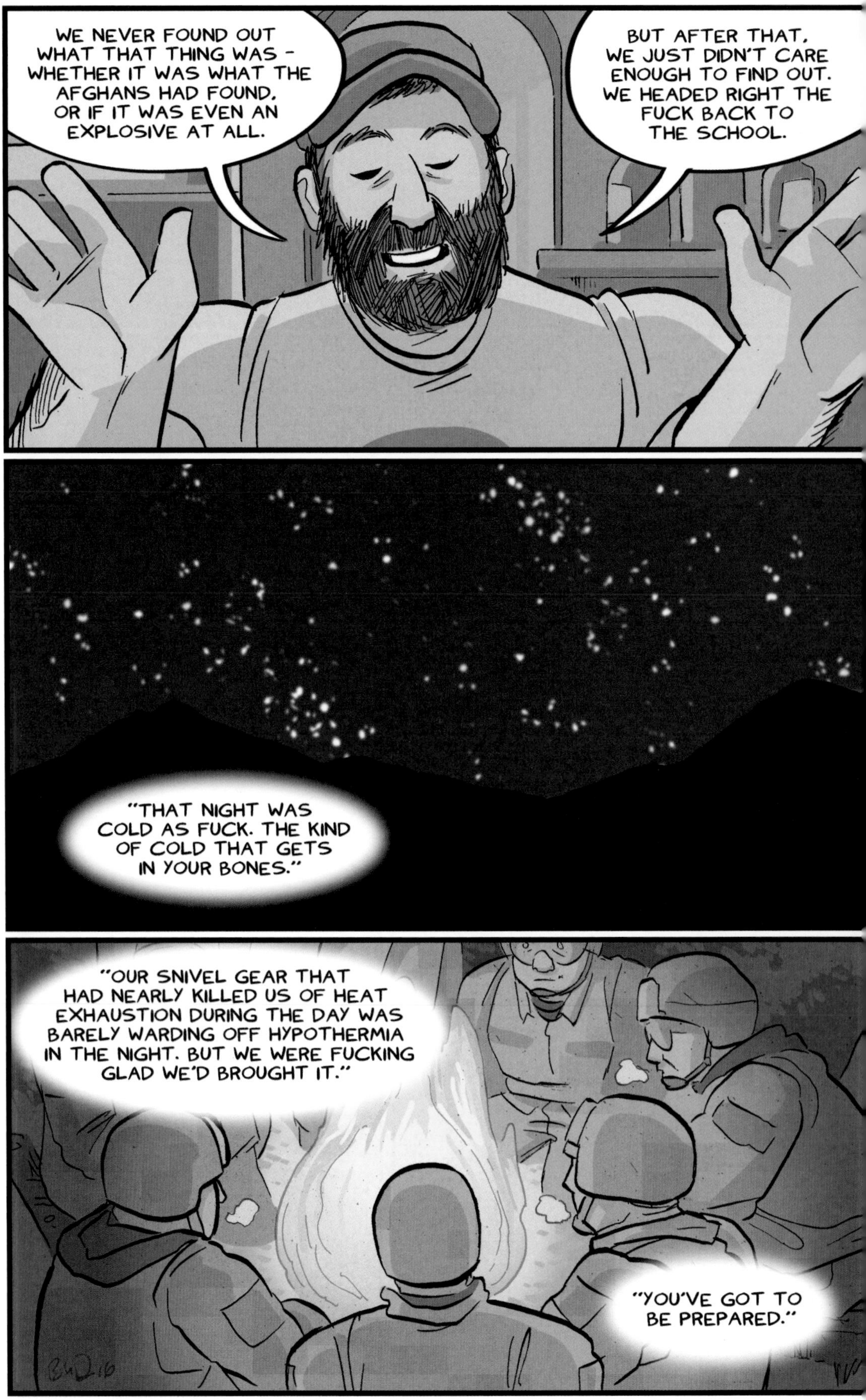
WE NEVER FOUND OUT WHAT THAT THING WAS - WHETHER IT WAS WHAT THE AFGHANS HAD FOUND, OR IF IT WAS EVEN AN EXPLOSIVE AT ALL.
BUT AFTER THAT, WE JUST DIDN'T CARE ENOUGH TO FIND OUT. WE HEADED RIGHT THE FUCK BACK TO THE SCHOOL.
"THAT NIGHT WAS COLD AS FUCK. THE KIND OF COLD THAT GETS IN YOUR BONES."
"OUR SNIVEL GEAR THAT HAD NEARLY KILLED US OF HEAT EXHAUSTION DURING THE DAY WAS BARELY WARDING OFF HYPOTHERMIA IN THE NIGHT. BUT WE WERE FUCKING GLAD WE'D BROUGHT IT."
"YOU'VE GOT TO BE PREPARED."

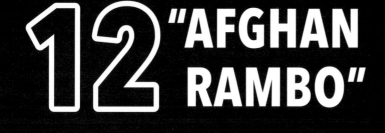

12 "AFGHAN RAMBO"

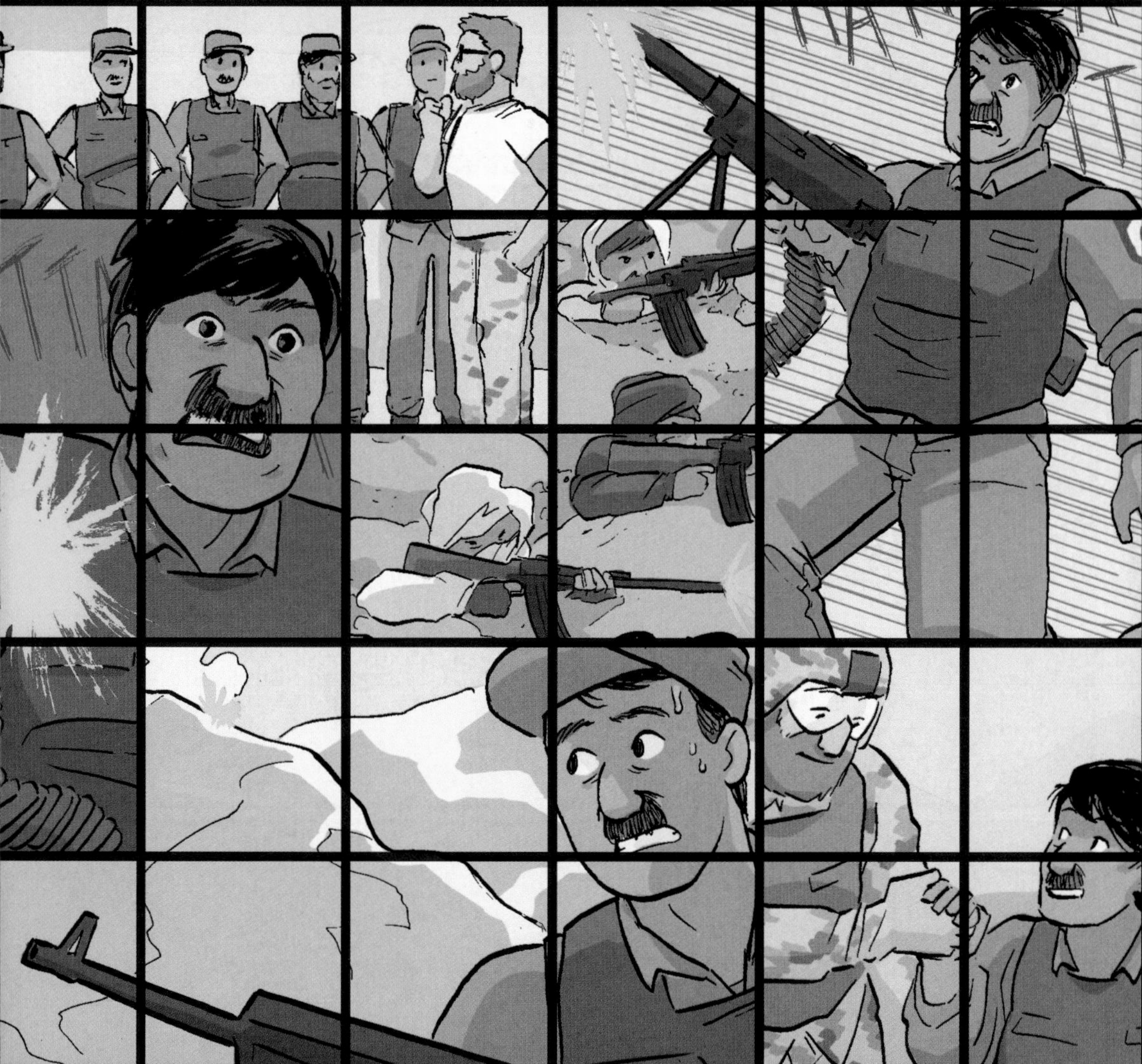

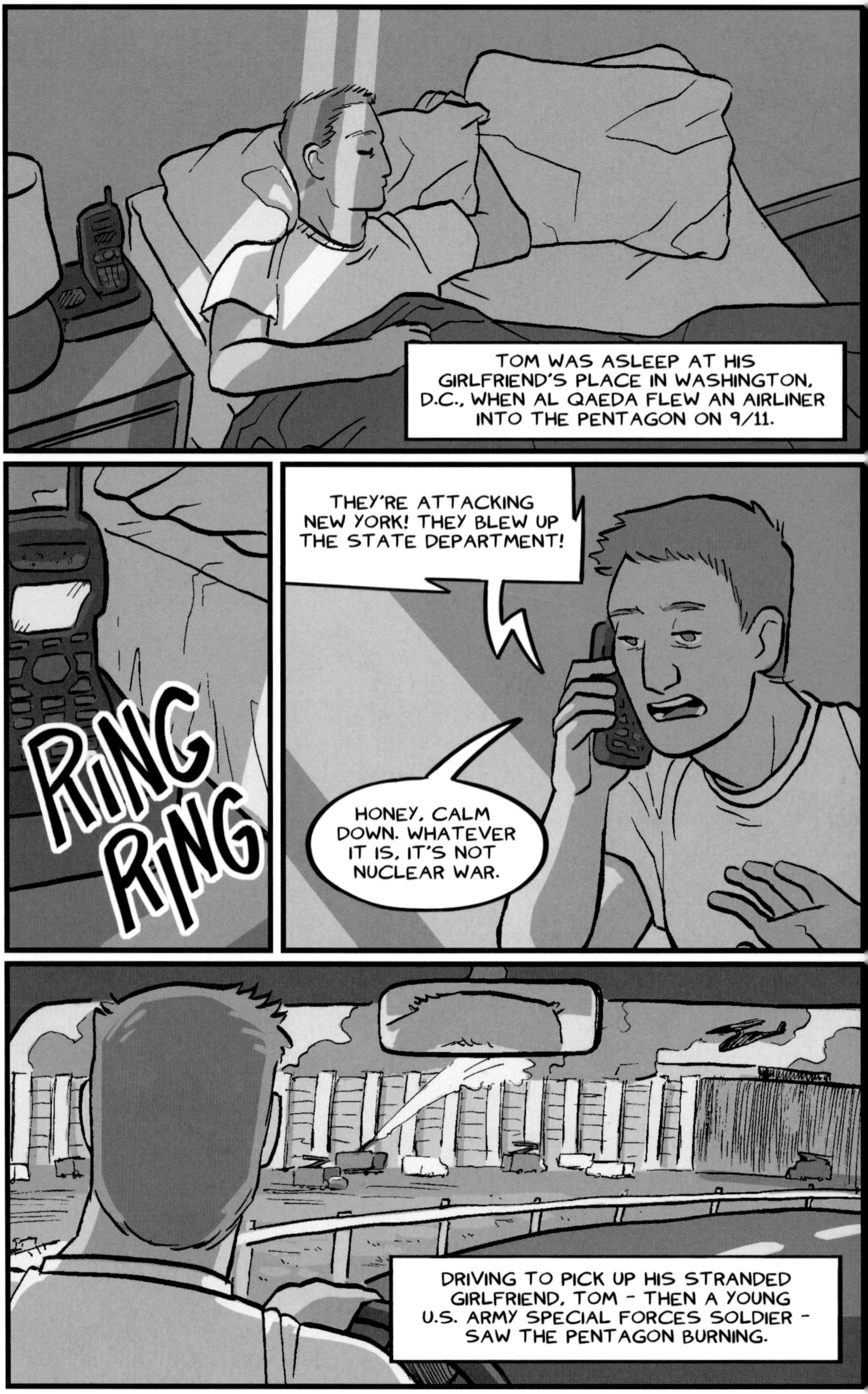
TOM WAS ASLEEP AT HIS GIRLFRIEND'S PLACE IN WASHINGTON, D.C., WHEN AL QAEDA FLEW AN AIRLINER INTO THE PENTAGON ON 9/11.
RING RING
THEY'RE ATTACKING NEW YORK! THEY BLEW UP THE STATE DEPARTMENT!
HONEY, CALM DOWN. WHATEVER IT IS, IT'S NOT NUCLEAR WAR.
DRIVING TO PICK UP HIS STRANDED GIRLFRIEND, TOM - THEN A YOUNG U.S. ARMY SPECIAL FORCES SOLDIER - SAW THE PENTAGON BURNING.

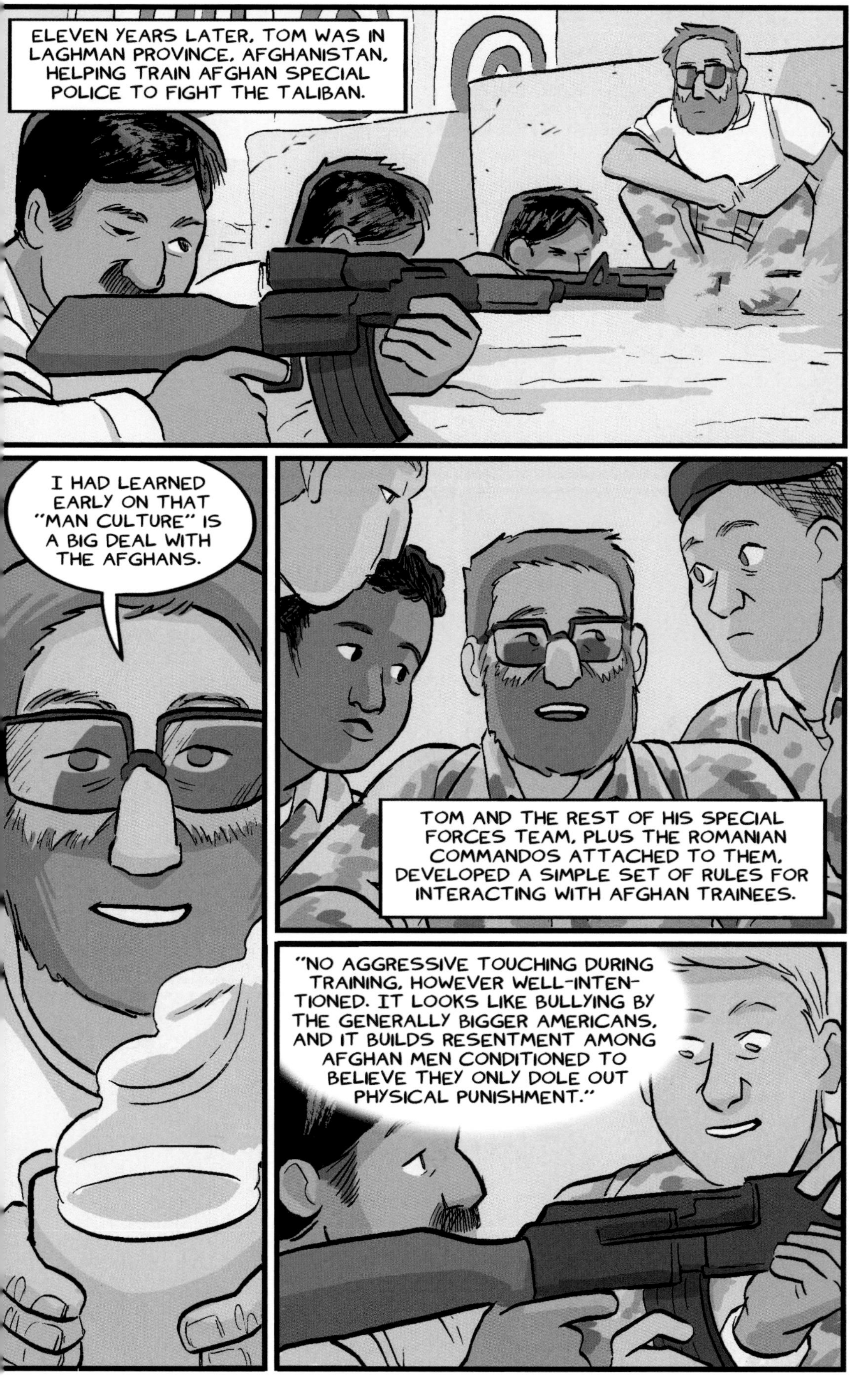
ELEVEN YEARS LATER, TOM WAS IN LAGHMAN PROVINCE, AFGHANISTAN, HELPING TRAIN AFGHAN SPECIAL POLICE TO FIGHT THE TALIBAN.
I HAD LEARNED EARLY ON THAT "MAN CULTURE" IS A BIG DEAL WITH THE AFGHANS.
TOM AND THE REST OF HIS SPECIAL FORCES TEAM, PLUS THE ROMANIAN COMMANDOS ATTACHED TO THEM, DEVELOPED A SIMPLE SET OF RULES FOR INTERACTING WITH AFGHAN TRAINEES.
"NO AGGRESSIVE TOUCHING DURING TRAINING, HOWEVER WELL-INTENTIONED. IT LOOKS LIKE BULLYING BY THE GENERALLY BIGGER AMERICANS, AND IT BUILDS RESENTMENT AMONG AFGHAN MEN CONDITIONED TO BELIEVE THEY ONLY DOLE OUT PHYSICAL PUNISHMENT."

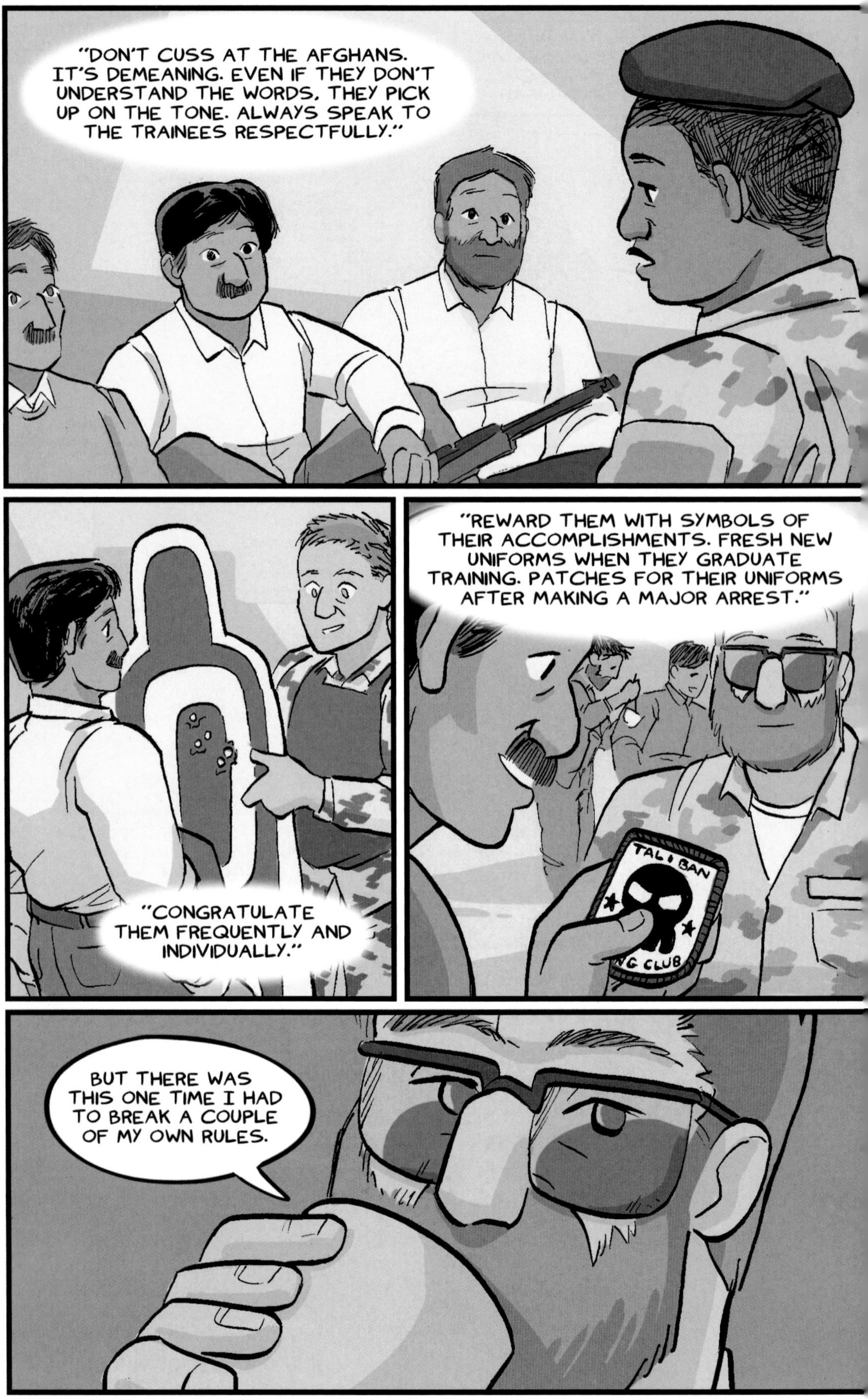
"DON'T CUSS AT THE AFGHANS. IT'S DEMEANING. EVEN IF THEY DON'T UNDERSTAND THE WORDS, THEY PICK UP ON THE TONE. ALWAYS SPEAK TO THE TRAINEES RESPECTFULLY."
"CONGRATULATE THEM FREQUENTLY AND INDIVIDUALLY."
"REWARD THEM WITH SYMBOLS OF THEIR ACCOMPLISHMENTS. FRESH NEW UNIFORMS WHEN THEY GRADUATE TRAINING. PATCHES FOR THEIR UNIFORMS AFTER MAKING A MAJOR ARREST."
BUT THERE WAS THIS ONE TIME I HAD TO BREAK A COUPLE OF MY OWN RULES.

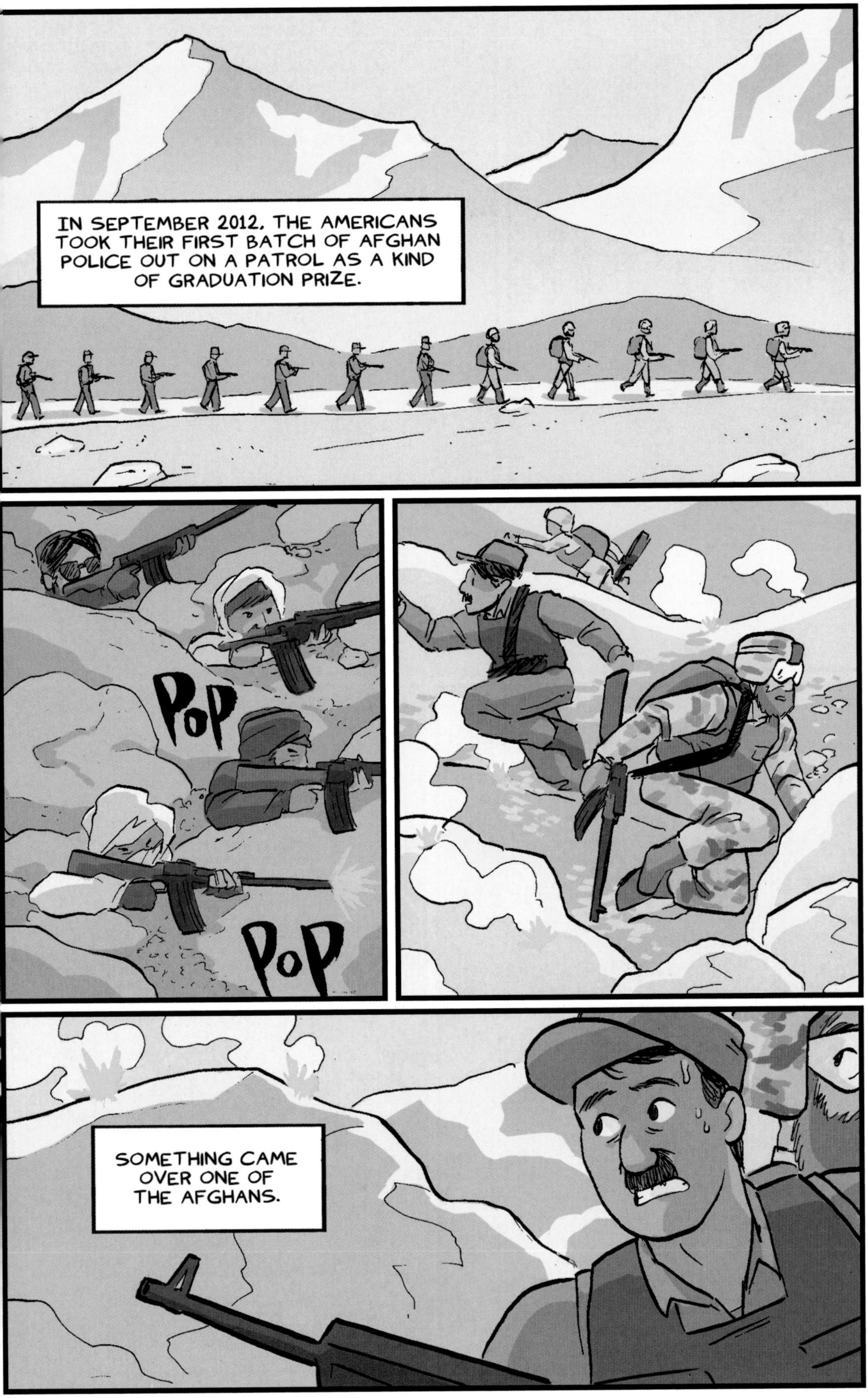
IN SEPTEMBER 2012, THE AMERICANS TOOK THEIR FIRST BATCH OF AFGHAN POLICE OUT ON A PATROL AS A KIND OF GRADUATION PRIZE.
POP
POP
SOMETHING CAME OVER ONE OF THE AFGHANS.

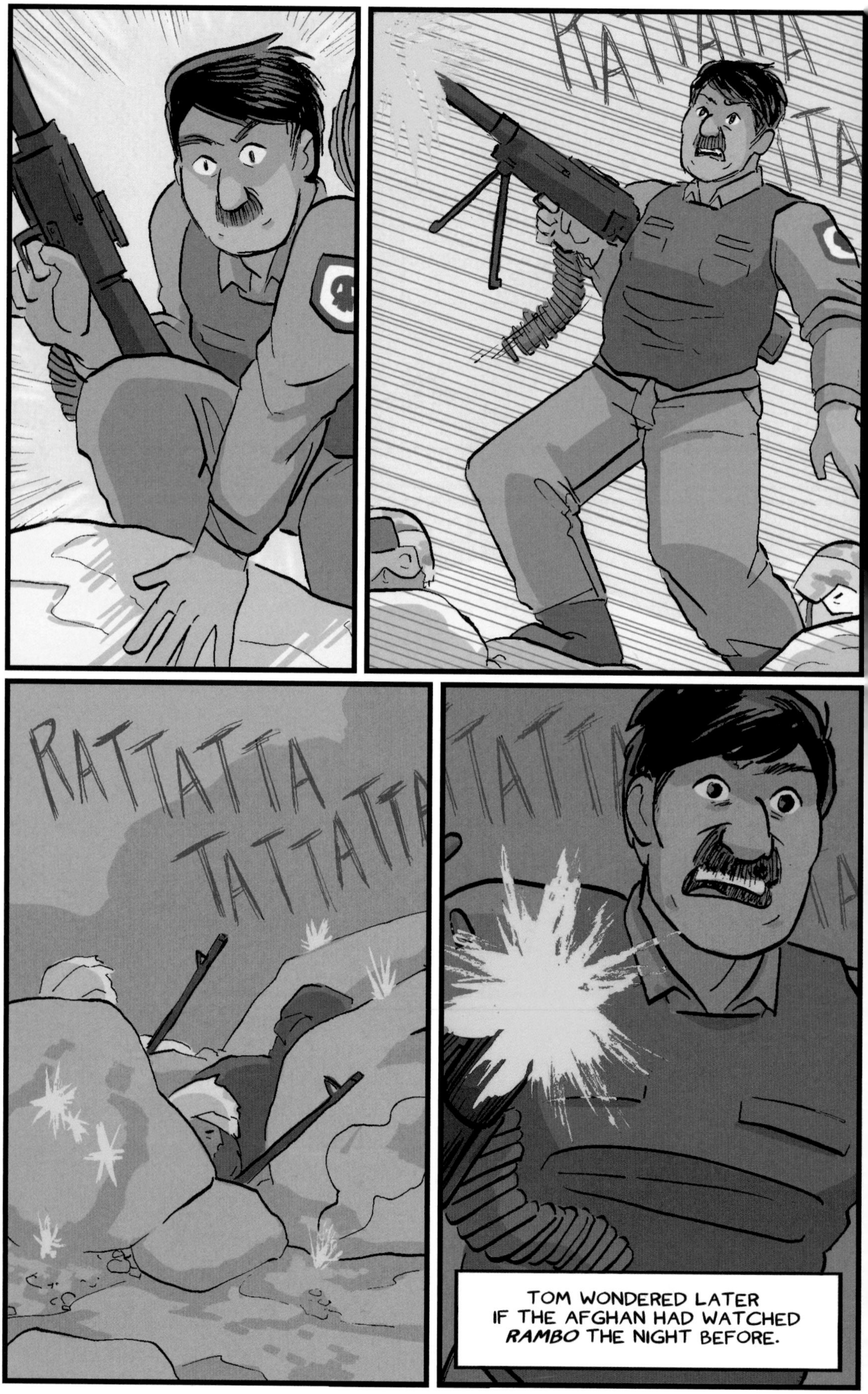
RATTATTA
TATTATTA
TOM WONDERED LATER
IF THE AFGHAN HAD WATCHED
RAMBO THE NIGHT BEFORE.

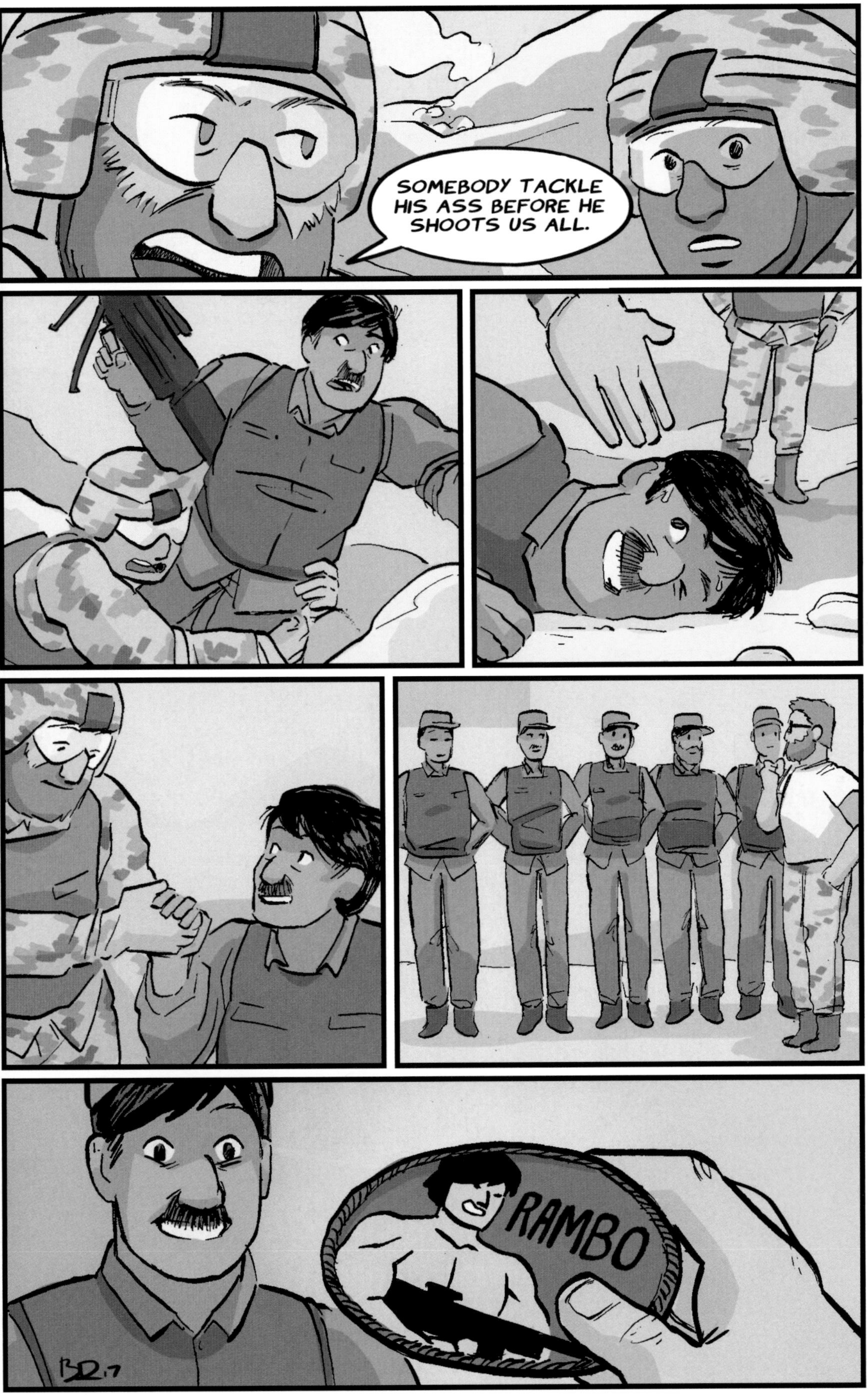
SOMEBODY TACKLE HIS ASS BEFORE HE SHOOTS US ALL.
RAMBO

13 "TALL TALES"

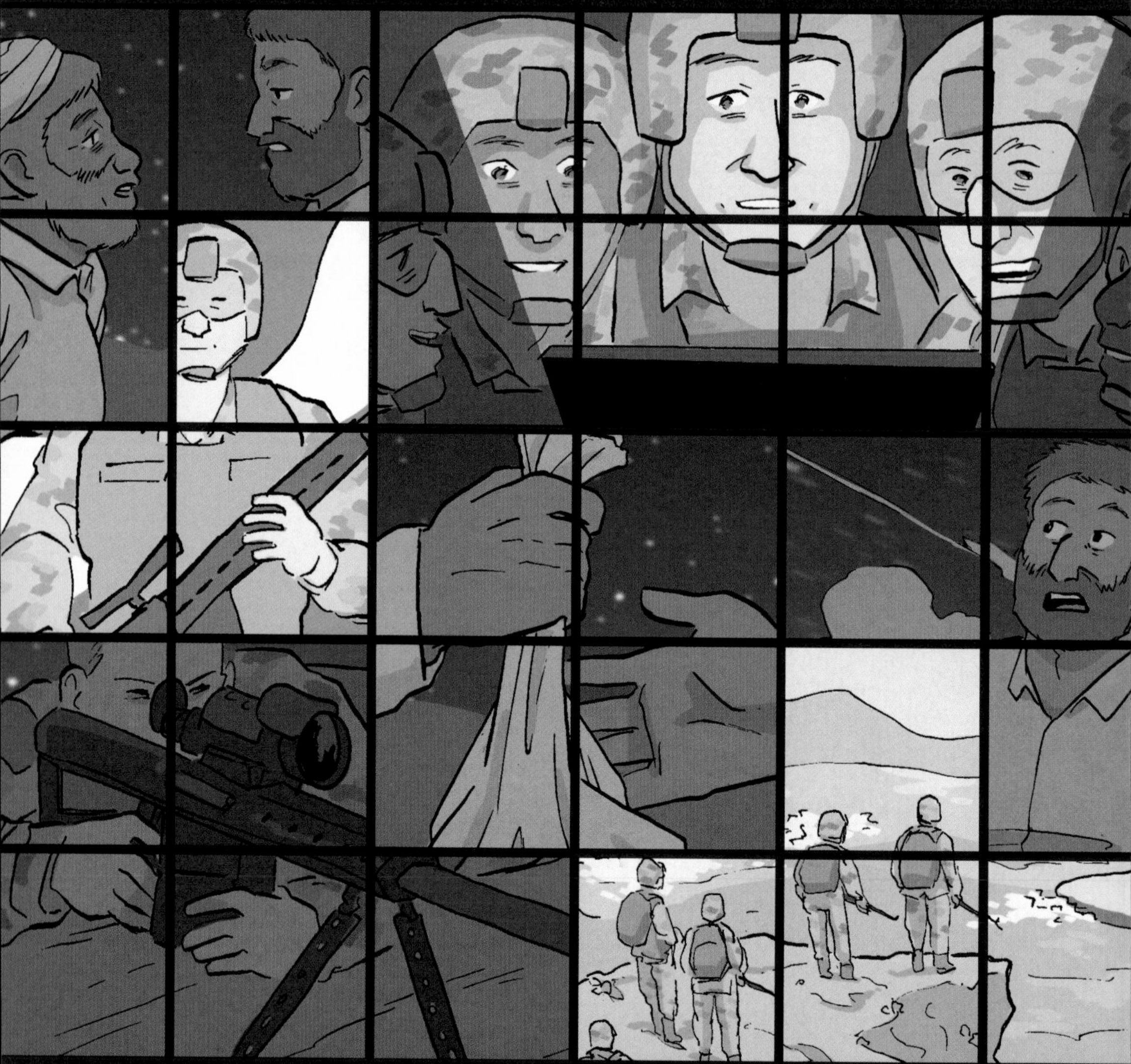

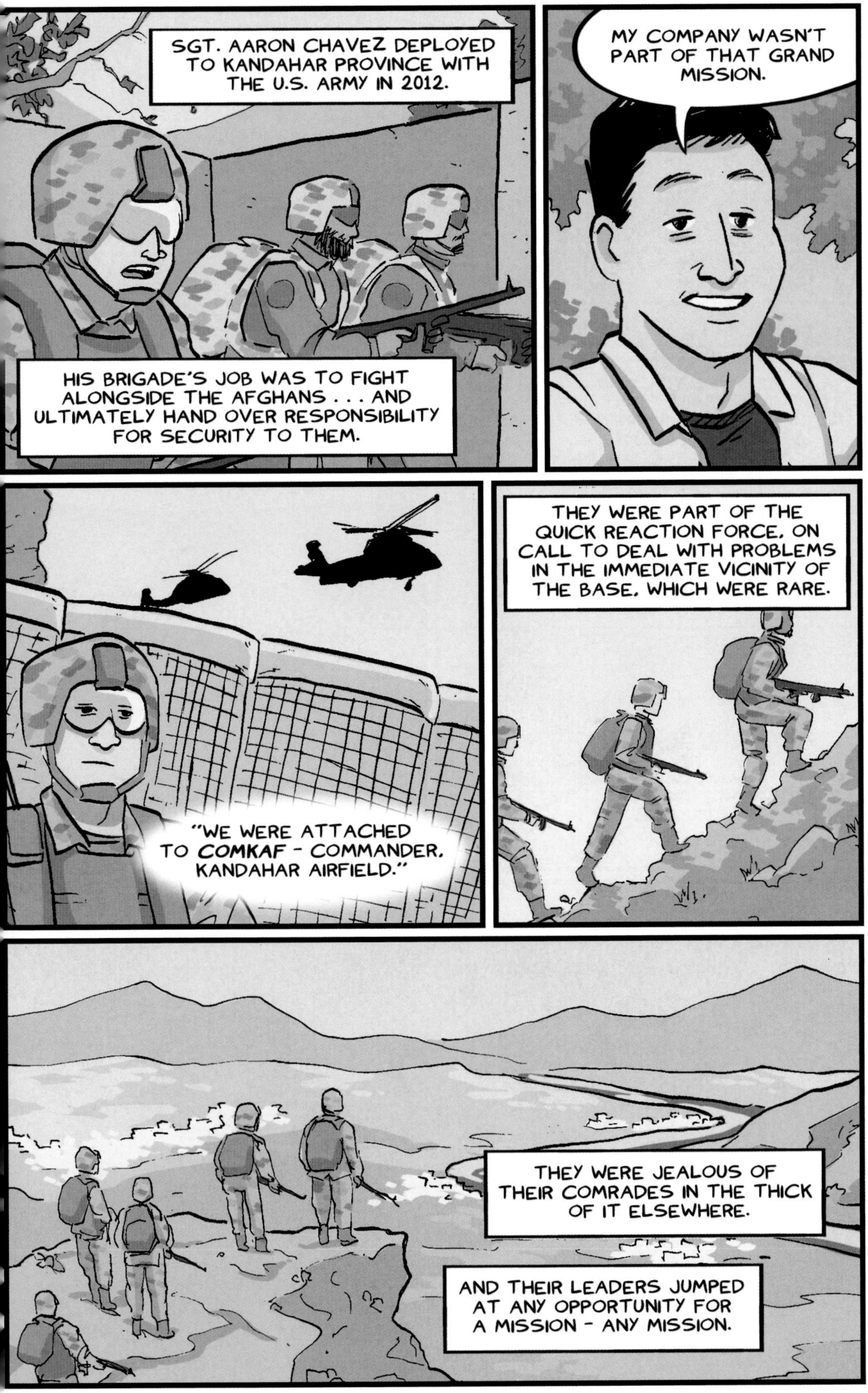
SGT. AARON CHAVEZ DEPLOYED TO KANDAHAR PROVINCE WITH THE U.S. ARMY IN 2012.
HIS BRIGADE'S JOB WAS TO FIGHT ALONGSIDE THE AFGHANS . . . AND ULTIMATELY HAND OVER RESPONSIBILITY FOR SECURITY TO THEM.
MY COMPANY WASN'T PART OF THAT GRAND MISSION.
"WE WERE ATTACHED TO *COMKAF* - COMMANDER, KANDAHAR AIRFIELD."
THEY WERE PART OF THE QUICK REACTION FORCE, ON CALL TO DEAL WITH PROBLEMS IN THE IMMEDIATE VICINITY OF THE BASE, WHICH WERE RARE.
THEY WERE JEALOUS OF THEIR COMRADES IN THE THICK OF IT ELSEWHERE.
AND THEIR LEADERS JUMPED AT ANY OPPORTUNITY FOR A MISSION - ANY MISSION.

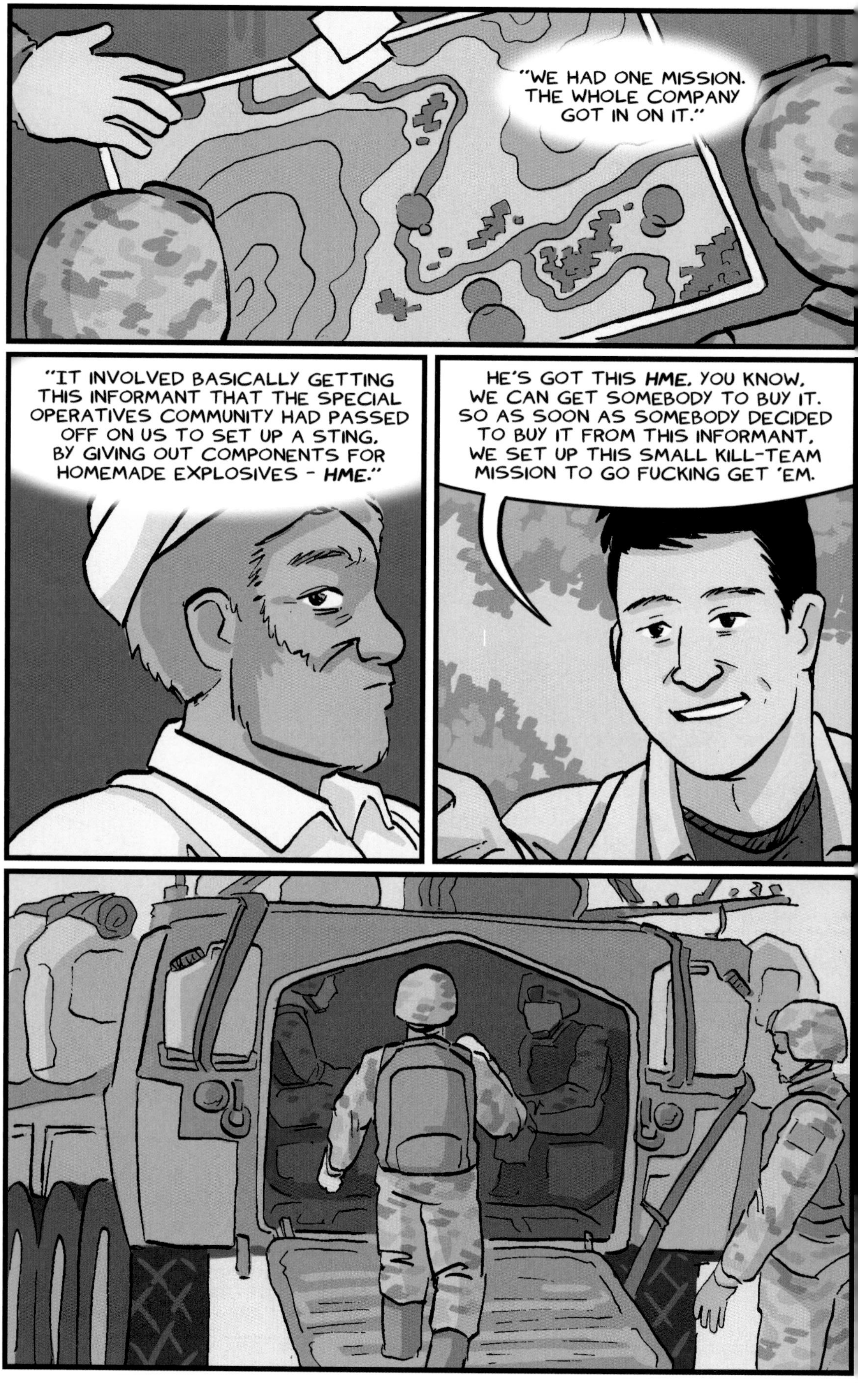
"WE HAD ONE MISSION. THE WHOLE COMPANY GOT IN ON IT."
"IT INVOLVED BASICALLY GETTING THIS INFORMANT THAT THE SPECIAL OPERATIVES COMMUNITY HAD PASSED OFF ON US TO SET UP A STING, BY GIVING OUT COMPONENTS FOR HOMEMADE EXPLOSIVES - HME."
HE'S GOT THIS HME. YOU KNOW, WE CAN GET SOMEBODY TO BUY IT. SO AS SOON AS SOMEBODY DECIDED TO BUY IT FROM THIS INFORMANT, WE SET UP THIS SMALL KILL-TEAM MISSION TO GO FUCKING GET 'EM.

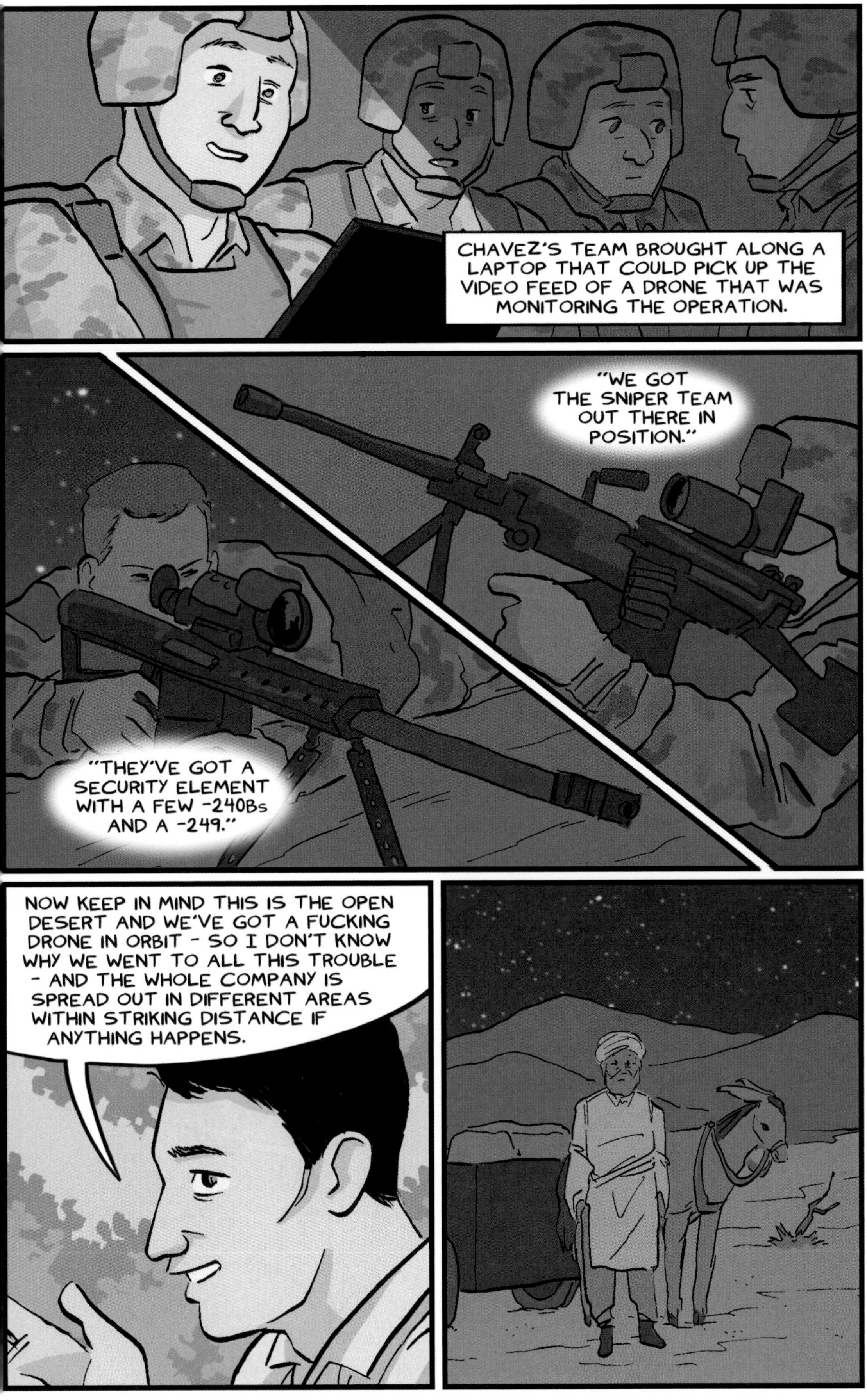
CHAVEZ'S TEAM BROUGHT ALONG A LAPTOP THAT COULD PICK UP THE VIDEO FEED OF A DRONE THAT WAS MONITORING THE OPERATION.
"WE GOT THE SNIPER TEAM OUT THERE IN POSITION."
"THEY'VE GOT A SECURITY ELEMENT WITH A FEW -240Bs AND A -249."
NOW KEEP IN MIND THIS IS THE OPEN DESERT AND WE'VE GOT A FUCKING DRONE IN ORBIT - SO I DON'T KNOW WHY WE WENT TO ALL THIS TROUBLE - AND THE WHOLE COMPANY IS SPREAD OUT IN DIFFERENT AREAS WITHIN STRIKING DISTANCE IF ANYTHING HAPPENS.

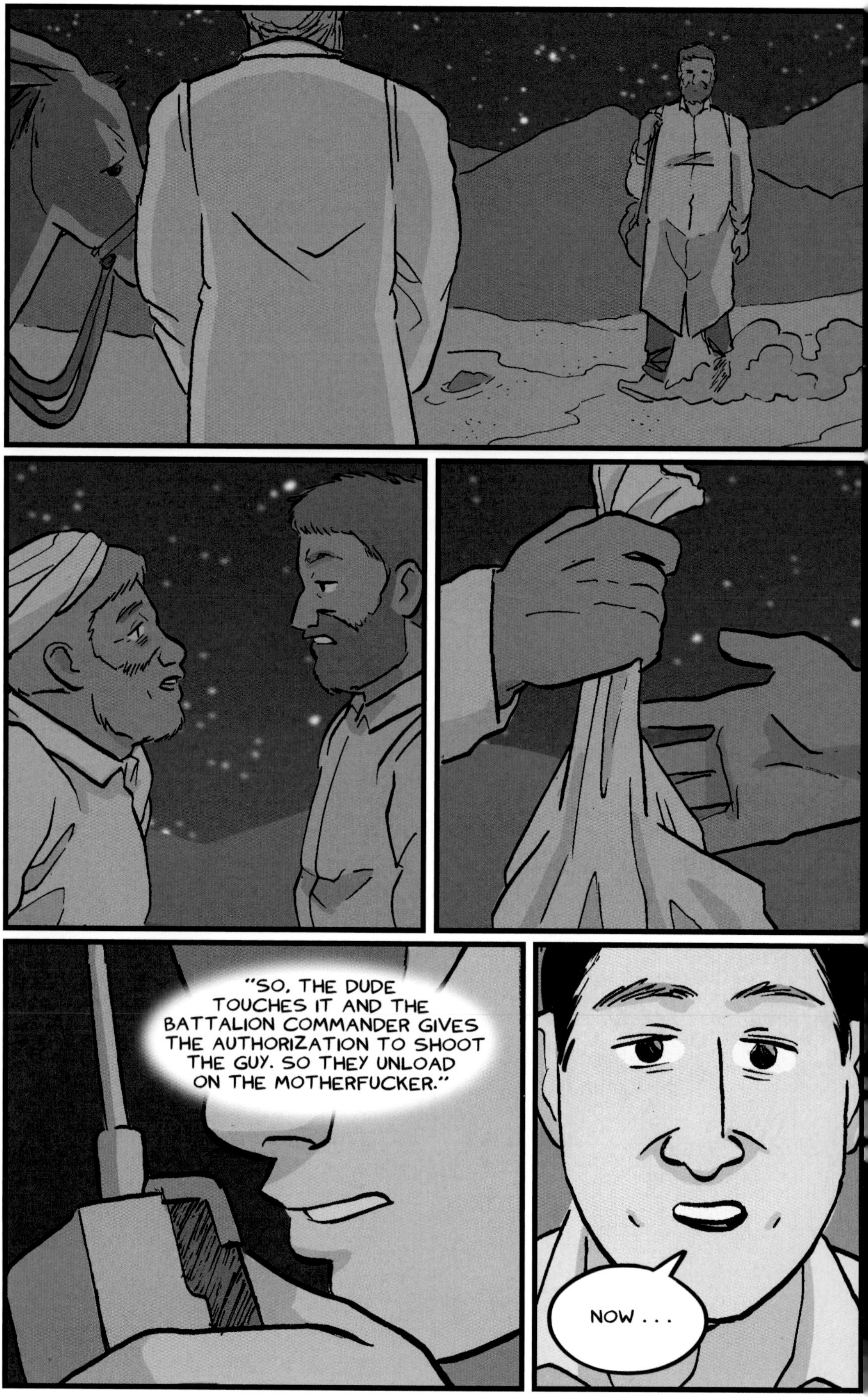
"SO, THE DUDE TOUCHES IT AND THE BATTALION COMMANDER GIVES THE AUTHORIZATION TO SHOOT THE GUY. SO THEY UNLOAD ON THE MOTHERFUCKER."
NOW . . .

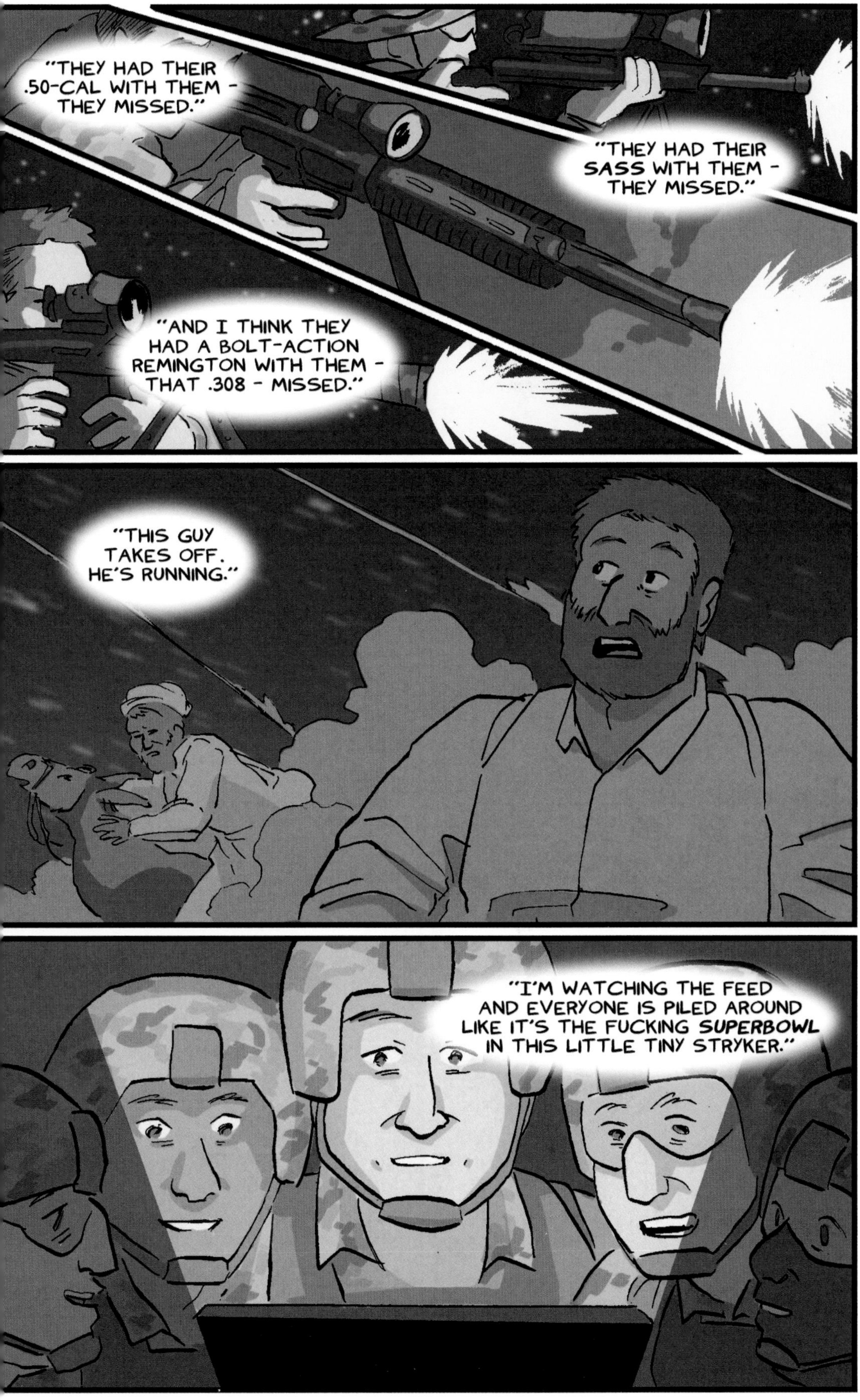
"THEY HAD THEIR .50-CAL WITH THEM - THEY MISSED."
"THEY HAD THEIR SASS WITH THEM - THEY MISSED."
"AND I THINK THEY HAD A BOLT-ACTION REMINGTON WITH THEM - THAT .308 - MISSED."
"THIS GUY TAKES OFF. HE'S RUNNING."
"I'M WATCHING THE FEED AND EVERYONE IS PILED AROUND LIKE IT'S THE FUCKING SUPERBOWL IN THIS LITTLE TINY STRYKER."

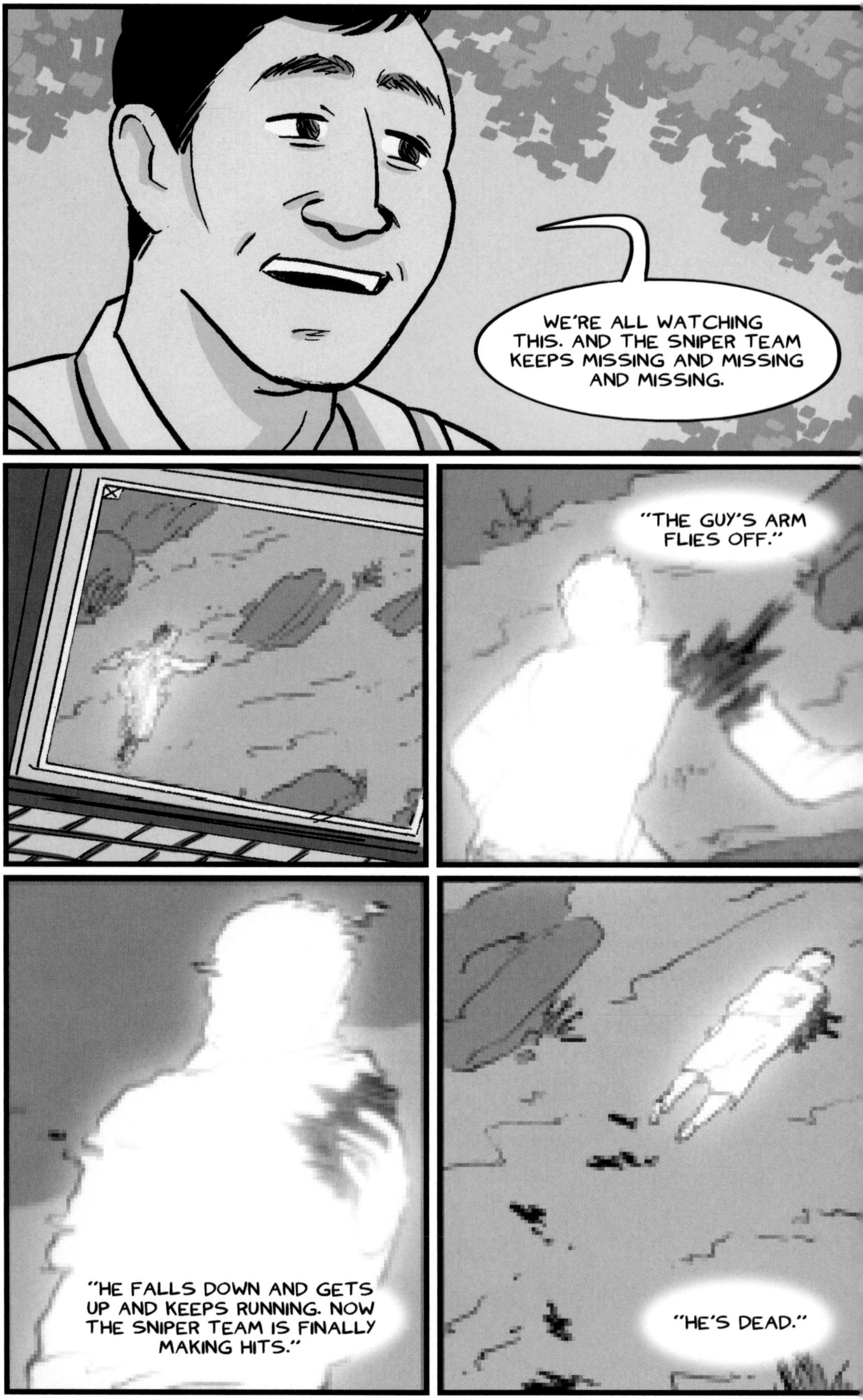
WE'RE ALL WATCHING THIS. AND THE SNIPER TEAM KEEPS MISSING AND MISSING AND MISSING.
"THE GUY'S ARM FLIES OFF."
"HE FALLS DOWN AND GETS UP AND KEEPS RUNNING. NOW THE SNIPER TEAM IS FINALLY MAKING HITS."
"HE'S DEAD."

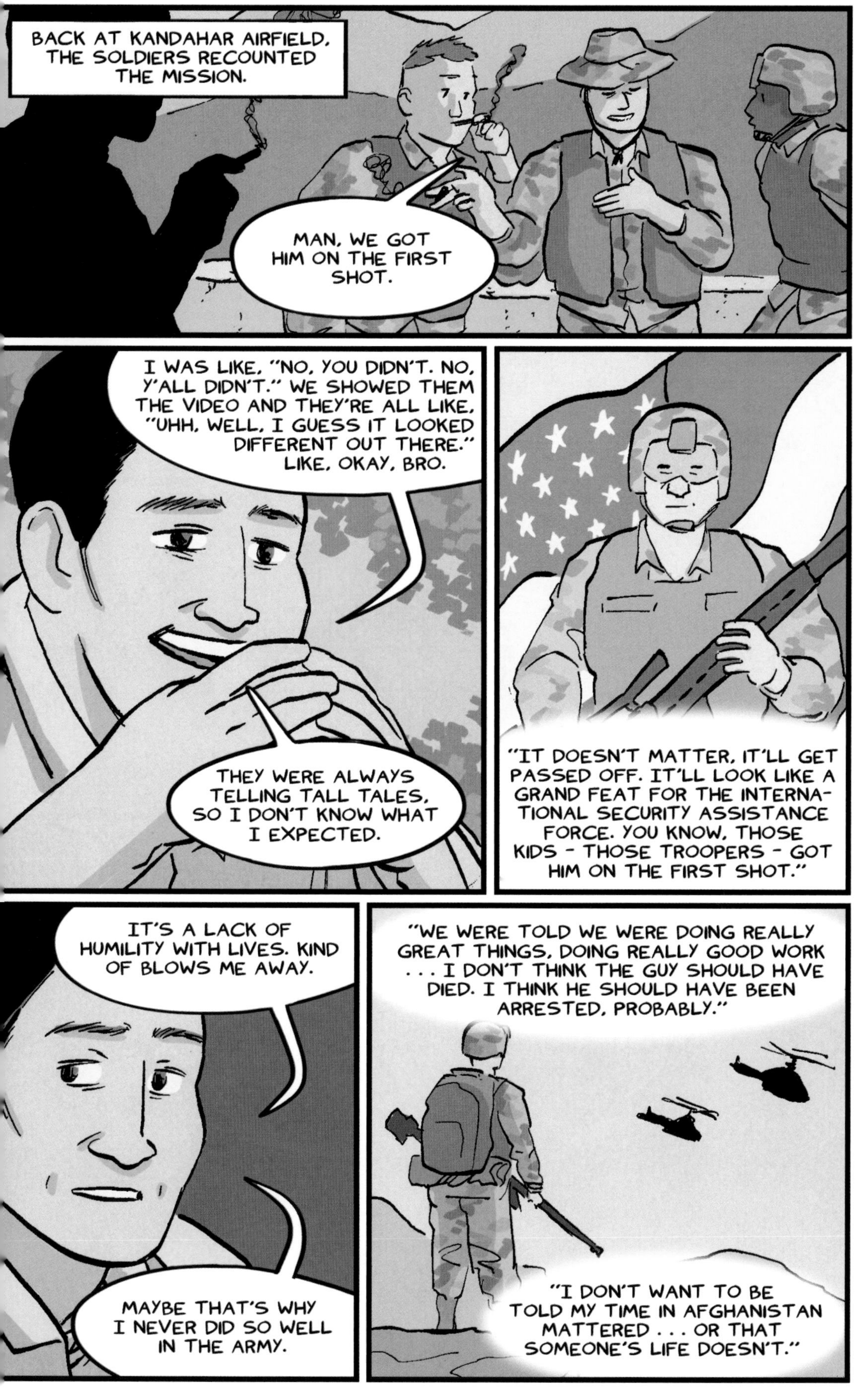
BACK AT KANDAHAR AIRFIELD, THE SOLDIERS RECOUNTED THE MISSION.
MAN, WE GOT HIM ON THE FIRST SHOT.
I WAS LIKE, "NO, YOU DIDN'T. NO, Y'ALL DIDN'T." WE SHOWED THEM THE VIDEO AND THEY'RE ALL LIKE, "UHH, WELL, I GUESS IT LOOKED DIFFERENT OUT THERE." LIKE, OKAY, BRO.
THEY WERE ALWAYS TELLING TALL TALES, SO I DON'T KNOW WHAT I EXPECTED.
"IT DOESN'T MATTER, IT'LL GET PASSED OFF. IT'LL LOOK LIKE A GRAND FEAT FOR THE INTERNATIONAL SECURITY ASSISTANCE FORCE. YOU KNOW, THOSE KIDS - THOSE TROOPERS - GOT HIM ON THE FIRST SHOT."
IT'S A LACK OF HUMILITY WITH LIVES. KIND OF BLOWS ME AWAY.
MAYBE THAT'S WHY I NEVER DID SO WELL IN THE ARMY.
"WE WERE TOLD WE WERE DOING REALLY GREAT THINGS, DOING REALLY GOOD WORK . . . I DON'T THINK THE GUY SHOULD HAVE DIED. I THINK HE SHOULD HAVE BEEN ARRESTED, PROBABLY."
"I DON'T WANT TO BE TOLD MY TIME IN AFGHANISTAN MATTERED . . . OR THAT SOMEONE'S LIFE DOESN'T."

14 "KABUL E.R." AND "THE ENTREPRENEUR"

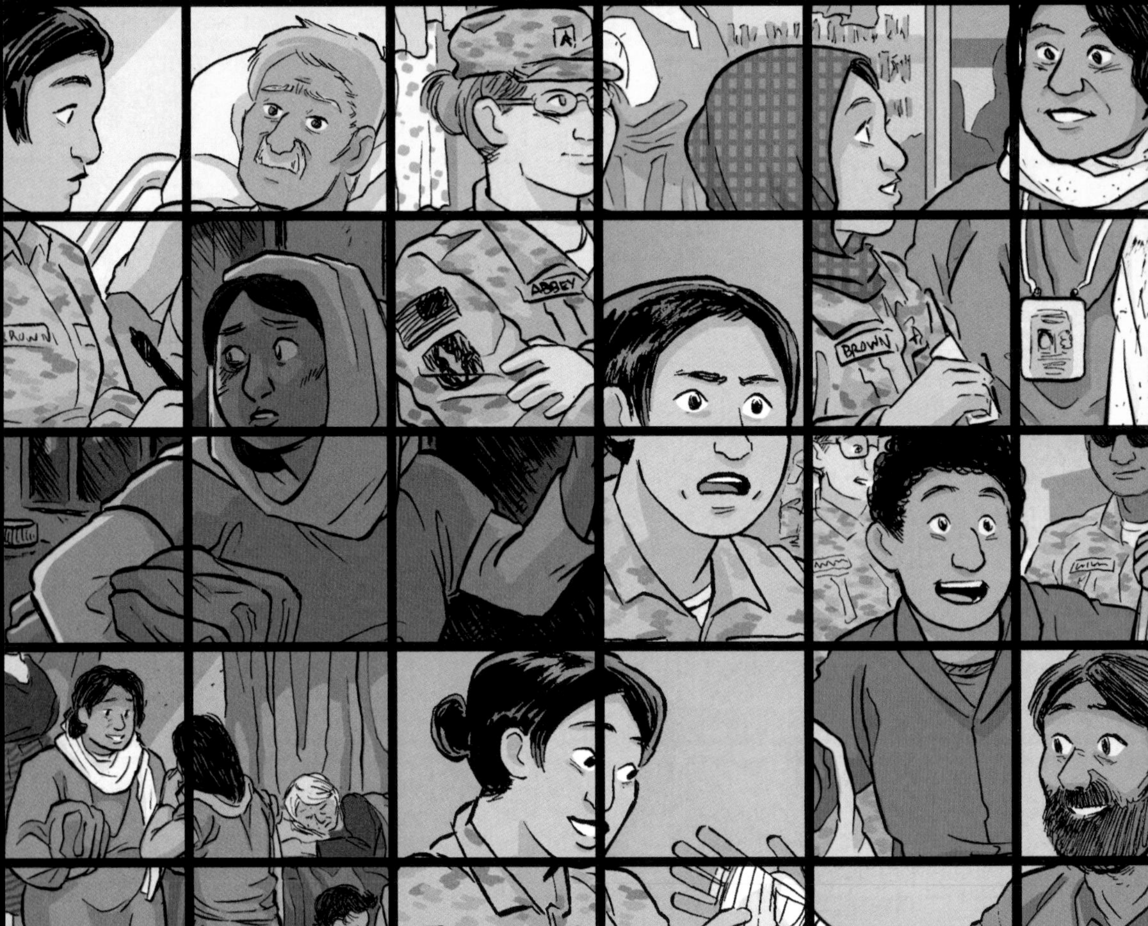
ABBEY
BROWN
BROWN

1st Lt. Corrine Brown, USA,
Kabul

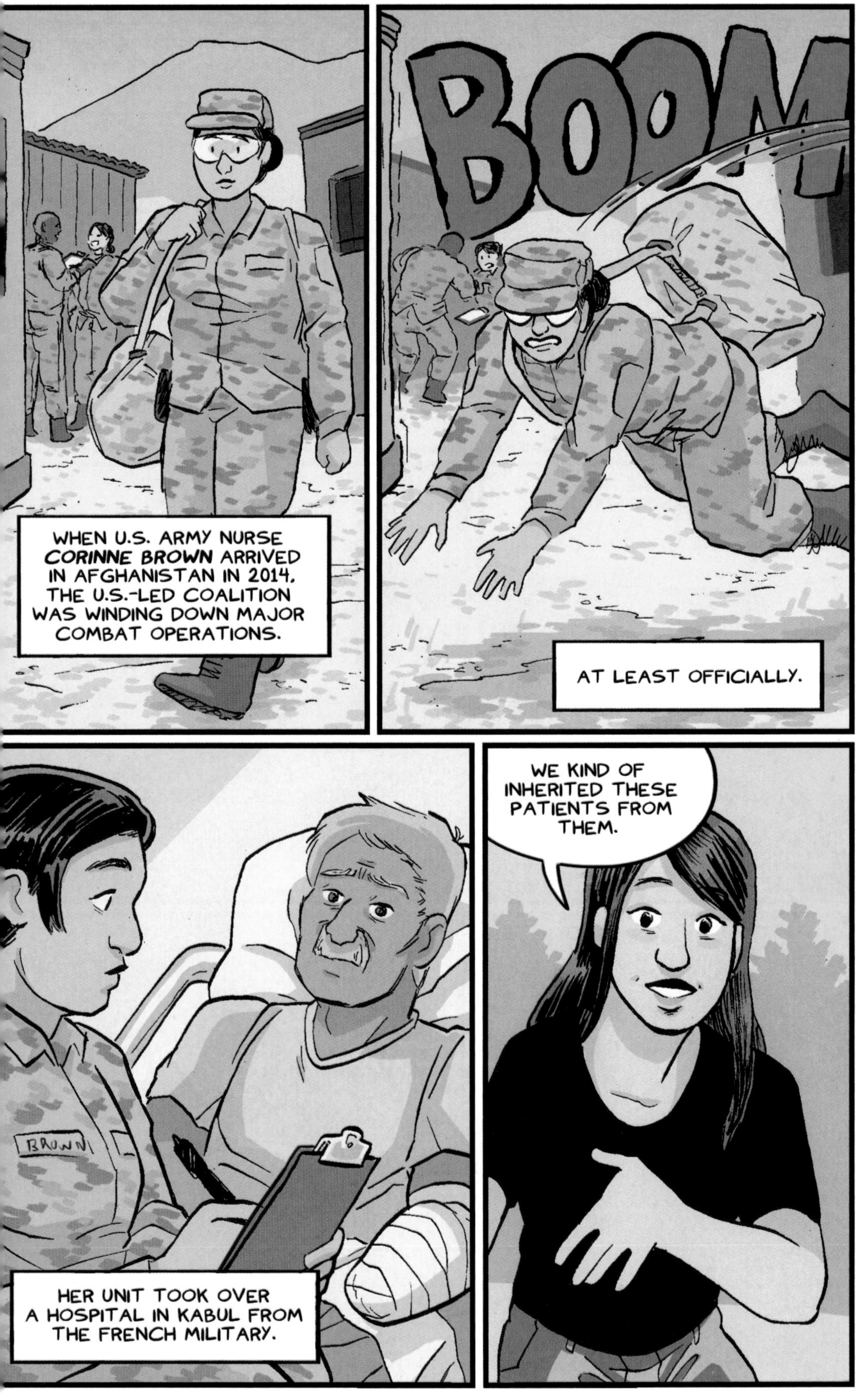
WHEN U.S. ARMY NURSE **CORINNE BROWN** ARRIVED IN AFGHANISTAN IN 2014, THE U.S.-LED COALITION WAS WINDING DOWN MAJOR COMBAT OPERATIONS.
BOOM
AT LEAST OFFICIALLY.
BROWN
HER UNIT TOOK OVER A HOSPITAL IN KABUL FROM THE FRENCH MILITARY.
WE KIND OF INHERITED THESE PATIENTS FROM THEM.

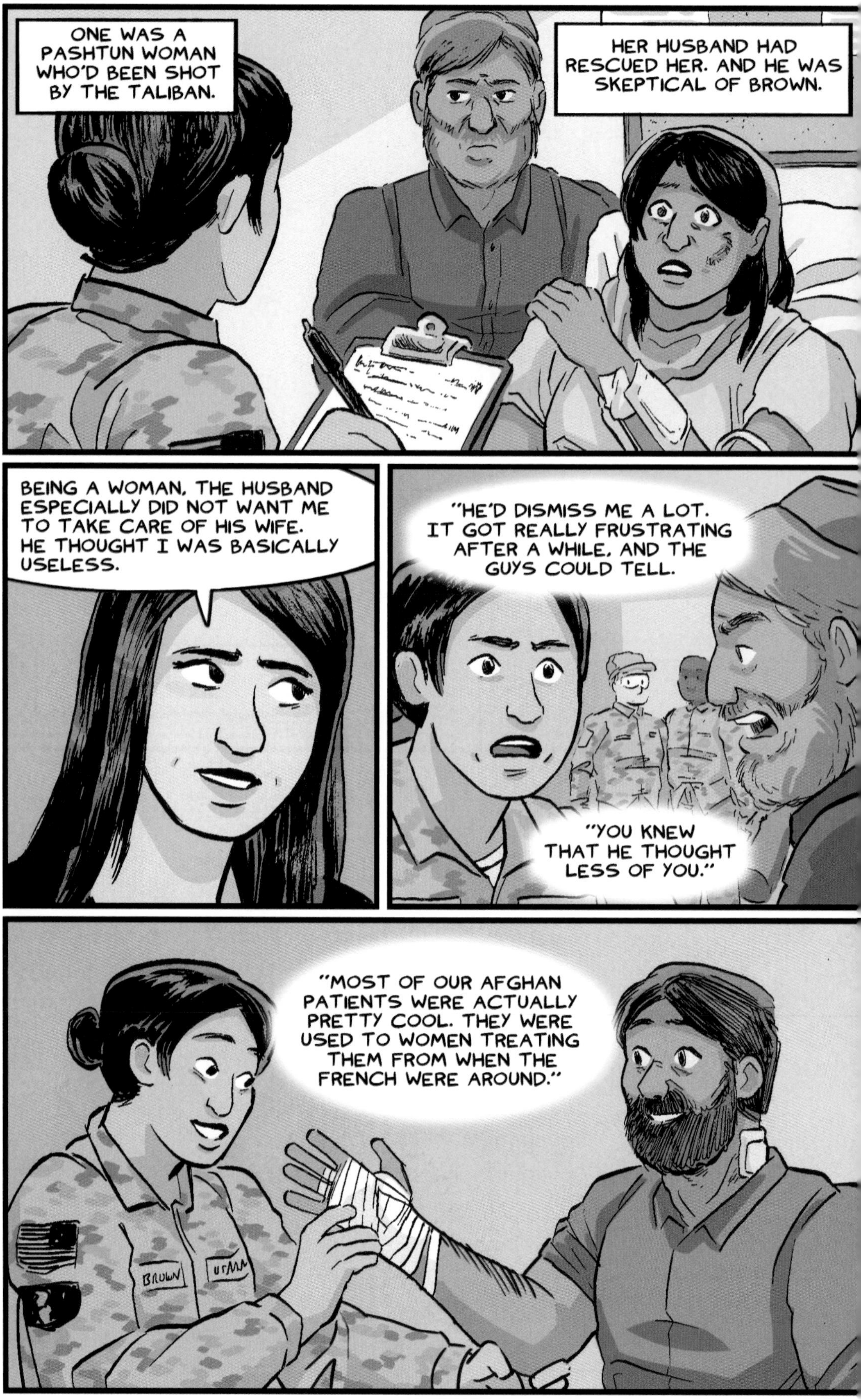
ONE WAS A PASHTUN WOMAN WHO'D BEEN SHOT BY THE TALIBAN.
HER HUSBAND HAD RESCUED HER. AND HE WAS SKEPTICAL OF BROWN.
BEING A WOMAN, THE HUSBAND ESPECIALLY DID NOT WANT ME TO TAKE CARE OF HIS WIFE. HE THOUGHT I WAS BASICALLY USELESS.
"HE'D DISMISS ME A LOT. IT GOT REALLY FRUSTRATING AFTER A WHILE, AND THE GUYS COULD TELL.
"YOU KNEW THAT HE THOUGHT LESS OF YOU."
"MOST OF OUR AFGHAN PATIENTS WERE ACTUALLY PRETTY COOL. THEY WERE USED TO WOMEN TREATING THEM FROM WHEN THE FRENCH WERE AROUND."
BROWN

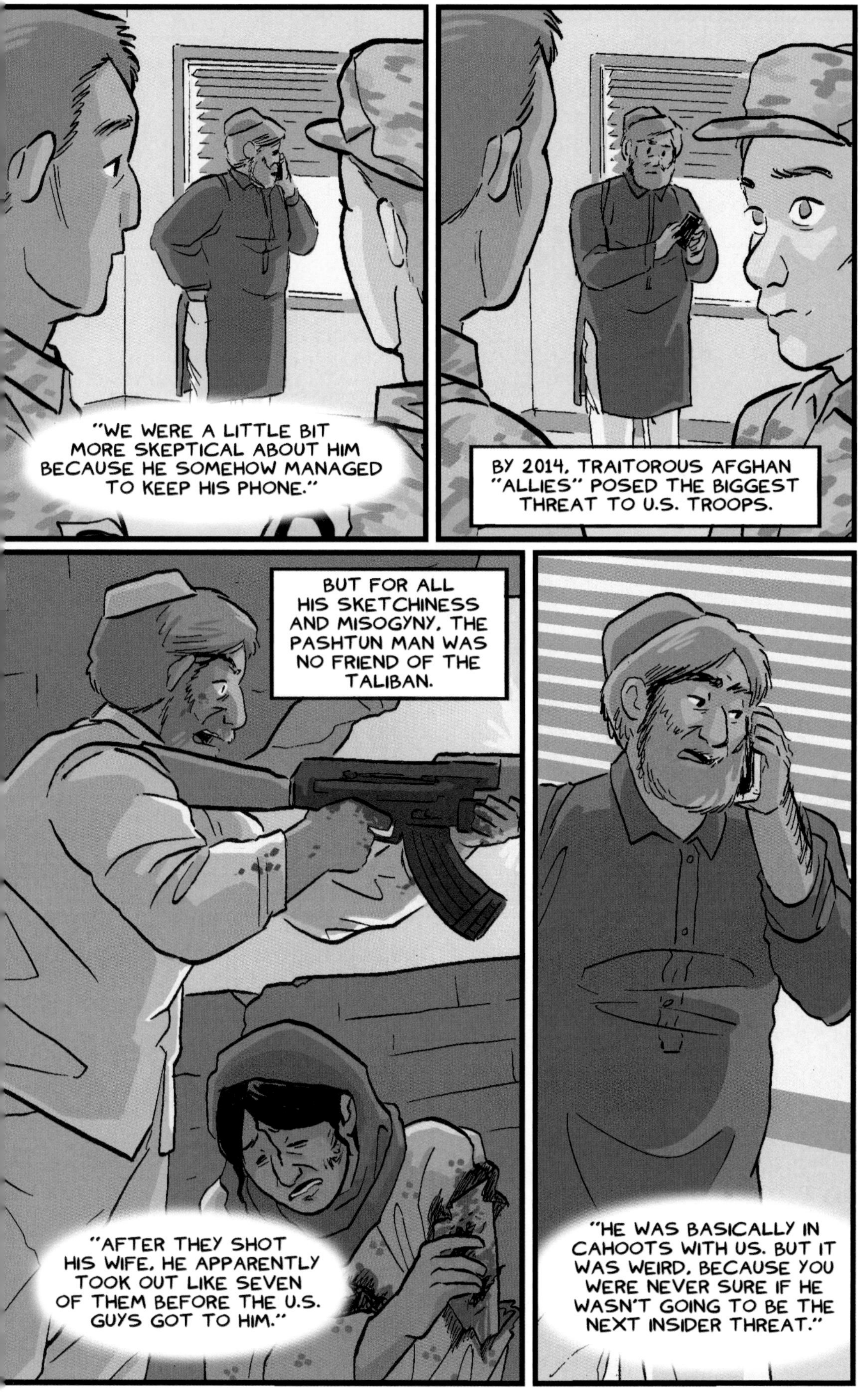
"WE WERE A LITTLE BIT MORE SKEPTICAL ABOUT HIM BECAUSE HE SOMEHOW MANAGED TO KEEP HIS PHONE."
BY 2014, TRAITOROUS AFGHAN "ALLIES" POSED THE BIGGEST THREAT TO U.S. TROOPS.
BUT FOR ALL HIS SKETCHINESS AND MISOGYNY, THE PASHTUN MAN WAS NO FRIEND OF THE TALIBAN.
"AFTER THEY SHOT HIS WIFE, HE APPARENTLY TOOK OUT LIKE SEVEN OF THEM BEFORE THE U.S. GUYS GOT TO HIM."
"HE WAS BASICALLY IN CAHOOTS WITH US. BUT IT WAS WEIRD, BECAUSE YOU WERE NEVER SURE IF HE WASN'T GOING TO BE THE NEXT INSIDER THREAT."

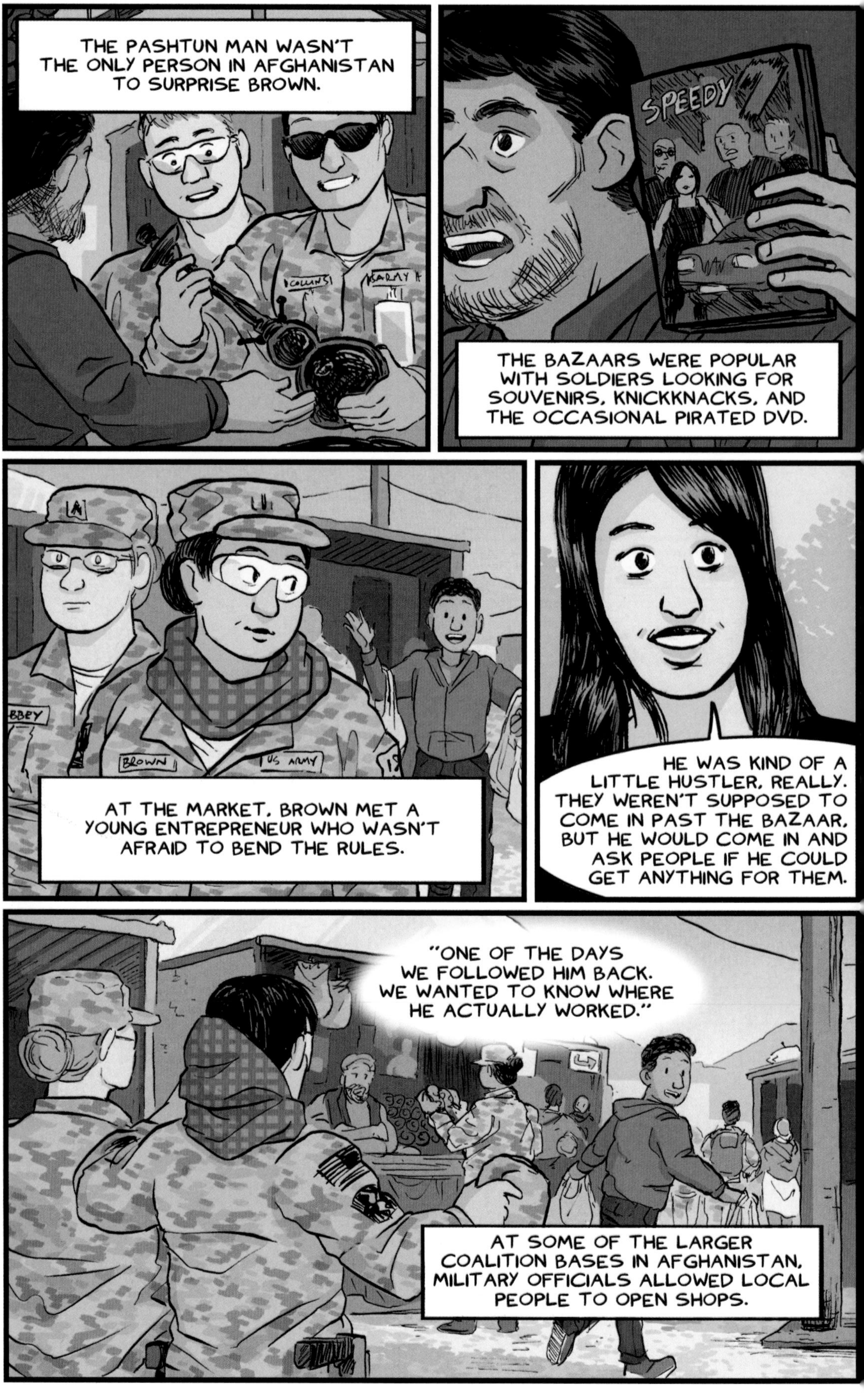
THE PASHTUN MAN WASN'T THE ONLY PERSON IN AFGHANISTAN TO SURPRISE BROWN.
COLLINS
ARMY
SPEEDY
THE BAZAARS WERE POPULAR WITH SOLDIERS LOOKING FOR SOUVENIRS, KNICKKNACKS, AND THE OCCASIONAL PIRATED DVD.
BROWN
US ARMY
AT THE MARKET, BROWN MET A YOUNG ENTREPRENEUR WHO WASN'T AFRAID TO BEND THE RULES.
HE WAS KIND OF A LITTLE HUSTLER, REALLY. THEY WEREN'T SUPPOSED TO COME IN PAST THE BAZAAR, BUT HE WOULD COME IN AND ASK PEOPLE IF HE COULD GET ANYTHING FOR THEM.
"ONE OF THE DAYS WE FOLLOWED HIM BACK. WE WANTED TO KNOW WHERE HE ACTUALLY WORKED."
AT SOME OF THE LARGER COALITION BASES IN AFGHANISTAN, MILITARY OFFICIALS ALLOWED LOCAL PEOPLE TO OPEN SHOPS.

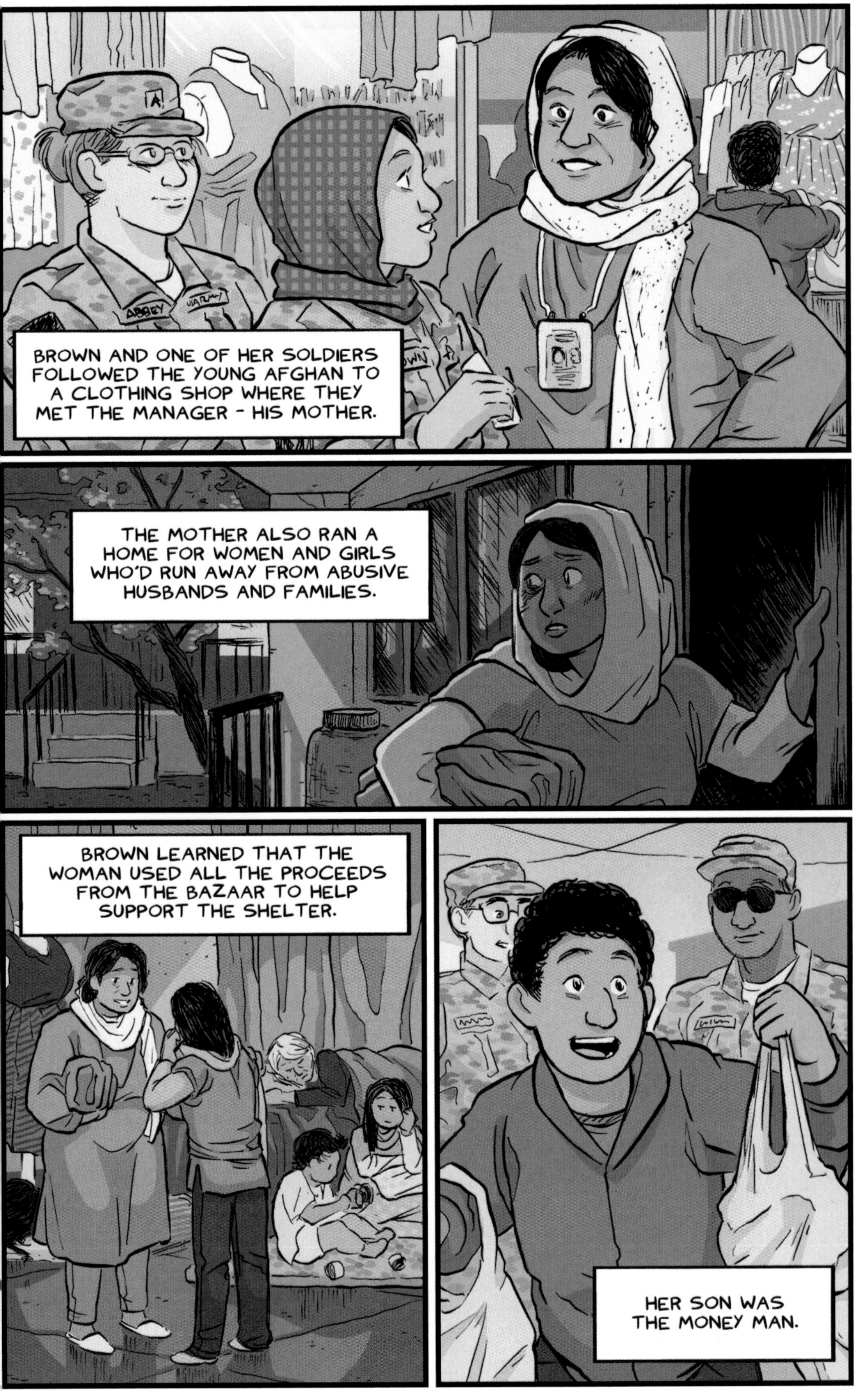
ABBEY
BROWN AND ONE OF HER SOLDIERS FOLLOWED THE YOUNG AFGHAN TO A CLOTHING SHOP WHERE THEY MET THE MANAGER - HIS MOTHER.
THE MOTHER ALSO RAN A HOME FOR WOMEN AND GIRLS WHO'D RUN AWAY FROM ABUSIVE HUSBANDS AND FAMILIES.
BROWN LEARNED THAT THE WOMAN USED ALL THE PROCEEDS FROM THE BAZAAR TO HELP SUPPORT THE SHELTER.
HER SON WAS THE MONEY MAN.

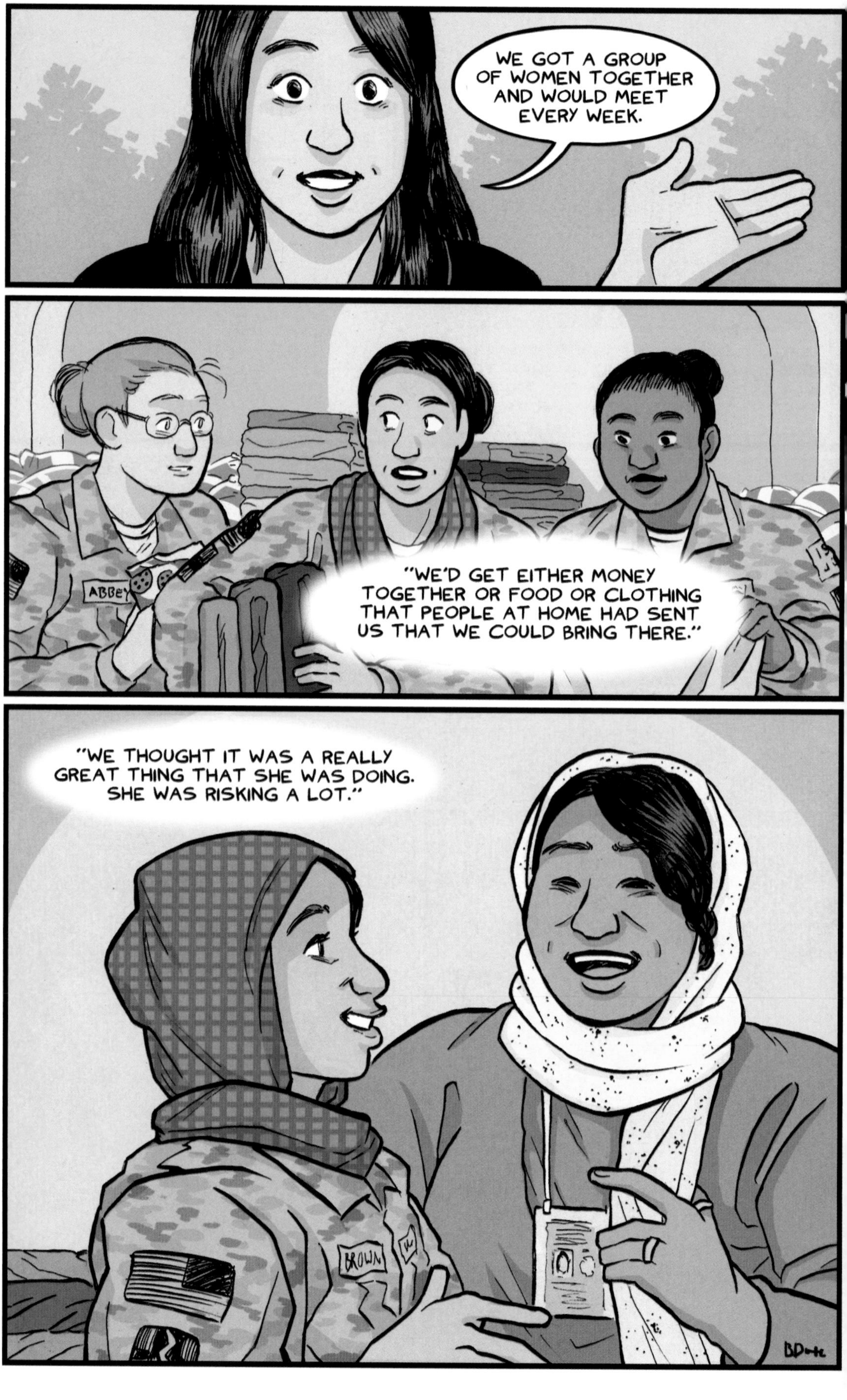
WE GOT A GROUP OF WOMEN TOGETHER AND WOULD MEET EVERY WEEK.
ABBEY
"WE'D GET EITHER MONEY TOGETHER OR FOOD OR CLOTHING THAT PEOPLE AT HOME HAD SENT US THAT WE COULD BRING THERE."
"WE THOUGHT IT WAS A REALLY GREAT THING THAT SHE WAS DOING. SHE WAS RISKING A LOT."
BROWN

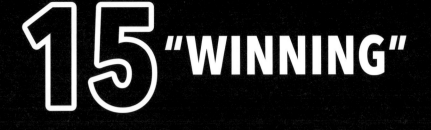

15 "WINNING"

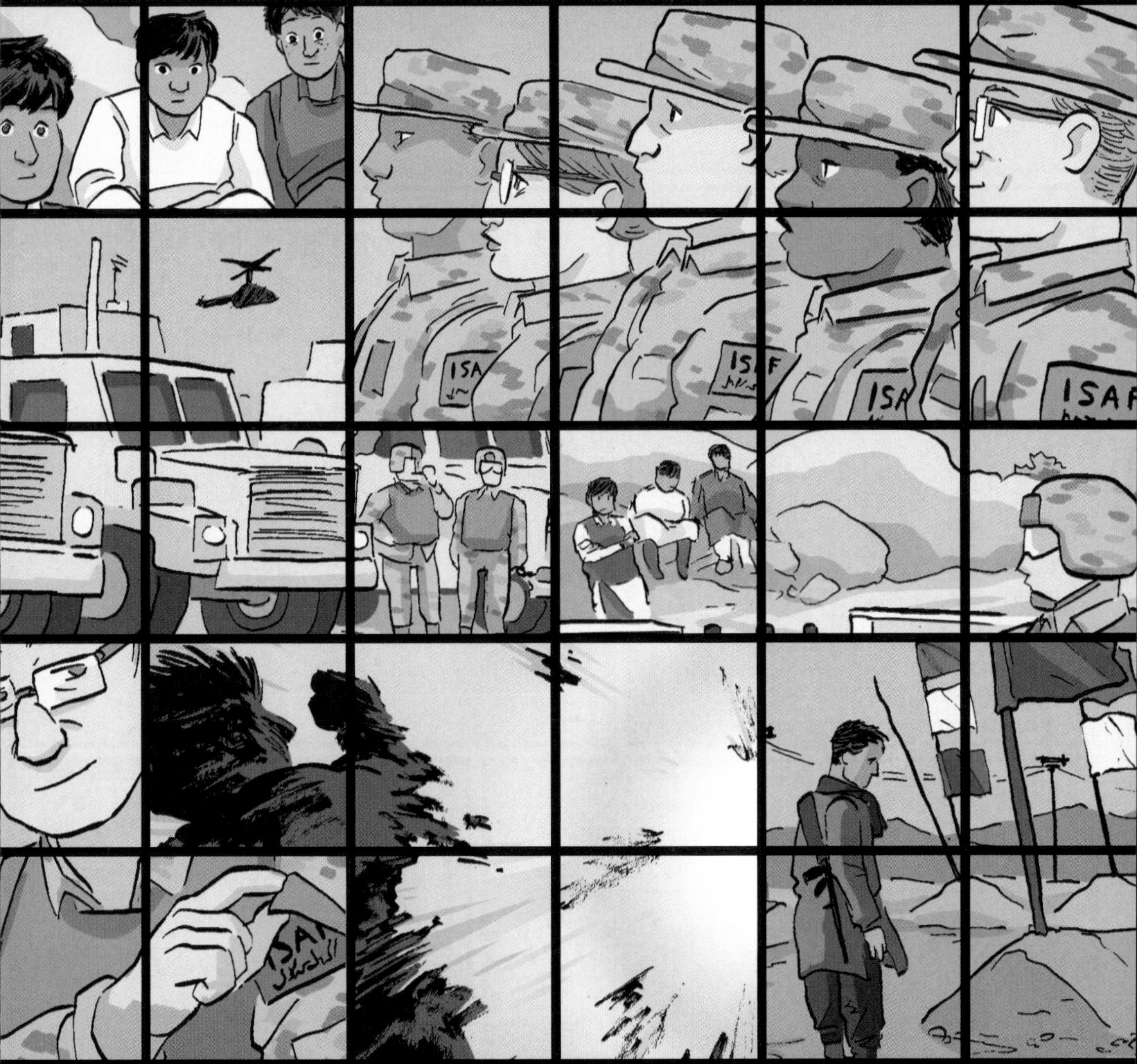
ISAF
ISAF

**SSgt. Ryan Nupen, USA,
Kunar and Laghman provinces**

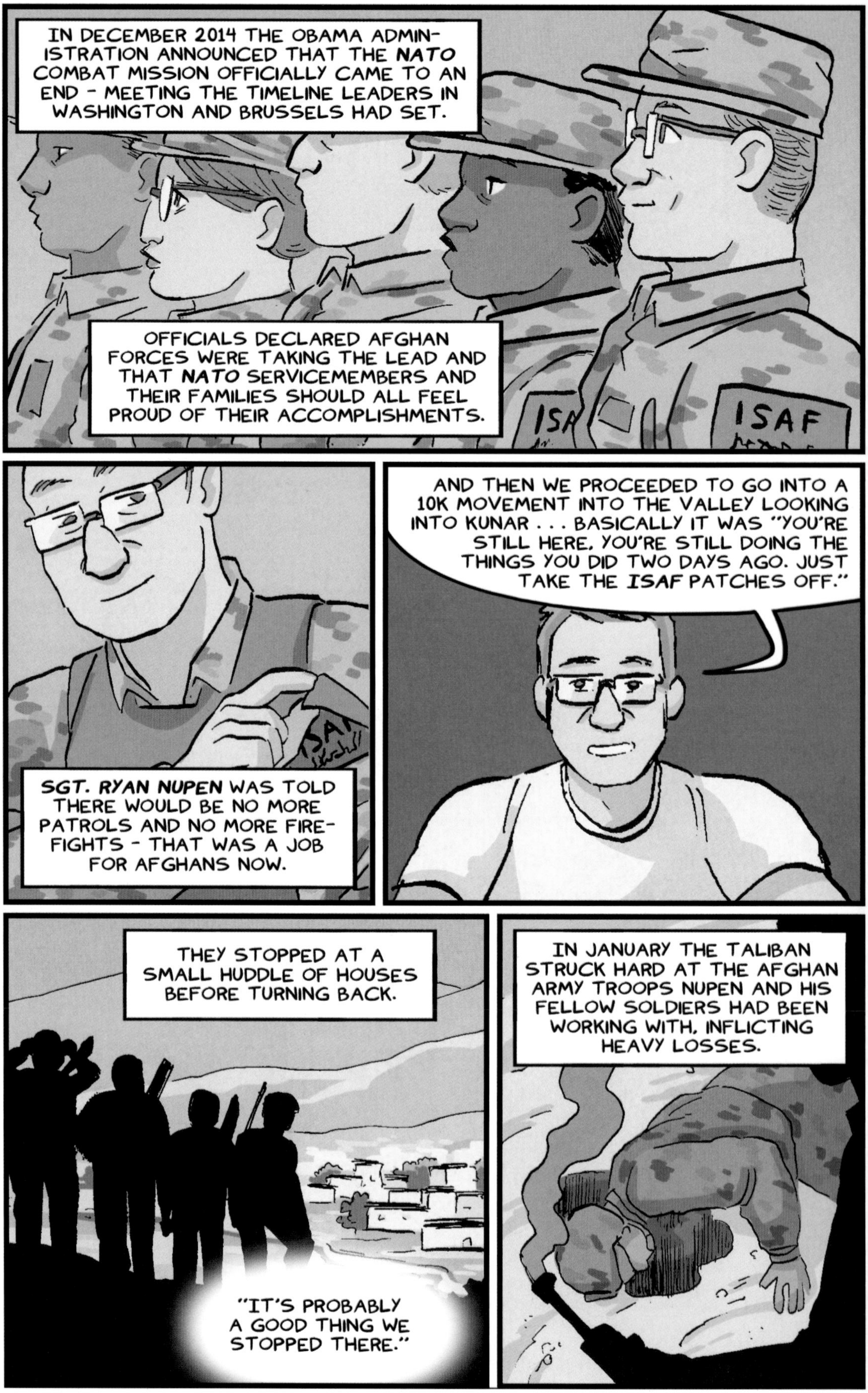
IN DECEMBER 2014 THE OBAMA ADMINISTRATION ANNOUNCED THAT THE NATO COMBAT MISSION OFFICIALLY CAME TO AN END - MEETING THE TIMELINE LEADERS IN WASHINGTON AND BRUSSELS HAD SET.
OFFICIALS DECLARED AFGHAN FORCES WERE TAKING THE LEAD AND THAT NATO SERVICEMEMBERS AND THEIR FAMILIES SHOULD ALL FEEL PROUD OF THEIR ACCOMPLISHMENTS.
ISAF
SGT. RYAN NUPEN WAS TOLD THERE WOULD BE NO MORE PATROLS AND NO MORE FIREFIGHTS - THAT WAS A JOB FOR AFGHANS NOW.
AND THEN WE PROCEEDED TO GO INTO A 10K MOVEMENT INTO THE VALLEY LOOKING INTO KUNAR . . . BASICALLY IT WAS "YOU'RE STILL HERE, YOU'RE STILL DOING THE THINGS YOU DID TWO DAYS AGO. JUST TAKE THE ISAF PATCHES OFF."
THEY STOPPED AT A SMALL HUDDLE OF HOUSES BEFORE TURNING BACK.
"IT'S PROBABLY A GOOD THING WE STOPPED THERE."
IN JANUARY THE TALIBAN STRUCK HARD AT THE AFGHAN ARMY TROOPS NUPEN AND HIS FELLOW SOLDIERS HAD BEEN WORKING WITH, INFLICTING HEAVY LOSSES.

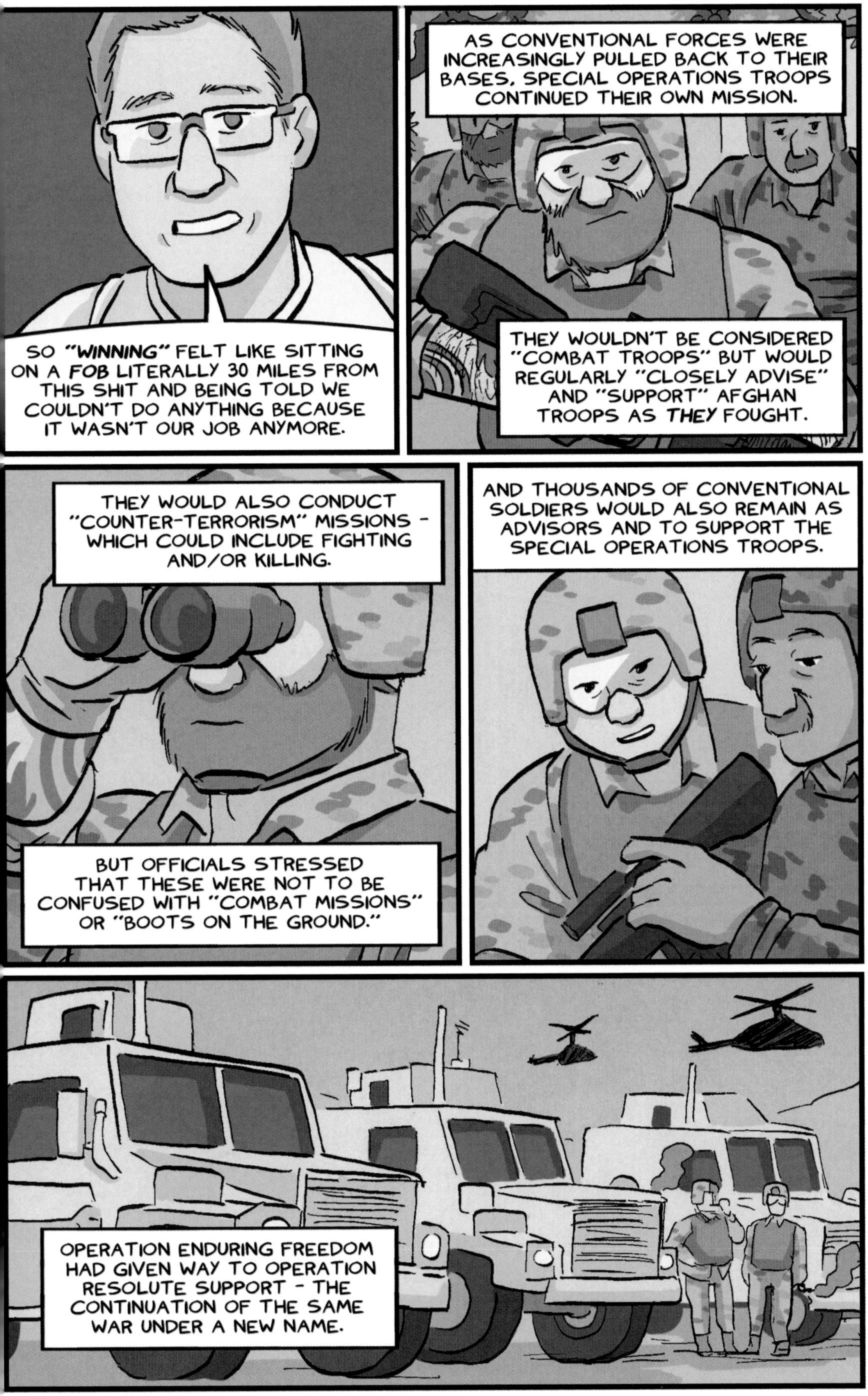
SO "WINNING" FELT LIKE SITTING ON A FOB LITERALLY 30 MILES FROM THIS SHIT AND BEING TOLD WE COULDN'T DO ANYTHING BECAUSE IT WASN'T OUR JOB ANYMORE.
AS CONVENTIONAL FORCES WERE INCREASINGLY PULLED BACK TO THEIR BASES, SPECIAL OPERATIONS TROOPS CONTINUED THEIR OWN MISSION.
THEY WOULDN'T BE CONSIDERED "COMBAT TROOPS" BUT WOULD REGULARLY "CLOSELY ADVISE" AND "SUPPORT" AFGHAN TROOPS AS THEY FOUGHT.
THEY WOULD ALSO CONDUCT "COUNTER-TERRORISM" MISSIONS - WHICH COULD INCLUDE FIGHTING AND/OR KILLING.
BUT OFFICIALS STRESSED THAT THESE WERE NOT TO BE CONFUSED WITH "COMBAT MISSIONS" OR "BOOTS ON THE GROUND."
AND THOUSANDS OF CONVENTIONAL SOLDIERS WOULD ALSO REMAIN AS ADVISORS AND TO SUPPORT THE SPECIAL OPERATIONS TROOPS.
OPERATION ENDURING FREEDOM HAD GIVEN WAY TO OPERATION RESOLUTE SUPPORT - THE CONTINUATION OF THE SAME WAR UNDER A NEW NAME.

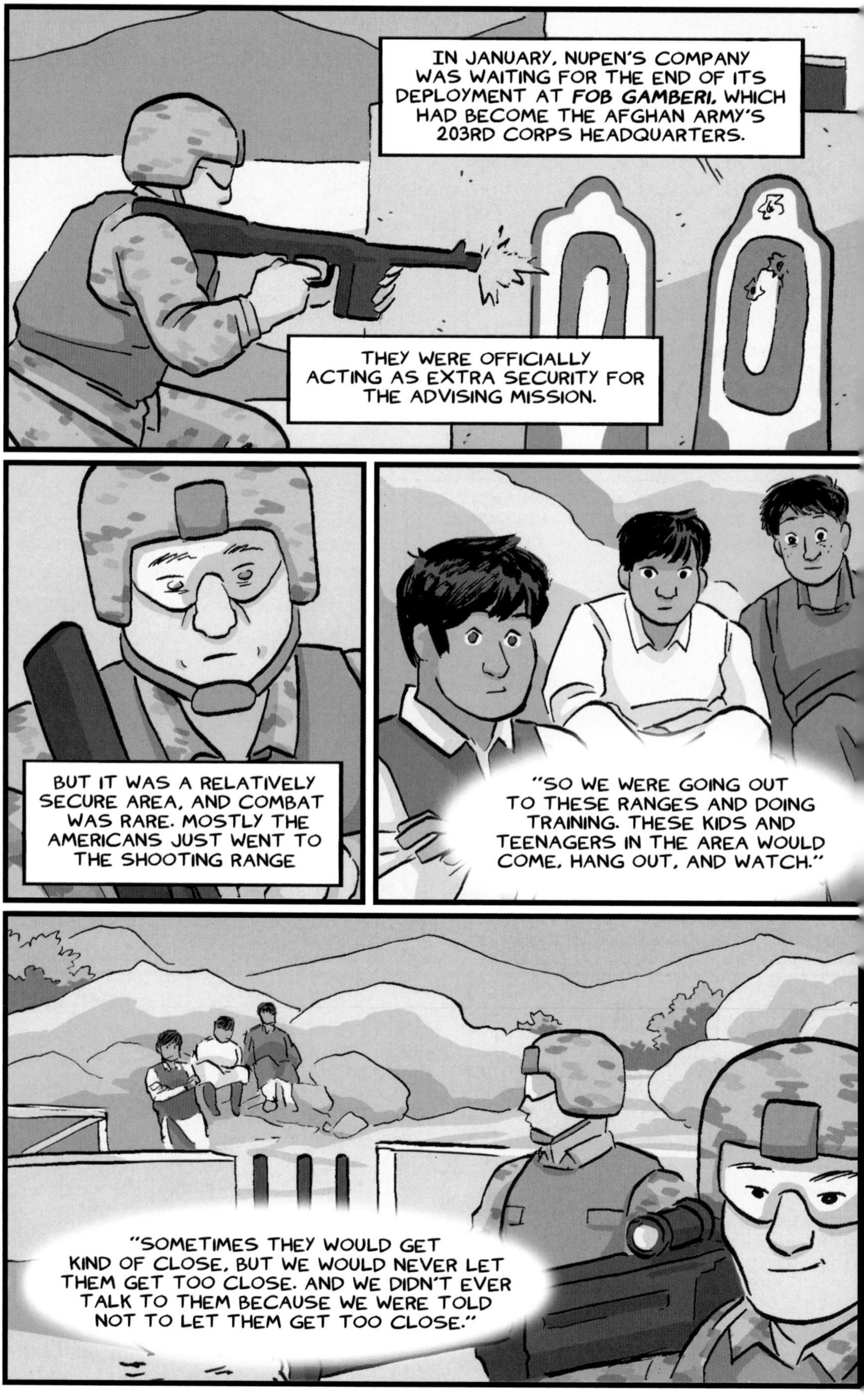
IN JANUARY, NUPEN'S COMPANY WAS WAITING FOR THE END OF ITS DEPLOYMENT AT FOB GAMBERI, WHICH HAD BECOME THE AFGHAN ARMY'S 203RD CORPS HEADQUARTERS.
THEY WERE OFFICIALLY ACTING AS EXTRA SECURITY FOR THE ADVISING MISSION.
BUT IT WAS A RELATIVELY SECURE AREA, AND COMBAT WAS RARE. MOSTLY THE AMERICANS JUST WENT TO THE SHOOTING RANGE
"SO WE WERE GOING OUT TO THESE RANGES AND DOING TRAINING. THESE KIDS AND TEENAGERS IN THE AREA WOULD COME, HANG OUT, AND WATCH."
"SOMETIMES THEY WOULD GET KIND OF CLOSE, BUT WE WOULD NEVER LET THEM GET TOO CLOSE. AND WE DIDN'T EVER TALK TO THEM BECAUSE WE WERE TOLD NOT TO LET THEM GET TOO CLOSE."

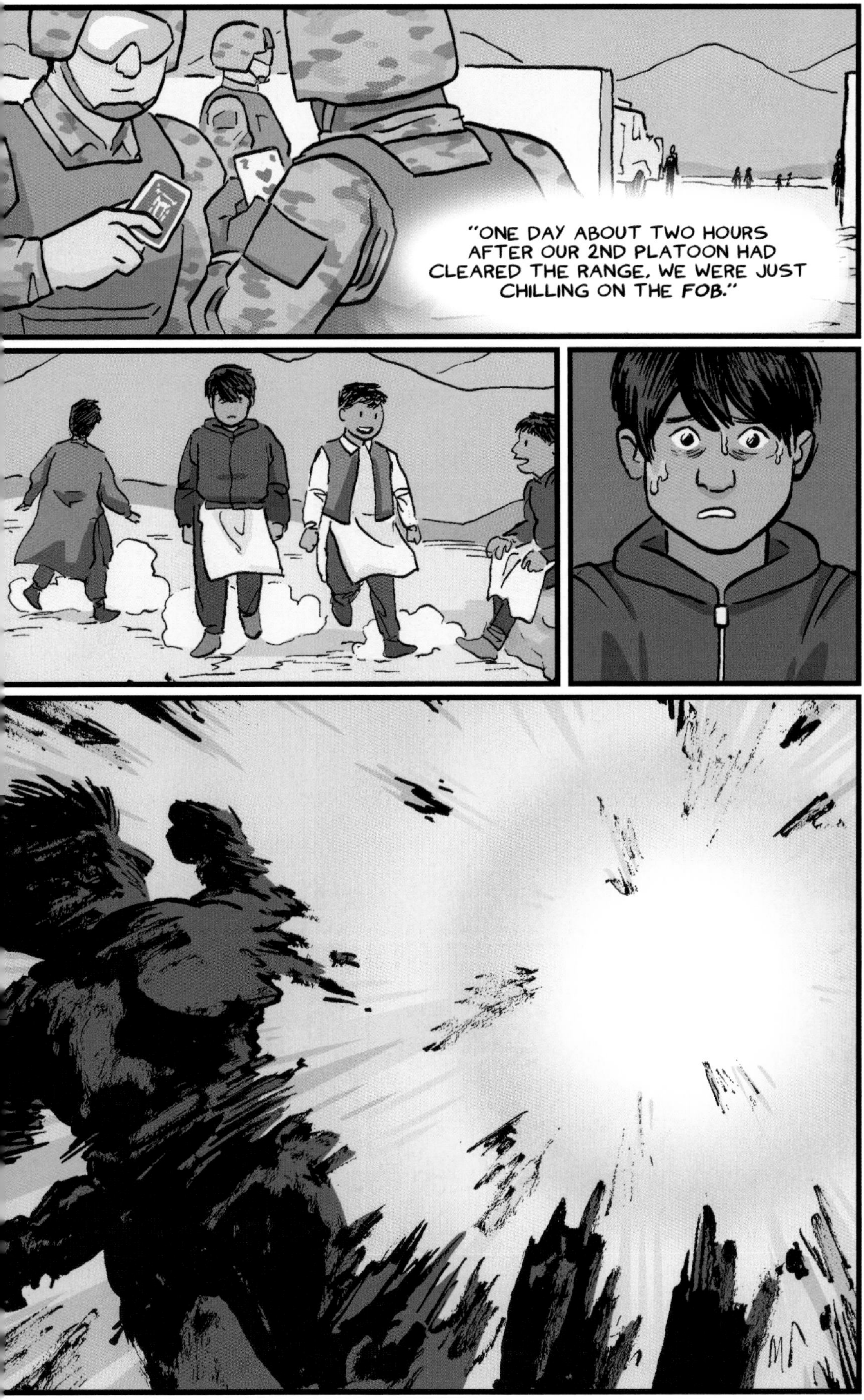
"ONE DAY ABOUT TWO HOURS AFTER OUR 2ND PLATOON HAD CLEARED THE RANGE, WE WERE JUST CHILLING ON THE FOB."

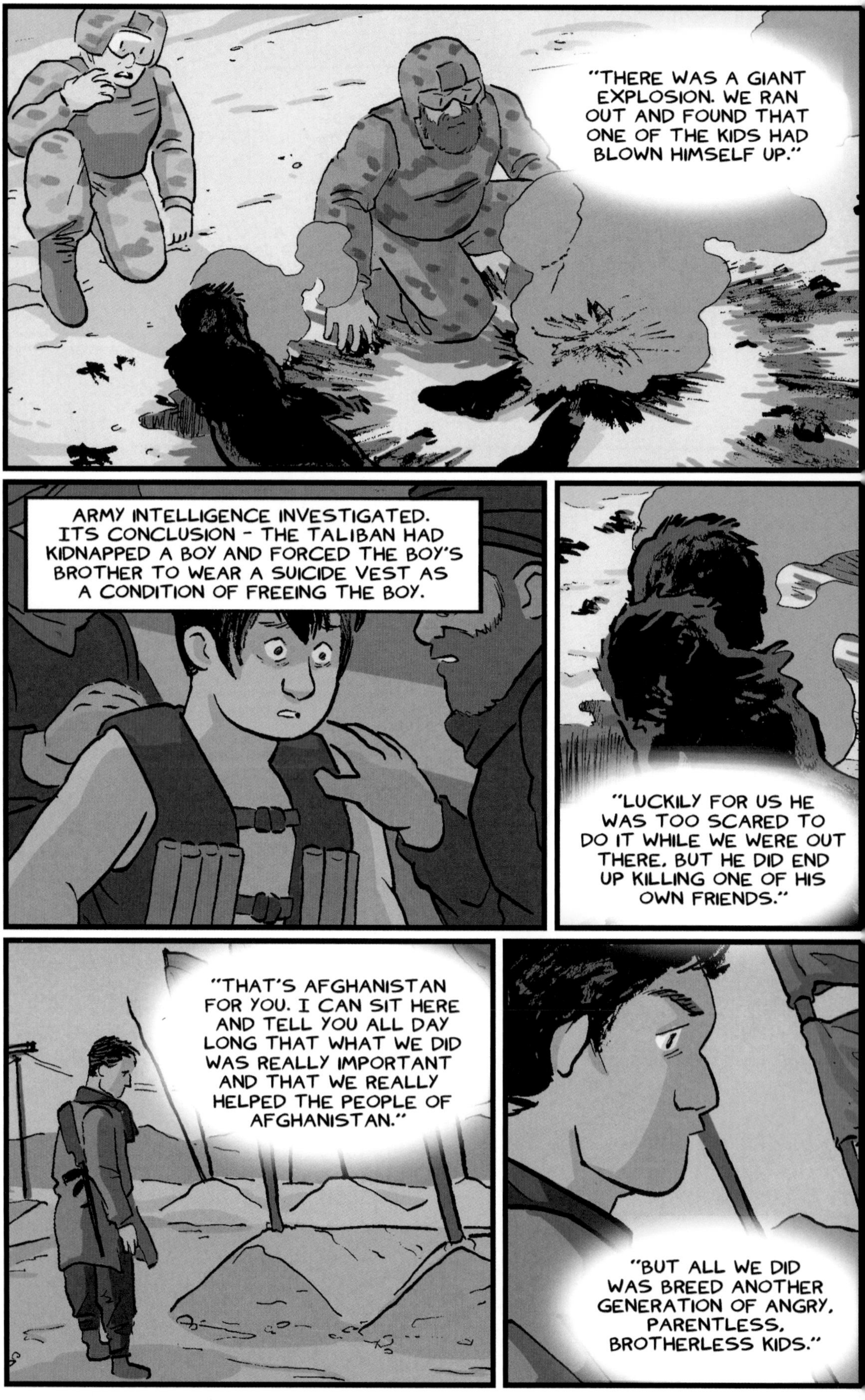
"THERE WAS A GIANT EXPLOSION. WE RAN OUT AND FOUND THAT ONE OF THE KIDS HAD BLOWN HIMSELF UP."
ARMY INTELLIGENCE INVESTIGATED. ITS CONCLUSION - THE TALIBAN HAD KIDNAPPED A BOY AND FORCED THE BOY'S BROTHER TO WEAR A SUICIDE VEST AS A CONDITION OF FREEING THE BOY.
"LUCKILY FOR US HE WAS TOO SCARED TO DO IT WHILE WE WERE OUT THERE, BUT HE DID END UP KILLING ONE OF HIS OWN FRIENDS."
"THAT'S AFGHANISTAN FOR YOU. I CAN SIT HERE AND TELL YOU ALL DAY LONG THAT WHAT WE DID WAS REALLY IMPORTANT AND THAT WE REALLY HELPED THE PEOPLE OF AFGHANISTAN."
"BUT ALL WE DID WAS BREED ANOTHER GENERATION OF ANGRY, PARENTLESS, BROTHERLESS KIDS."

16 "LEFT BEHIND"

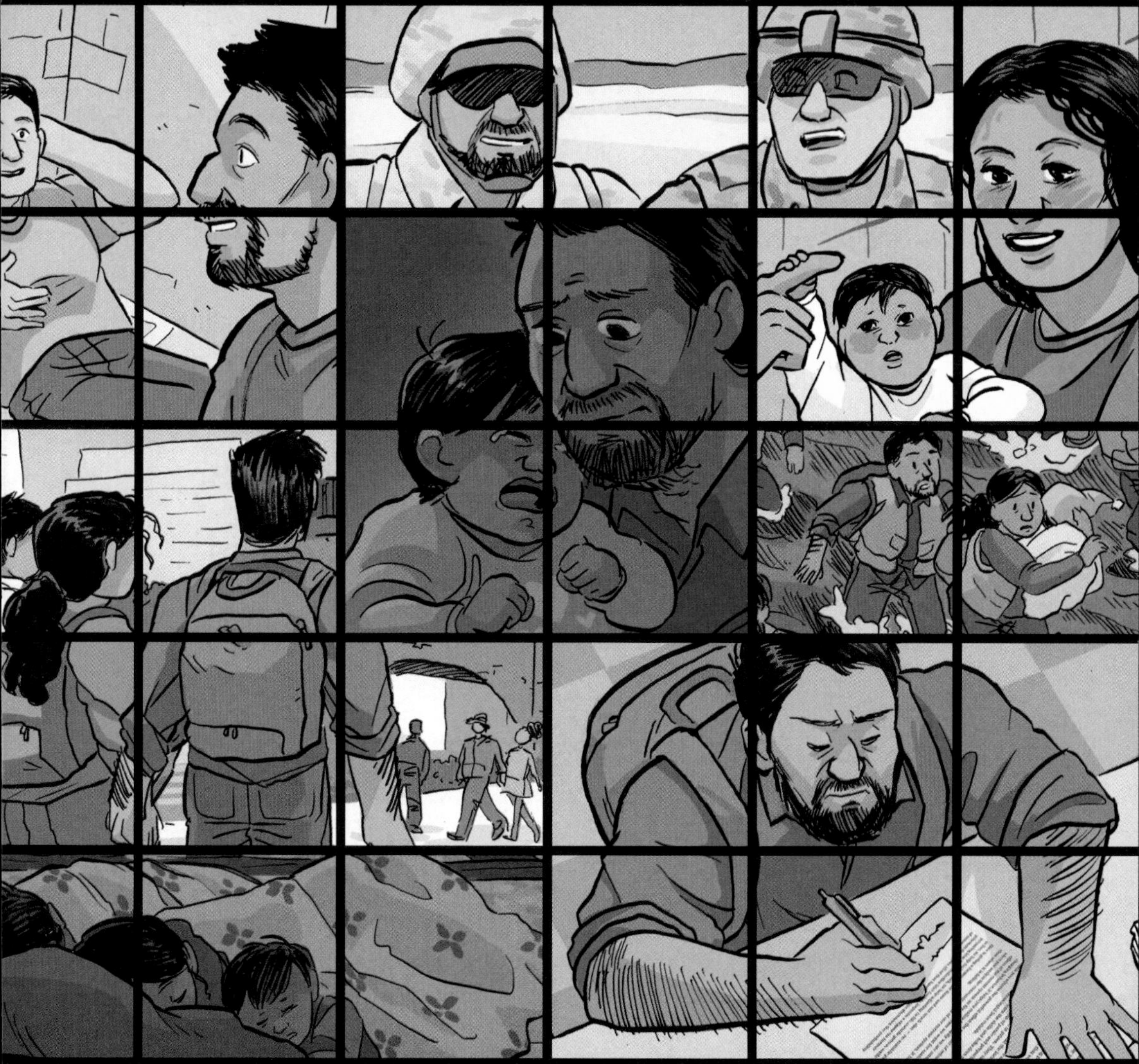

Sami Kazikhani, Afghan interpreter and Sgt. Aaron Fleming, USMC, Turkey, the Mediterranean Sea, Greece, Macedonia, Croatia, and Germany

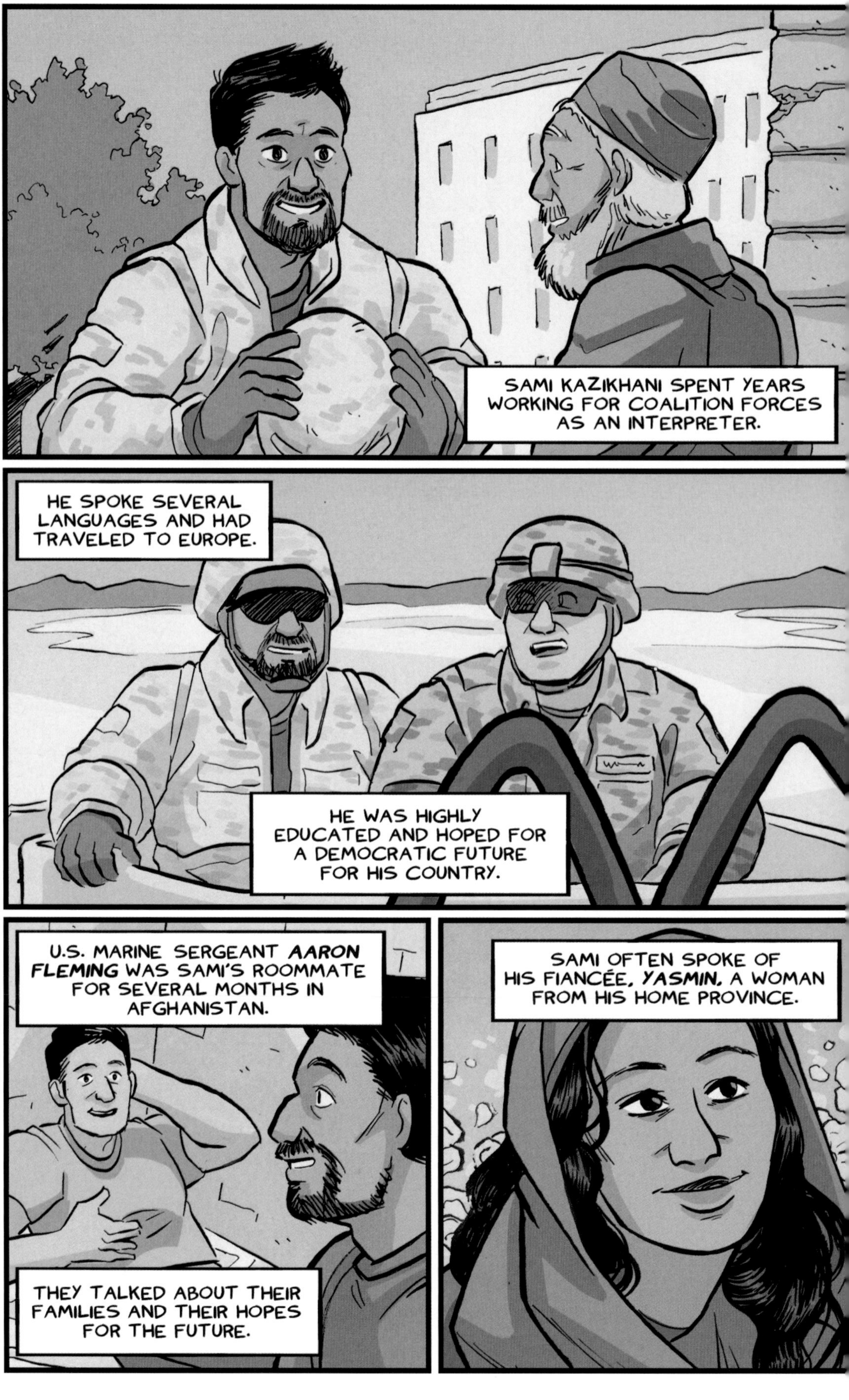
SAMI KAZIKHANI SPENT YEARS WORKING FOR COALITION FORCES AS AN INTERPRETER.
HE SPOKE SEVERAL LANGUAGES AND HAD TRAVELED TO EUROPE.
HE WAS HIGHLY EDUCATED AND HOPED FOR A DEMOCRATIC FUTURE FOR HIS COUNTRY.
U.S. MARINE SERGEANT ***AARON FLEMING*** WAS SAMI'S ROOMMATE FOR SEVERAL MONTHS IN AFGHANISTAN.
THEY TALKED ABOUT THEIR FAMILIES AND THEIR HOPES FOR THE FUTURE.
SAMI OFTEN SPOKE OF HIS FIANCÉE, ***YASMIN,*** A WOMAN FROM HIS HOME PROVINCE.

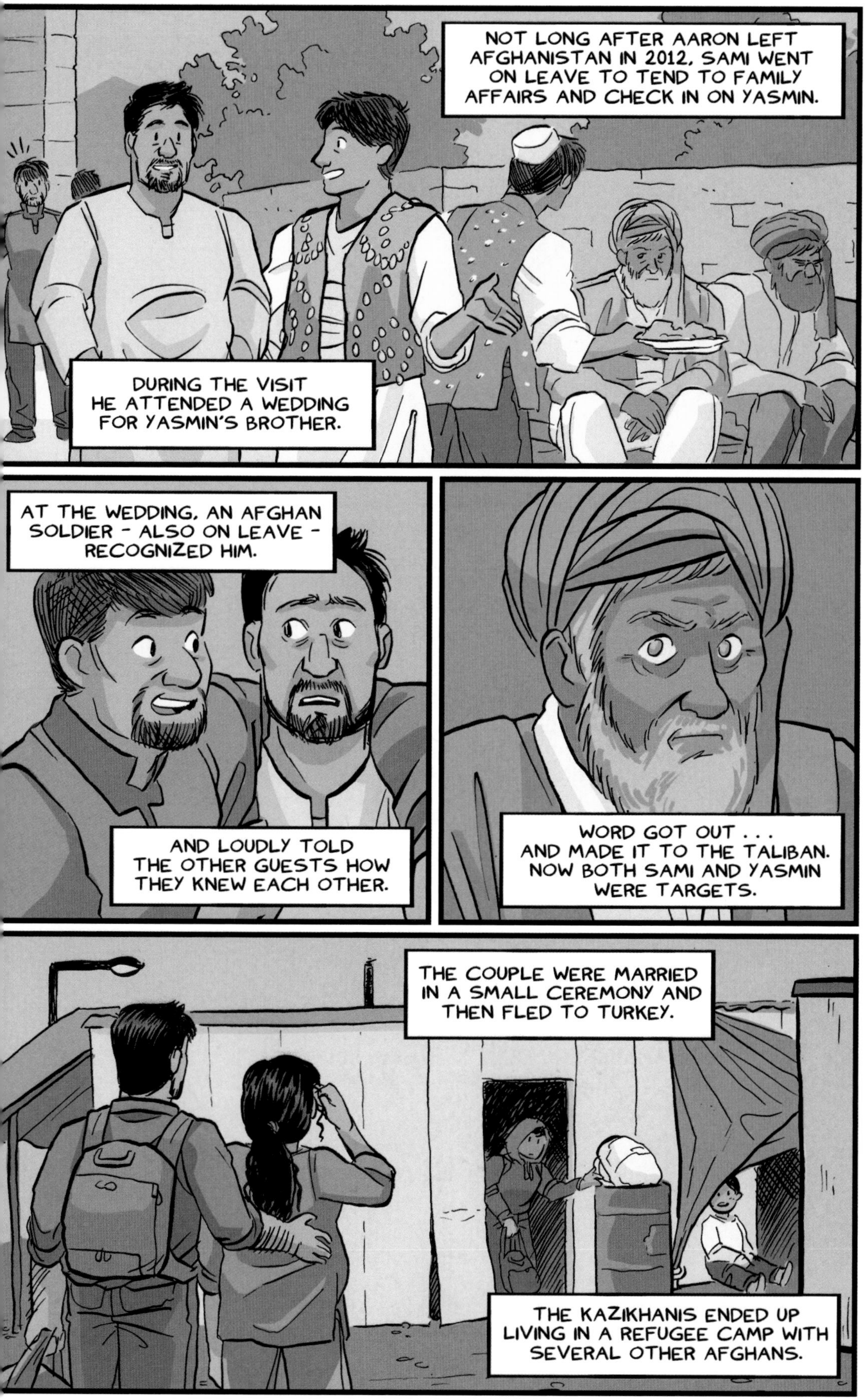
NOT LONG AFTER AARON LEFT AFGHANISTAN IN 2012, SAMI WENT ON LEAVE TO TEND TO FAMILY AFFAIRS AND CHECK IN ON YASMIN.
DURING THE VISIT HE ATTENDED A WEDDING FOR YASMIN'S BROTHER.
AT THE WEDDING, AN AFGHAN SOLDIER - ALSO ON LEAVE - RECOGNIZED HIM.
AND LOUDLY TOLD THE OTHER GUESTS HOW THEY KNEW EACH OTHER.
WORD GOT OUT . . . AND MADE IT TO THE TALIBAN. NOW BOTH SAMI AND YASMIN WERE TARGETS.
THE COUPLE WERE MARRIED IN A SMALL CEREMONY AND THEN FLED TO TURKEY.
THE KAZIKHANIS ENDED UP LIVING IN A REFUGEE CAMP WITH SEVERAL OTHER AFGHANS.

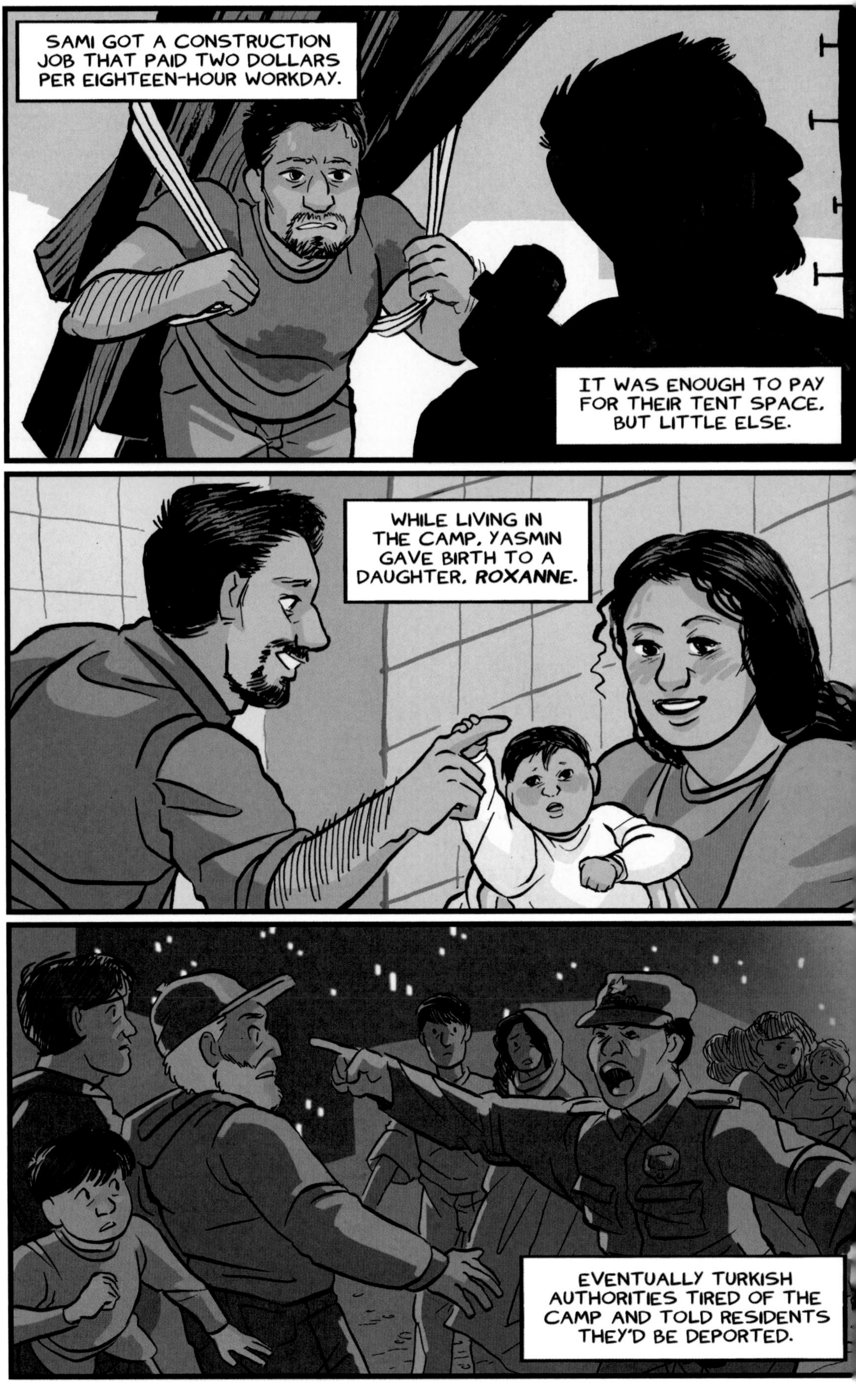
SAMI GOT A CONSTRUCTION JOB THAT PAID TWO DOLLARS PER EIGHTEEN-HOUR WORKDAY.
IT WAS ENOUGH TO PAY FOR THEIR TENT SPACE, BUT LITTLE ELSE.
WHILE LIVING IN THE CAMP, YASMIN GAVE BIRTH TO A DAUGHTER, **ROXANNE**.
EVENTUALLY TURKISH AUTHORITIES TIRED OF THE CAMP AND TOLD RESIDENTS THEY'D BE DEPORTED.

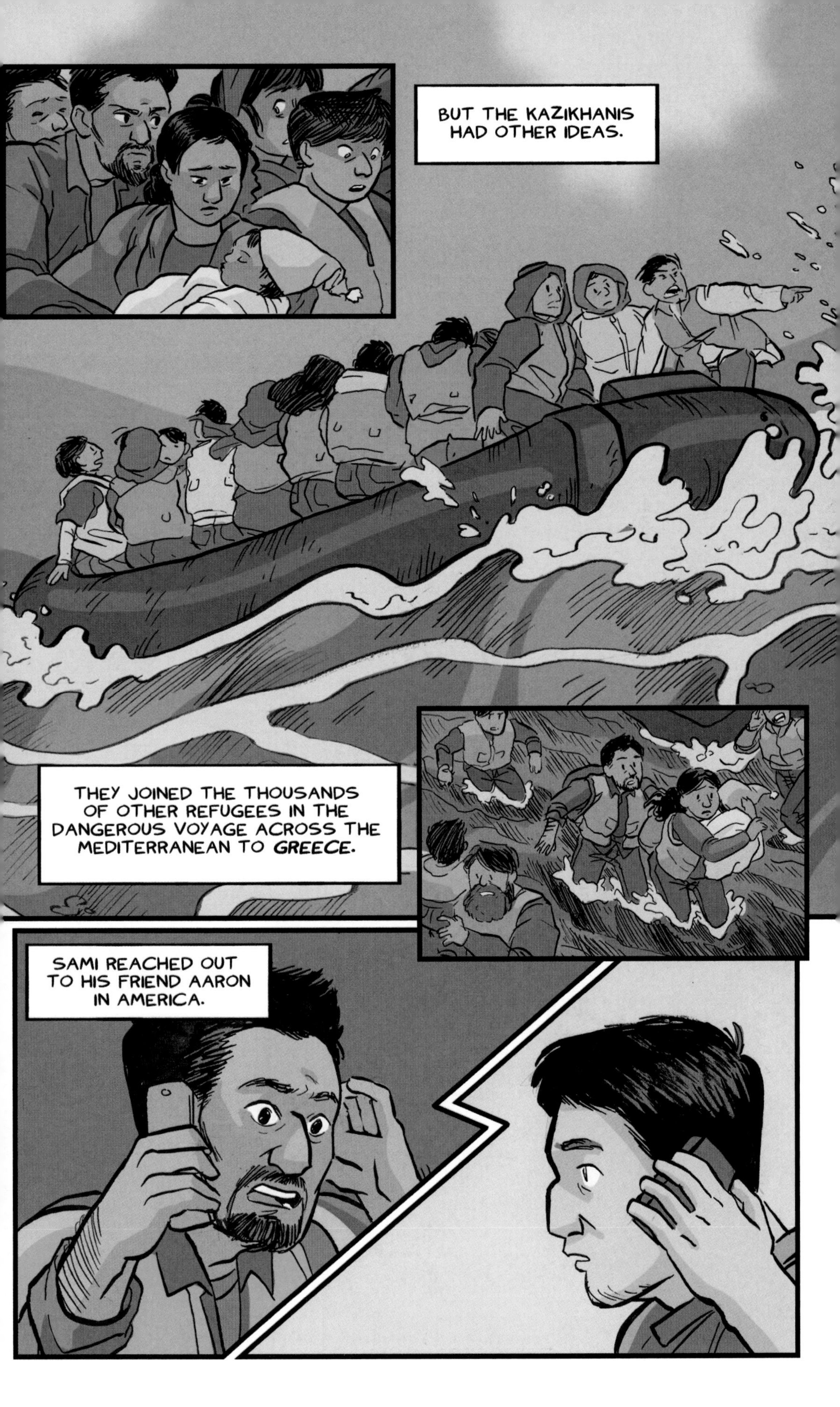
BUT THE KAZIKHANIS HAD OTHER IDEAS.
THEY JOINED THE THOUSANDS OF OTHER REFUGEES IN THE DANGEROUS VOYAGE ACROSS THE MEDITERRANEAN TO *GREECE*.
SAMI REACHED OUT TO HIS FRIEND AARON IN AMERICA.

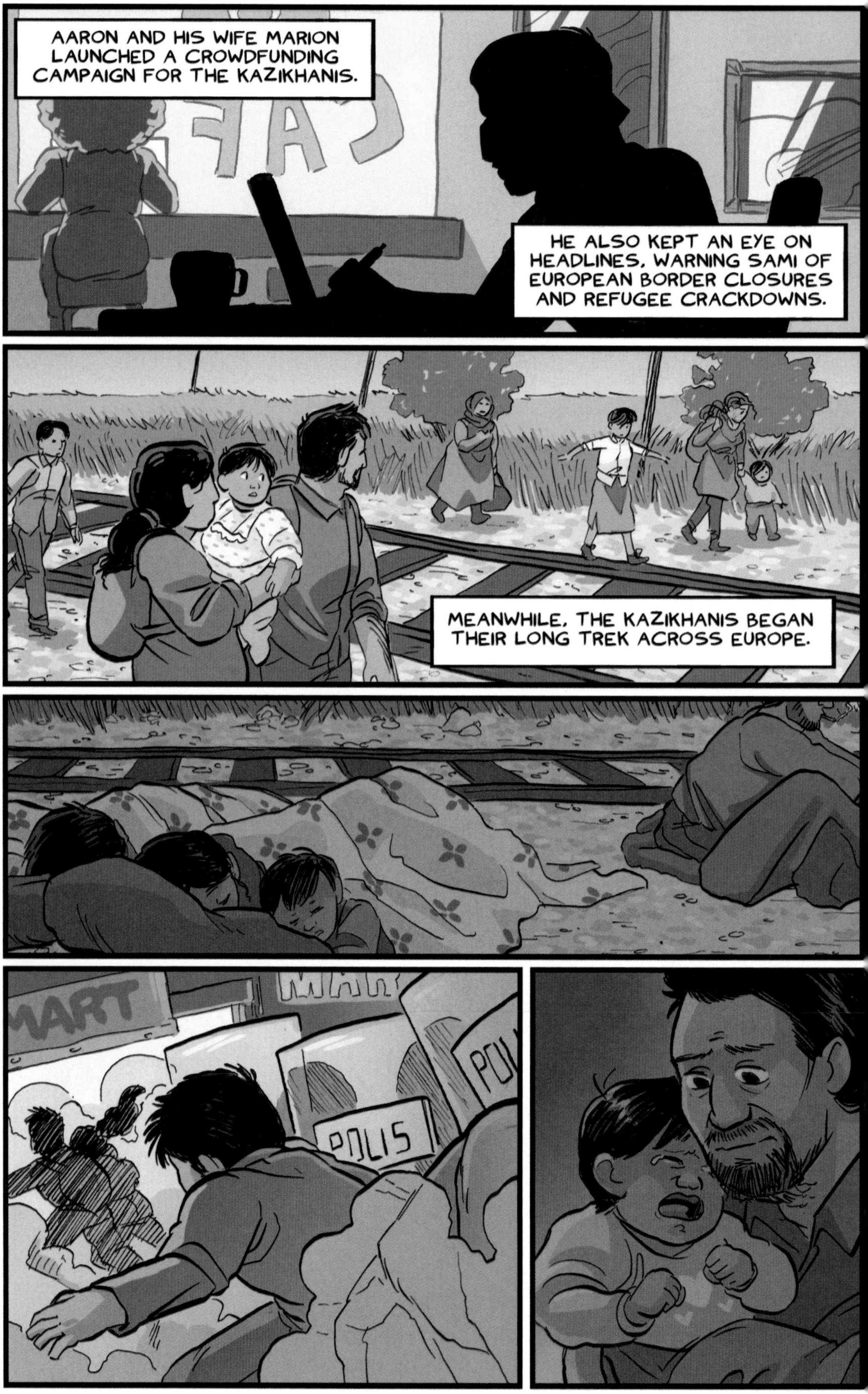
AARON AND HIS WIFE MARION LAUNCHED A CROWDFUNDING CAMPAIGN FOR THE KAZIKHANIS.
HE ALSO KEPT AN EYE ON HEADLINES, WARNING SAMI OF EUROPEAN BORDER CLOSURES AND REFUGEE CRACKDOWNS.
MEANWHILE, THE KAZIKHANIS BEGAN THEIR LONG TREK ACROSS EUROPE.
MART
POLIS

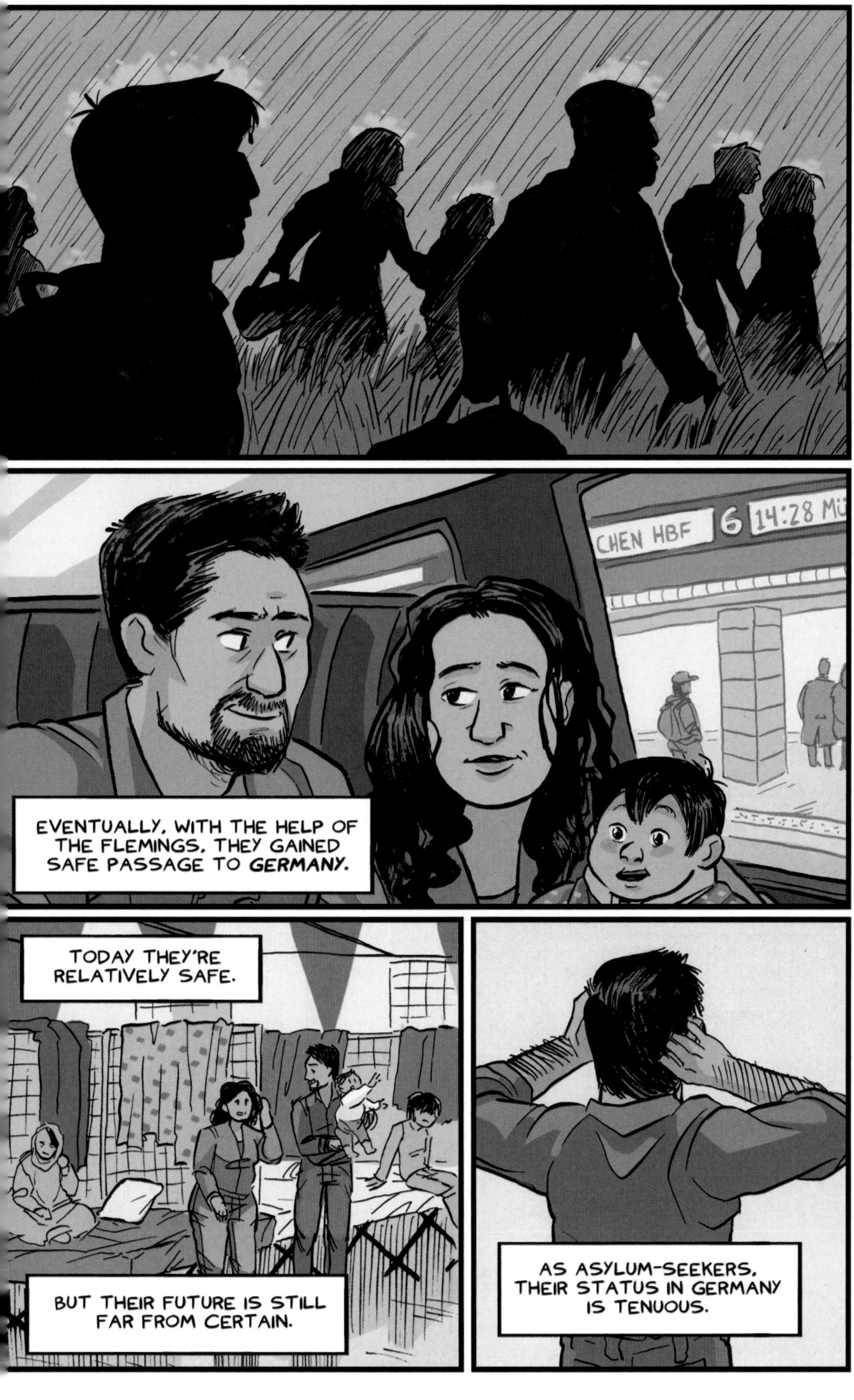
CHEN HBF
6
14:28 MÜ
EVENTUALLY, WITH THE HELP OF THE FLEMINGS, THEY GAINED SAFE PASSAGE TO GERMANY.
TODAY THEY'RE RELATIVELY SAFE.
BUT THEIR FUTURE IS STILL FAR FROM CERTAIN.
AS ASYLUM-SEEKERS, THEIR STATUS IN GERMANY IS TENUOUS.

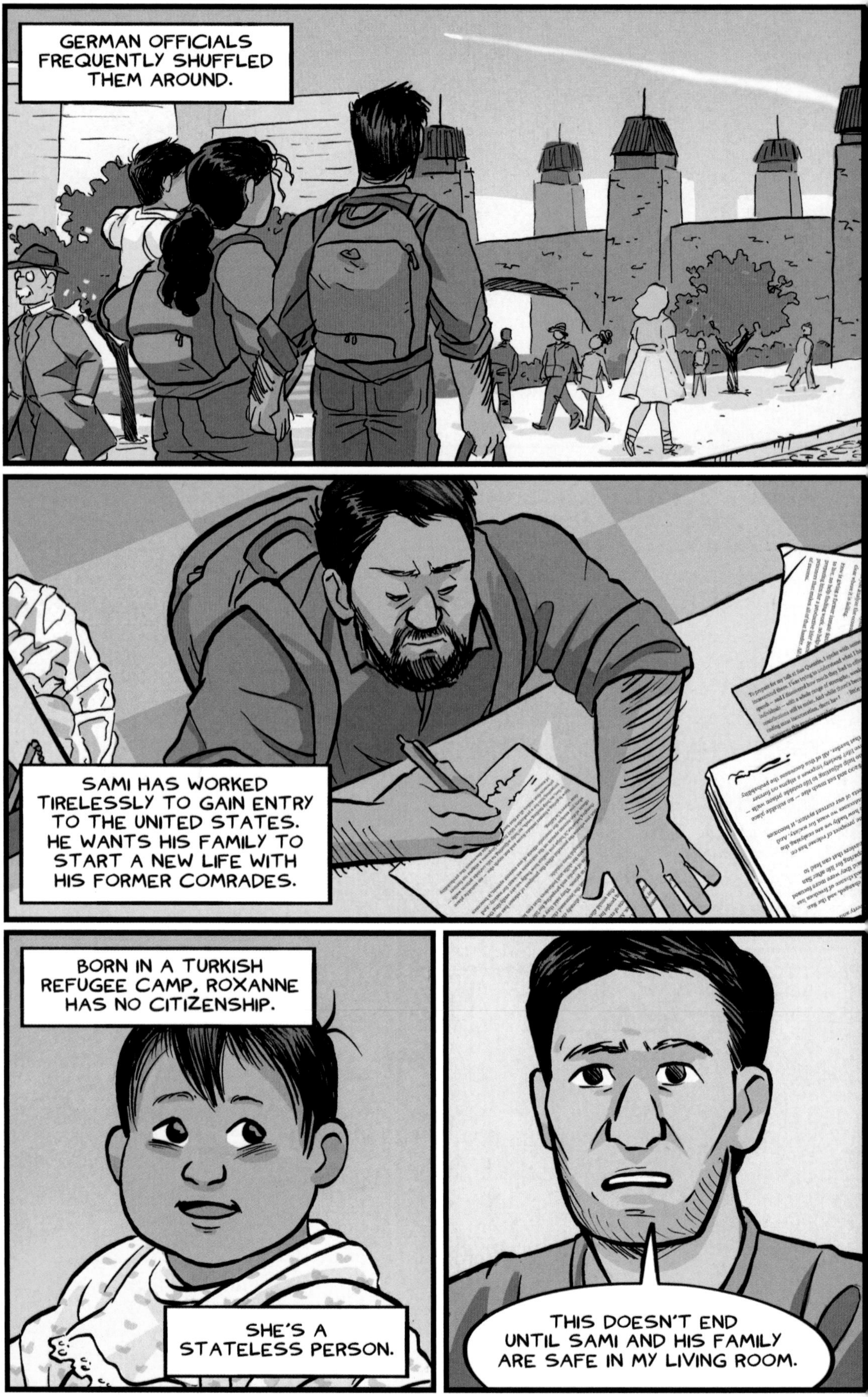
GERMAN OFFICIALS FREQUENTLY SHUFFLED THEM AROUND.
SAMI HAS WORKED TIRELESSLY TO GAIN ENTRY TO THE UNITED STATES. HE WANTS HIS FAMILY TO START A NEW LIFE WITH HIS FORMER COMRADES.
BORN IN A TURKISH REFUGEE CAMP, ROXANNE HAS NO CITIZENSHIP.
SHE'S A STATELESS PERSON.
THIS DOESN'T END UNTIL SAMI AND HIS FAMILY ARE SAFE IN MY LIVING ROOM.

17 "WAR AND FIREWORKS"

Kevin Knodell, freelance journalist,
Parkland, Washington

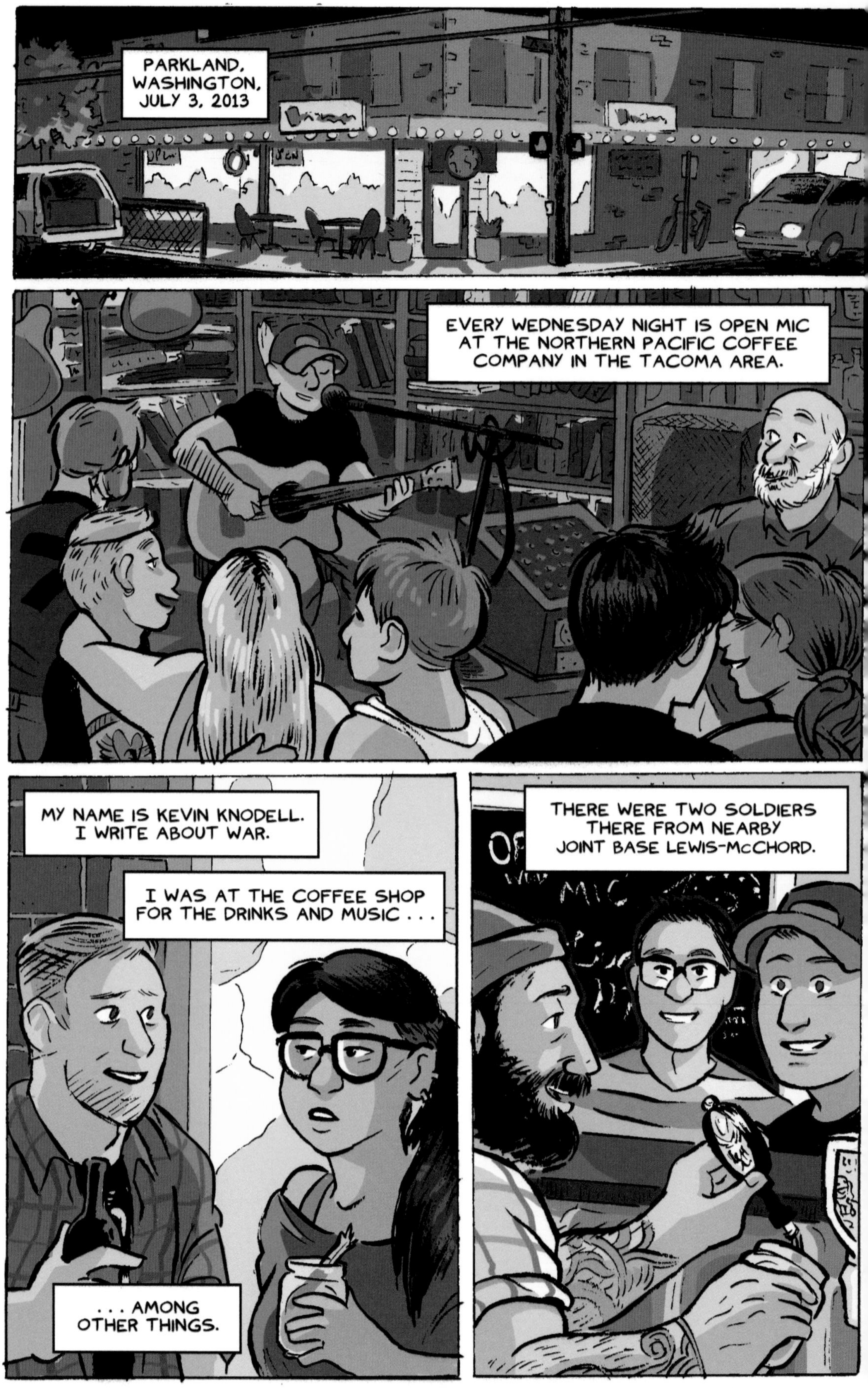
PARKLAND, WASHINGTON, JULY 3, 2013
EVERY WEDNESDAY NIGHT IS OPEN MIC AT THE NORTHERN PACIFIC COFFEE COMPANY IN THE TACOMA AREA.
MY NAME IS KEVIN KNODELL. I WRITE ABOUT WAR.
I WAS AT THE COFFEE SHOP FOR THE DRINKS AND MUSIC . . .
. . . AMONG OTHER THINGS.
THERE WERE TWO SOLDIERS THERE FROM NEARBY JOINT BASE LEWIS-McCHORD.

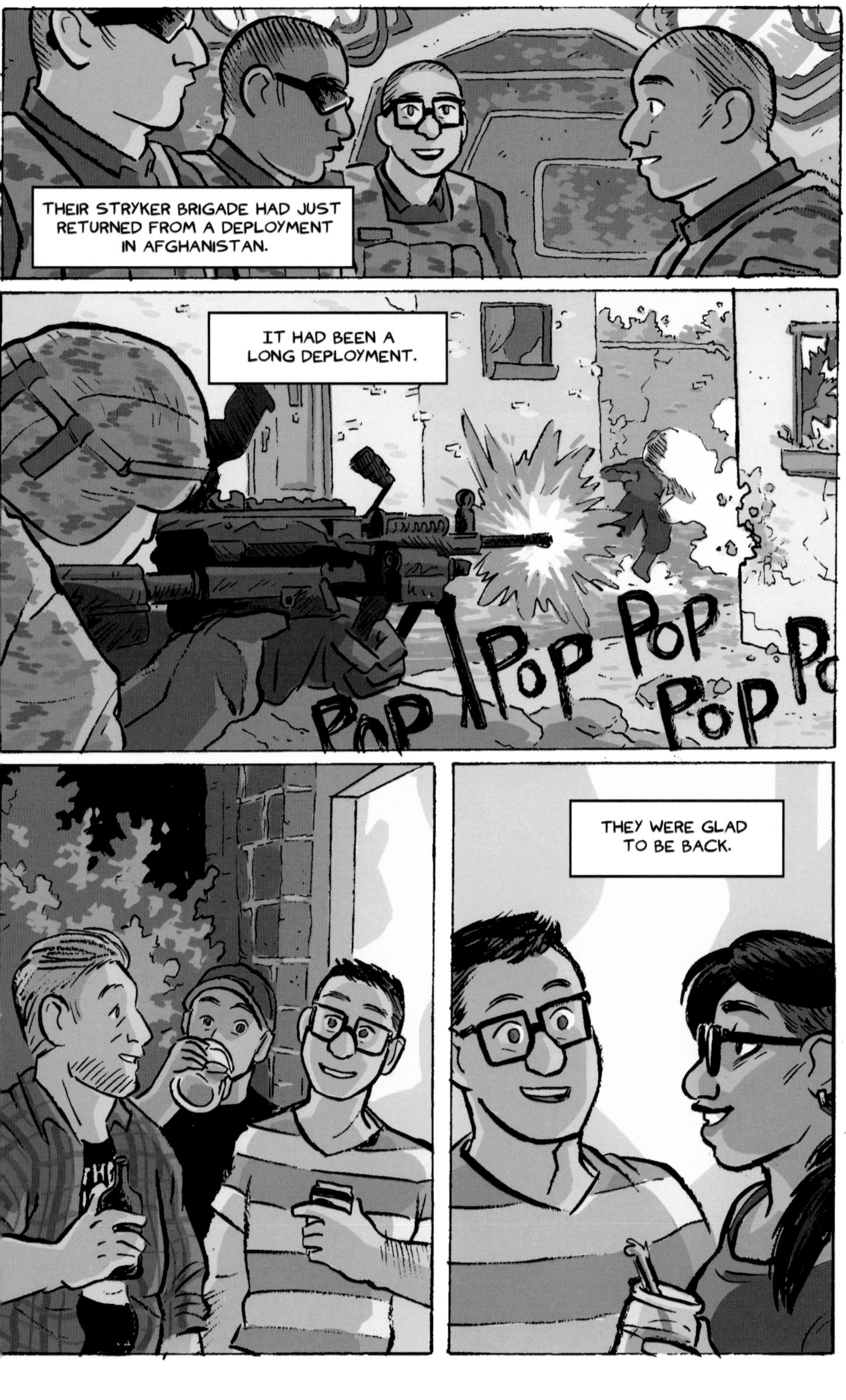
THEIR STRYKER BRIGADE HAD JUST RETURNED FROM A DEPLOYMENT IN AFGHANISTAN.
IT HAD BEEN A LONG DEPLOYMENT.
POP POP POP POP
THEY WERE GLAD TO BE BACK.

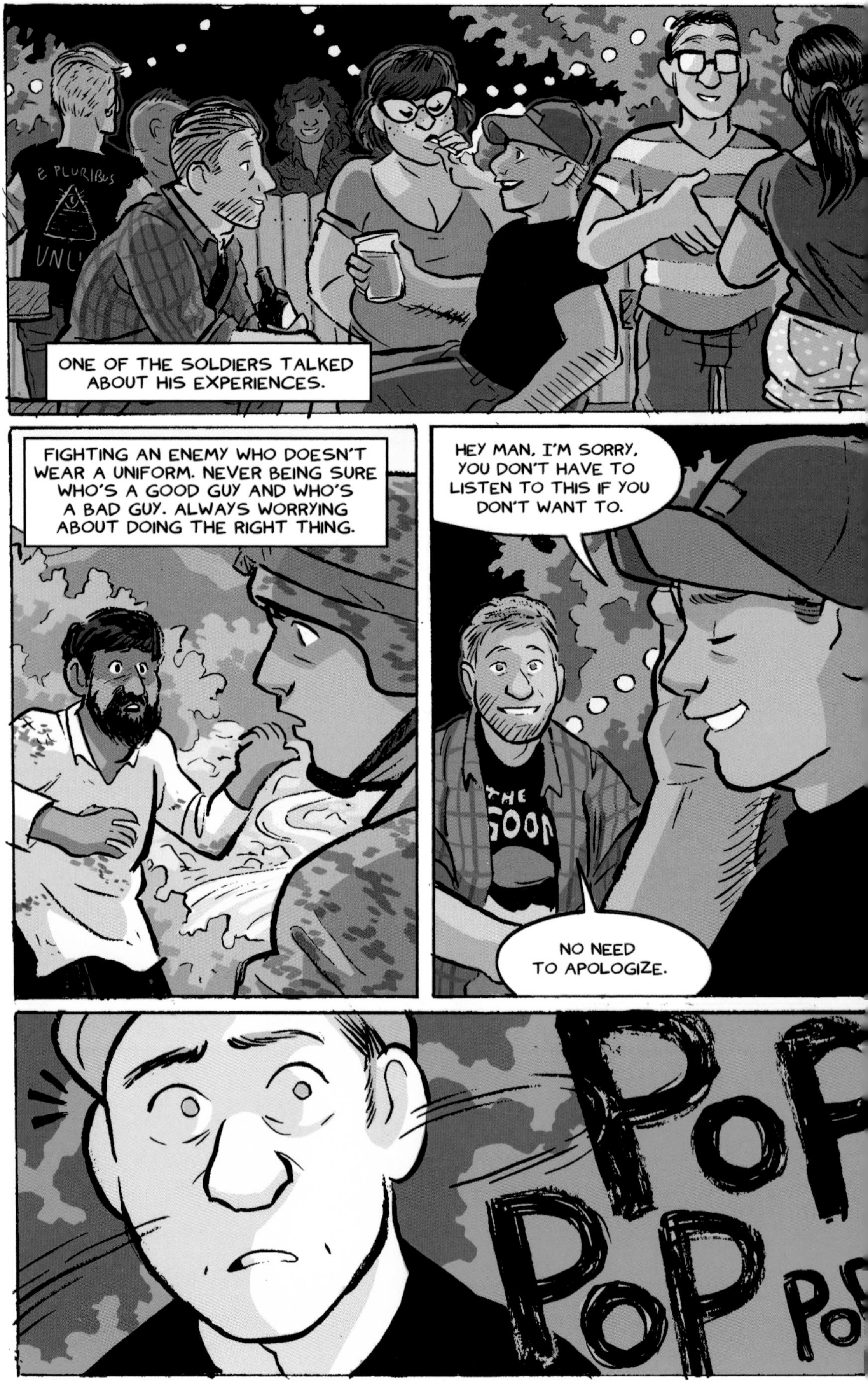
E PLURIBUS
UNU
ONE OF THE SOLDIERS TALKED ABOUT HIS EXPERIENCES.
FIGHTING AN ENEMY WHO DOESN'T WEAR A UNIFORM. NEVER BEING SURE WHO'S A GOOD GUY AND WHO'S A BAD GUY. ALWAYS WORRYING ABOUT DOING THE RIGHT THING.
HEY MAN, I'M SORRY, YOU DON'T HAVE TO LISTEN TO THIS IF YOU DON'T WANT TO.
THE GOOD
NO NEED TO APOLOGIZE.
POP
POP

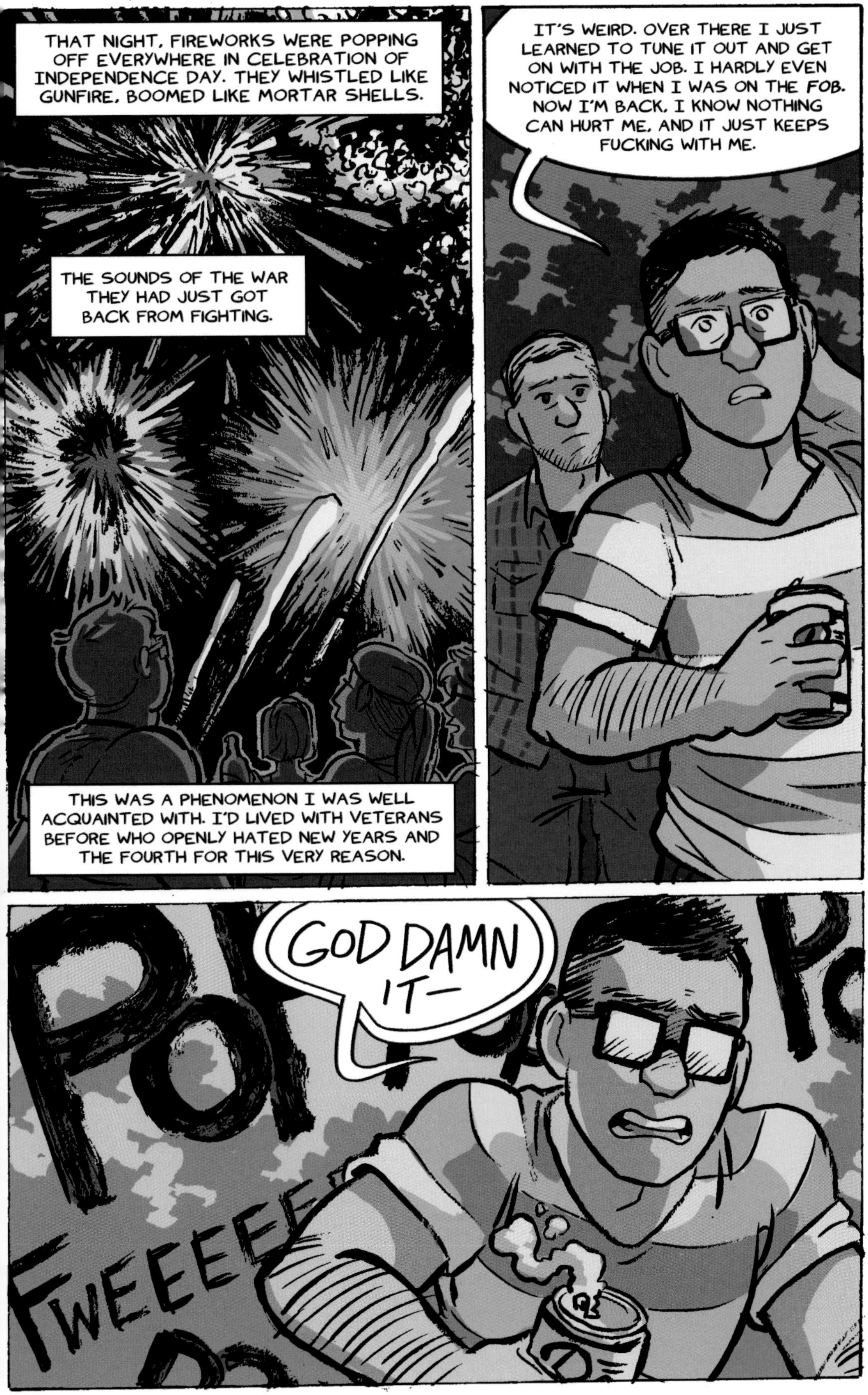
THAT NIGHT, FIREWORKS WERE POPPING OFF EVERYWHERE IN CELEBRATION OF INDEPENDENCE DAY. THEY WHISTLED LIKE GUNFIRE, BOOMED LIKE MORTAR SHELLS.
THE SOUNDS OF THE WAR THEY HAD JUST GOT BACK FROM FIGHTING.
THIS WAS A PHENOMENON I WAS WELL ACQUAINTED WITH. I'D LIVED WITH VETERANS BEFORE WHO OPENLY HATED NEW YEARS AND THE FOURTH FOR THIS VERY REASON.
IT'S WEIRD. OVER THERE I JUST LEARNED TO TUNE IT OUT AND GET ON WITH THE JOB. I HARDLY EVEN NOTICED IT WHEN I WAS ON THE *FOB*. NOW I'M BACK, I KNOW NOTHING CAN HURT ME, AND IT JUST KEEPS FUCKING WITH ME.
GOD DAMN IT—
FWEEEE

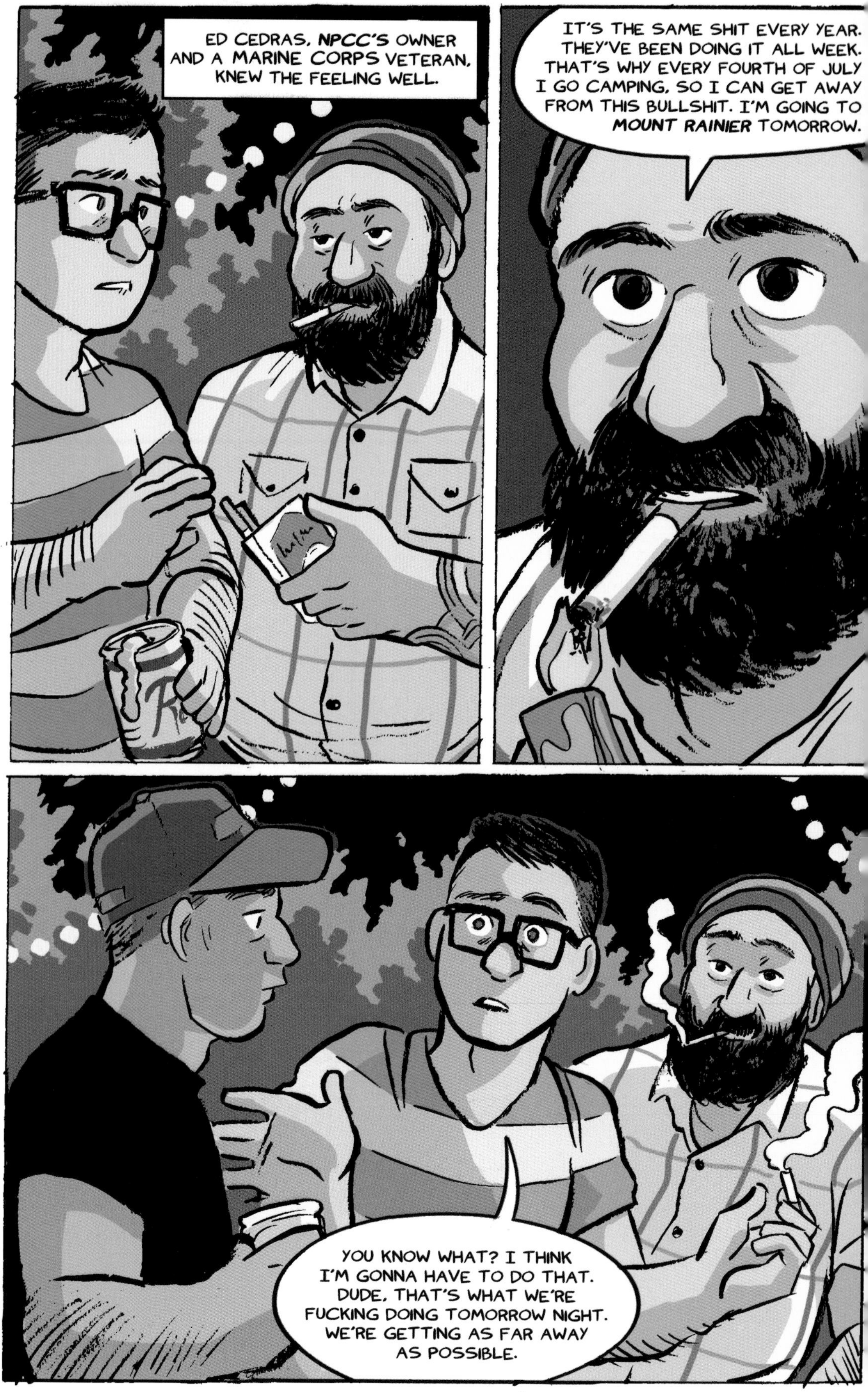
ED CEDRAS, NPCC'S OWNER AND A MARINE CORPS VETERAN, KNEW THE FEELING WELL.
IT'S THE SAME SHIT EVERY YEAR. THEY'VE BEEN DOING IT ALL WEEK. THAT'S WHY EVERY FOURTH OF JULY I GO CAMPING, SO I CAN GET AWAY FROM THIS BULLSHIT. I'M GOING TO MOUNT RAINIER TOMORROW.
YOU KNOW WHAT? I THINK I'M GONNA HAVE TO DO THAT. DUDE, THAT'S WHAT WE'RE FUCKING DOING TOMORROW NIGHT. WE'RE GETTING AS FAR AWAY AS POSSIBLE.

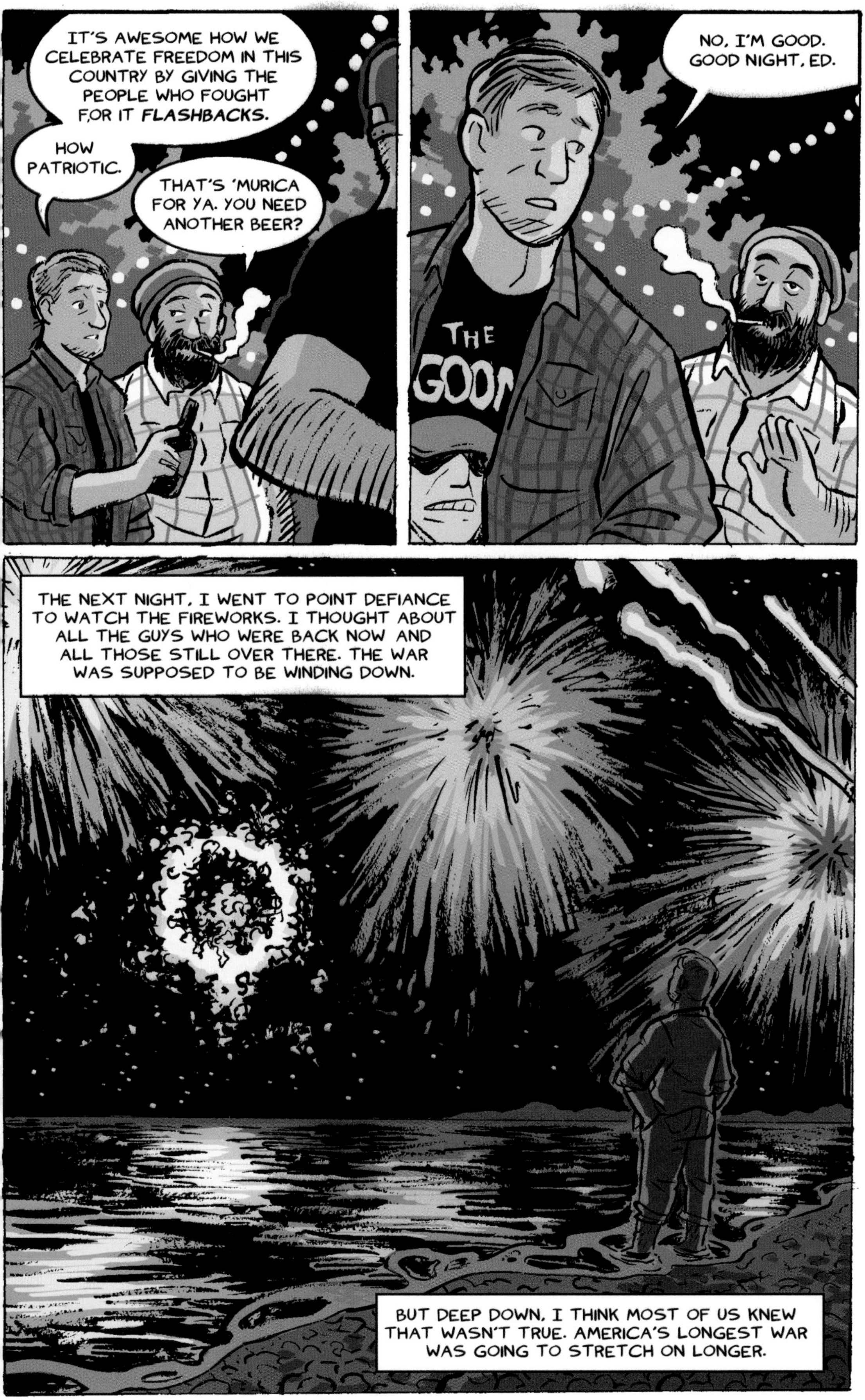
IT'S AWESOME HOW WE CELEBRATE FREEDOM IN THIS COUNTRY BY GIVING THE PEOPLE WHO FOUGHT FOR IT FLASHBACKS.
HOW PATRIOTIC.
THAT'S 'MURICA FOR YA. YOU NEED ANOTHER BEER?
NO, I'M GOOD. GOOD NIGHT, ED.
THE GOOD
THE NEXT NIGHT, I WENT TO POINT DEFIANCE TO WATCH THE FIREWORKS. I THOUGHT ABOUT ALL THE GUYS WHO WERE BACK NOW AND ALL THOSE STILL OVER THERE. THE WAR WAS SUPPOSED TO BE WINDING DOWN.
BUT DEEP DOWN, I THINK MOST OF US KNEW THAT WASN'T TRUE. AMERICA'S LONGEST WAR WAS GOING TO STRETCH ON LONGER.

ABOUT THE CREATORS

Kevin Knodell is a journalist who covers conflict, culture, and crime. His work has appeared in *Playboy*, *Week*, *Vice*, *Soldier of Fortune*, *News Tribune*, and other publications. He is a former contributing editor at Warisboring.com and writes the *Acts of Valor* comic series for *Naval History Magazine*.

David Axe is a writer, editor, and filmmaker living in Columbia, South Carolina. A former war correspondent, he has written for *Vice*, *Daily Beast*, *Village Voice* and many other publications. He is the writer of the graphic novel *War Is Boring* and the 2017 movie *The Theta Girl*.

Blue Delliquanti is a cartoonist and illustrator who likes to write about robots, insects, and unconventional families. She is the creator of the online comic *O Human Star* and the co-creator of the graphic novel *Meal* with Soleil Ho. Blue lives in Minneapolis with a woman and a cat.